Apprenticies, Poor Children and Bastards Loudoun County, Virginia 1757-1850

Louisa Skinner Hutchinson

HERITAGE BOOKS
2008

HERITAGE BOOKS
AN IMPRINT OF HERITAGE BOOKS, INC.

Books, CDs, and more—Worldwide

For our listing of thousands of titles see our website at
www.HeritageBooks.com

Published 2008 by
HERITAGE BOOKS, INC.
Publishing Division
100 Railroad Ave. #104
Westminster, Maryland 21157

Copyright © 2000 Louisa Skinner Hutchison

Other books by the author:
Index to Loudoun County, Virginia Wills 1757-1850

All rights reserved. No part of this book may be reproduced or transmitted in any form or by any means, electronic or mechanical, including photocopying, recording or by any information storage and retrieval system without written permission from the author, except for the inclusion of brief quotations in a review.

International Standard Book Numbers
Paperbound: 978-1-58549-637-2
Clothbound: 978-0-7884-7072-1

Table of Contents

INTRODUCTION III

ABBREVIATIONS V

RECORDS FOUND IN COURT ORDER BOOKS 1

INDENTURES ON FILE (NO ORDERS FOUND).. 139

BASTARD CHILDREN 149

INDEX 165

Introduction

About two years ago I began searching the Order (Minute) Books of Loudoun County for additional information on a servant who had been mentioned in a will written in 1776. Although I did not have success there, I discovered that dates of birth or ages were given for many apprentices, poor children and orphans bound out to learn a trade. Realizing this would be a help in genealogical research, I decided to compile a list from 1757 to 1850.

I have used information from the Order Books and from loose papers which include actual indentures and numerous small pieces of paper with bits of information evidently intended to be used in writing the orders. Up until the General Assembly of Virginia transferred their powers and duties to the Overseers of the Poor of the counties, the Churchwardens of the Parishes had been responsible for binding out the children. In April 1786 Overseers of the Poor were elected in Loudoun and the first entry noting their powers was on April 10.

Children were bound out until they became of age, males at 21 and females at 18, unless otherwise noted in the indenture. They were to be taught to read and write as early as 1770 and later arithmetic to the rule of three was included for boys. Often the indentures of girls included being taught spinning, knitting and sewing along with housekeeping.

It should be remembered that the term "orphan" was often used when the father was deceased and the mother was still living. Also, the use of "Jr." did not necessarily indicate a son but was used to indicate a younger person with the same name.

The references listed refer to Order (Minute) Books unless otherwise noted. There was a confusing numbering system used for which no explanation has been found. Books A-Z include orders from July 1757 to July 1807, Books 1-7 from August 1807 to July 1815, Books 1-8 from August 1815 to February 1828, Book 1 (only) from June 1829 to October 1830 and Books 1-30 from November 1830 to January 1904.

Introduction

The section on bastards has been gleaned from Order Books and loose papers, some of which have been difficult to interpret, but I have attempted to include all the information that will be of value to the genealogist. In the early years the mother of the child was fined 500 pounds of tobacco, and cask, or fifty shillings current money payable to the Churchwardens. However, a fine in a like amount was assessed against the person in whose house she was delivered if such person failed to report the birth to the churchwardens before the mother left. Thus, with a suit by the Churchwardens for this amount the defendant could be the mother or the homeowner.

In one case in 1811, the Court determined that no married woman could be allowed to swear her child to any man so as to bind him to the support of it, that the Act of Assembly only embraced the case of single women.

Payments for the support of bastard children were to be paid to the Churchwardens or the Overseers of the Poor, as the case might be, and they in turn were to see the children were provided with necessities. Payments were to be made on a quarterly basis and often suits were brought to enforce collection of overdue amounts. The term of payments was often qualified by "if the child shall live so long."

This list includes only those who were determined likely to become a burden on the parish or county. I am sure there were those who were raised by grandparents or other relatives and do not appear in the court records.

It is my hope that some information from this work will be valuable to searchers for their ancestors or relatives.

I wish to express my appreciation to Elizabeth R. Frain without whose encouragement and assistance this work would not have been completed.

Louisa Skinner Hutchison
September 2000

Abbreviations

ads.	adversus
als.	Alias
b.	born
CHWDNS	Churchwardens
dau	daughter
D.B.	Deed Book
dec'd	deceased
D.P.P.	Deeds Partially Proven
O.P.	Overseers of the Poor
vs.	versus
W.B.	Will Book

Apprentices, Poor Children and Bastards 1

Records Found in Court Order Books

A:6	9 Aug 1757	John FRYER, poor infant, 16 yrs on 2 Mar 1758, to John ETHELL, to be a blacksmith
A:6	9 Aug 1757	William FRYER, poor infant, 10 yrs on 25 Jul 1757, to Obed HARRIS, to be a house carpenter
A:8	9 Aug 1757	Sarah PROCTOR, baseborn, 8 yrs old in March 1757, to Thomas OWSLEY
A:11	10 Aug 1757	Peter JENNINGS, baseborn, 3 yrs old in Oct. 1757, to William DODD, to be a shoemaker
A:17	1 Sep 1757	Jane RUSSELL, mulatto, dau. of Anne Russell, to Thomas AWBREY
A:17	1 Sep 1757	Henry MAGESS, mulatto, son of Elizabeth Magess, to Thomas AWBREY
A:17	1 Sep 1757	Rebecca MACON, alias Rinah, mulatto, to John GIBSON. A:36, 12 Oct 1757, Rebecca RYAN vs John GIBSON, John Gibson to appear why Rebecca Ryan, orphan, should not be removed to another master or delivered to her mother. A:106, Rebecca MACON, alias Rinah, alias Ryan (or Rian)
A:17	1 Sep 1757	Thomas WILLIAMS, baseborn, 7 yrs old on 15 Mar 1757, to George NORMAN, cordwainer
A:17	1 Sep 1757	Joseph GREEN, 6 yrs old on 6 Jun 1757, to Samuel MOBLEY, cordwainer
A:57	14 Dec 1757	John CARUTHERS to William BROWN, to be a leather dresser
A:57	14 Dec 1757	Phillis MANLEY, indenture to serve Thomas FIELDS, seven years
A:63	14 Dec 1757	Rebecca RYAN, who is bound to John Gibson, vs John GIBSON, her mother, Margaret Parker and Anthony Parker, Margaret's husband, complaint against Gibson dismissed
A:67	14 Mar 1758	Mary GREEN, servant of William NODDING, to serve 1 yr 3 mo over her indenture for having a baseborn child. Nodding paying her fine to CHWDNS
A:85	11 Apr 1758	Catharine MECABE to Mary JANEY

Records Found in Court Order Books

A:94	12 Apr 1758	Conrad SHANKS & Margaret, his wife, vs Thomas AWBREY, sued for Freedom Dues. See A:109, Freedom Dues granted
A:100	9 May 1758	Isaac MANUEL, servant, of John MORRIS, to serve his master additional time to reimburse expense, he being a runaway
A:103	9 May 1758	William BREWER, servant of John BENTLEY, to serve 6 mos additional time
A:111	13 Jun 1758	Diana SAMPLE, age 4 yrs in March 1758, to William HATCHER
A:122	14 Jun 1758	Hugh MCGUIRE vs George CHILTON, for Freedom Dues, Chilton to pay
A:124	15 Jun 1758	Reuben WILLARD, runaway servant of David DAVIS, vs David DAVIS. Became a servant by contract and was an infant incapable of making contract so was discharged from further service
D.B. A:167	11 Jul 1758	Jacob BEESON, 17 yrs old on 17 Jun 1758, to Owen ROBERTS, indenture recorded, to be a tanner & currier until age 21
A:136	21 Jul 1758	James SHRIVES to Daniel DAVIS, indenture of apprentiship to be recorded. See D.B. A:199. To serve 3 yrs 9 mos
A:166	13 Sep 1758	John PARSONS, age 14 on 25 Sep 1758, son of Catharine Parsons, removed from Samuel AWBREY
A:166	13 Sep 1758	John PARSONS to Aeneas CAMPBELL, to be a carpenter
A:166	13 Sep 1758	Mary ORTON, orphan, to James HAMILTON
A:178	14 Nov 1758	Thomas GORE and David HUDSON, indenture of apprenticeship. [Which is the apprentice?]
A:178	14 Nov 1758	John RYLEY to Henry BREWER, discharged from further service
A:183	12 Dec 1758	Elizabeth JENKINS, orphan, to Francis WILKS
A:188	12 Feb 1759	William CRAWFORD, orphan, 15 yrs old, to Samuel COMBS, to be a shoemaker
A:188	12 Feb 1759	Isaac MANUEL vs John MORRIS, for Freedom Dues [book says 1758, evidently an error]
A:190	13 Feb 1759	John MUSCHET to William ROBINSON, to be a shoemaker
A:191	14 Feb 1759	Amey BARE to John MORRIS

Apprentices, Poor Children and Bastards 3

A:194	14 Feb 1759	William ORTON to Josias CLAPHAM, to be a carpenter
A:209	13 Mar 1759	Margaret GIBBS vs Thomas FIELDS, for unlawfully detaining her in his service
A:237	9 May 1759	Joseph SCOTT, son of George Scott, to John WESTBY, discharged from service
A:238	9 May 1759	Mary NOLAND, orphan, 9 yrs old, to Elizabeth DAVIS
A:265	14 Aug 1759	William BOLTON to Andrew ADAMS, to be a merchant
A:265	14 Aug 1759	Sarah PRESTON to Samuel COMBS
A:265	14 Aug 1759	Aaron REDMOND to Peter WILSON, to be a shoemaker
A:271	15 Aug 1759	Daniel PRESTON, 4 yrs old on 12 Dec 1758, to Thomas WATSON, to be a carpenter Loose Papers: b. 12 Dec 1754, son of Martha Preston in MD
A:295	13 Sep 1759	James Carr BARRETT to James LANE, to be a house carpenter
A:301	13 Nov 1759	Jonathan HALL, 7 yrs old, to William SMITH, to be a cooper
A:321	12 Dec 1759	Susanna GRIMES vs John DAVIS, sues for her freedom - granted
A:324	11 Mar 1760	Mary ROBERTS to William SMITH
A:346	14 May 1760	Margaret ROBERTS to William SMITH
A:347	14 May 1760	John ROBERTS, 10 yrs old, to Philip NOLAND, to be a house carpenter
A:349	14 May 1760	Henry George GREEN, 2 yrs old on 16 Jan 1760, to William NODING, to be a tile cooper
A:403	11 Nov 1760	William FLEMING, orphan, to James WHALEY, to be a cord winder
A:453	9 Jun 1761	Henry FRANKS, orphan, 10 yrs 3 mos, to Thomas STUMP, to be a cord winder
A:479	14 Jul 1761	Jane MCDANIEL, a runaway servant, sued by Cornelius VAUNE
A:479	14 Jul 1761	Margaret WATSON, a runaway servant, sued by Cornelius VAUNE
A:484	11 Aug 1761	Jesse MCNEAL, orphan, to Thomas LEWELLING, to be a cordwainer
A:493	8 Sep 1761	Joseph LOCKLAN, mulatto, 10 yrs old, to John GIST, until 21 yrs, to be a cordwainer, son of Priscilla Locklan

Records Found in Court Order Books

A:493	8 Sep 1761	Henry LOCKLAN, mulatto, 12 yrs old, to John GIST, until 21 yrs, to be a cordwainder, son of Priscilla Locklan
A:494	8 Sep 1761	John Winn HAYS, 3 yrs old 1 May 1761, to John HALL
A:532	11 Nov 1761	Mary MCNAB, baseborn child 2 yrs old on 13 Nov 1761, to John CARR
A:554	9 Feb 1762	John PROCTOR, mulatto, baseborn, to Thomas KELLY
A:567	10 Mar 1762	John RAWDERY, orphan, to John TRAMMELL, to be a cooper
A:584	11 May 1762	James BINKS, orphan, 9 yrs old in Feb. 1762, to Kitchen PRIM, to be a house carpenter
A:584	11 May 1762	James PRIM, orphan, 5 yrs old in Dec. 1761, to Kitchen PRIM, to be a house carpenter
A:594	12 May 1762	Leonard DYALL, orphan, to John MCGINNIS, until 21, to be a taylor
A:622	14 May 1762	Jesse HALL vs Thomas AWBREY, for ill usage
A:630	9 Jun 1762	Perregrin ALLAN, baseborn, 8 yrs old, to Craven PEYTON, to be a house carpenter
A:633	9 Jun 1762	Winifred ENGLISH, orphan, 8 yrs old in July 1762, to Robert POPKINS
B:29	10 Aug 1762	Tobias ALLAN, baseborn, to Thomas MIDDLETON, Jr., to be a cordwinder
B:29	10 Aug 1762	Mary JACKSON, baseborn, to Abel JANNEY
B:77	14 Dec 1762	Christian WOODHOUSE, a servant of Minor WINN, to serve additional 9 mos.
B:88	12 Apr 1763	James FREELAND, 10 yrs old, to Thomas GORE, to be a skin dresser
B:105	13 Apr 1763	Thomas WINSOR, 9 yrs old in Feb. 1763, to Thomas CONNELL, to be a house carpenter
B:108	13 Apr 1763	James MCCOY, 6 yrs old, to William FIELDER, to be a stone mason
B:109	13 Apr 1763	Jesse HALL, formerly bound to Thomas Awbrey, to John MOSS, Sr., to be a house carpenter
B:121	10 May 1763	Thomas MASKEL, or Mashel, to John O'CAIN, to be a weaver
B:124	10 May 1763	Rebecca CRAIG, 11 yrs old, to James HENDERSON

Apprentices, Poor Children and Bastards 5

B:195	9 Aug 1763	Frances RUCARD, (Reecard?), 6 yrs old in Sep. 1763, to William HOGE
B:196	9 Aug 1763	James WATTS, 2 yrs old, child of __ Watts who is a run away, to Jacob SCHACHEN, to be a weaver
B:196	9 Aug 1763	Elizabeth WATTS, 5 yrs old, child of __ Watts who is a run away, to Jacob SCHACHEN
B:207	11 Aug 1763	John COATS to Christopher PERFECT, indenture of apprentiship recorded D.B. C:687, to serve until 25 Dec 1764
B:232	13 Sep 1763	William CRAWFORD to John REIGER, released from indenture of apprentiship to Samuel Combs and agreed to serve 1 yr 3 mo, to be a cordwainer
B:251	15 Sep 1763	Phillis STYLES vs John CHAMP, Jr., for Freedom Dues
B:269	13 Dec 1763	Barrett TRAVERSE vs Robert WATSON, for ill usage
B:274	15 Feb 1764	Richard PASCALS, orphan, 17 yrs old on 9 Mar 1764, to James HAMILTON, to be a cordwainer or taylor
B:275	15 Feb 1764	James Carr BARRET, baseborn, 7 yrs old, to John GODDARD, to be a joiner
B:279	13 Mar 1764	Cruse MERCER, 3 yrs old in Sep. 1763, to Richard MERCER, to be a cooper
B:280	13 Mar 1764	Rebecca OLDRIDGE, 5 yrs old, to John MOSS, Jr.,
B:281	14 Mar 1764	Moren WOODHOUSE, 15 mo. old, to Minor WINN
B:285	14 Mar 1764	James ALDRIDGE, 9 yrs old, to Alexander WIDNER, to be a wheelwright
B:287	15 Mar 1764	Charles SECRES, 15 yrs old, to Joseph JANNEY, to be a cooper
B:353	8 May 1764	John PATTERSON, 16 yrs old 19 May 1764, to William PATTERSON, to be a blacksmith
B:353	8 May 1764	Joseph PATTERSON, 8 yrs old 8 Sep 1764, to William PATTERSON, to be a blacksmith
B:373	14 Jun 1764	Mary CONNER, orphan, 11 yrs old 26 Dec 1763, to William MEAD
B:373	14 Jun 1764	David EDWARD to Robert POPKINS, to be a joiner, for 3 yrs and 4 mos. Indenture recorded D.B. D:232

B:382	14 Jun 1764	William PHILLIPS to Minor WINN, Jr., indenture of apprenticeship ordered to be recorded. D.B. D:233 to serve 4 yrs. 6 mo.
B:467	14 Sep 1764	Rachel MCNAB to Benjamin EDWARDS
B:473	8 Oct 1764	James BUCKLEY, orphan, 3 yrs old in June 1764, to William BUCKLEY, to be a cordwainer
B:487	10 Oct 1764	Mary BRANE vs Robert WATSON, for ill treatment, removed from service
B:495	13 Nov 1764	Tobias ALLAN, formerly bound to Thomas Middleton Jr. who is since run away, to Moses BOTTS, to be a cooper
B:506	15 Nov 1764	Jeremiah FRYER, 14 yrs old 1 Sep 1764, to Thomas WATSON, to be a carpenter
B:523	12 Mar 1765	Reuben VINES, 8 yrs old 1 Feb 1765, to William HOGE, to be a cordwainer
B:527	12 Mar 1765	Job JENKINS, orphan of Harness Jenkins, dec'd, 12 yrs old in Feb 1765, to John MORRIS, to be a tight cooper
B:551	10 Apr 1765	Voluntine HOLIFIELD, orphan, 9 yrs old, to Robert SANFORD, to be a weaver
B:554	10 Apr 1765	Henry LOYD vs William MEAD, for detaining him as a servant, dismissed
B:571	13 May 1765	Thomas MARTIN, baseborn, 8 yrs old on 25 Dec 1764, to Ralph MARTIN, to be a weaver
B:572	13 May 1765	Tobias ALLAN to be returned to Thomas MIDDLETON, his former master
B:572	13 May 1765	Catharine MCKAY, 11 yrs old in Aug 1764, to Margaret JENKINS
B:622	10 Jun 1765	Sarah FINASS, 4 yrs old 22 Dec 1765, to John CAVENS
C:5	12 Aug 1765	Stephen COX, 12 yrs old 12 Sep 1765, to Samuel SMITH, to be a cord wainer
C:5	12 Aug 1765	William DOUGLASS, baseborn, 15 yrs old in Mar. 1765, to John TRAMMEL, to be a cooper
C:36	10 Sep 1765	Hezekiah Butler WINDSOR, baseborn, 9 yrs old on 7 Jul 1765, to Benjamin SHREVE, to be a carpenter
C:60	14 Oct 1765	Peter PICKLER to John HOUGH, agreed to serve 18 mos. Additional time and Mary Magdalene, wife of Peter, released from further service. D.B. D:666

Apprentices, Poor Children and Bastards 7

C:63	15 Oct 1765	John TALBUT, 15 yrs old in Dec. 1764, to Jason MORLAN, to be a joyner
C:68	16 Oct 1765	John MCKENZEY, 7 yrs old, to John REIGER, to be a tanner and cordwainer
C:83	9 Jun 1766	Jane WELLS, 12 yrs old in Sep 1765, to Samuel ARWIN
C:83	9 Jun 1766	Jane MELVIN, baseborn mulatto, 2 yrs old 19 Nov 1766, to Fielding TURNER
C:83	9 Jun 1766	Isaac EATON, orphan, 16 yrs 6 mo, to Joshua JONES, to be a tanner Loose Papers: petition by William and Bridget Cummins to remove her son from J. Jones granted Sep 1766
C:109	11 Jun 1766	James ALDRIDGE, poor orphan 11 yrs old in Feb 1766, to William MEAD, to be a malster [maltster]
C:148	11 Aug 1766	Zachariah JENKINS, 10 yrs old in Apr 1766, to John GORAM, to be a shoemaker
C:148	11 Aug 1766	Elizabeth BARRETT, 6 yrs old in Oct 1766, to John GORAM
C:148	11 Aug 1766	Mary BRAWNER, baseborn mulatto, to Robert WATSON
C:155	13 Aug 1766	Nicolle (Nicholas) BIVITE (BIVET), 9 yrs old, to John MILLER
C:175	14 Aug 1766	John PHILLIPS, 13 yrs old, to William DICKSON, to be a blacksmith
C:211	14 Oct 1766	William KEITH, orphan, to Abraham WARFORD, to be a blacksmith
C:219	10 Nov 1766	Stacey LANHAM, 13 yrs old in Jan 1767, to John PILES
C:219	10 Nov 1766	Jane LANHAM, 8 yrs old in Apr 1767, to John PILES
C:219	10 Nov 1766	Henry LANHAM, 11 yrs old in Aug 1767, to John PILES, to be a cooper
C:231	8 Dec 1766	John STEPHENS, about 15 yrs old, to Joseph PARKER, to be a blacksmith
C:240	10 Mar 1767	John MCKENSIE, about 7 yrs old, to John MOSS, to be a cooper
C:240	10 Mar 1767	William MCKENSIE, about 5 yrs old, to John MOSS, to be a cooper
C:240	10 Mar 1767	Daniel HATCH, servant, to Farlan BALL, to serve additional time for being a runaway

C:241	11 Mar 1767	Henry PEYTON, Jr., son of Henry Peyton, to Charles BINNS, see D.B. E:300, to serve until 14 Jan 1770
C:279	8 Jun 1767	Aaron REDMOND, about 9 yrs 6 mo old, to Henry FERGUSON
C:279	8 Jun 1767	John Peyton HARRISON, 16 yrs old 29 Jun 1767, to Levin POWELL
C:292	10 Aug 1767	William JAMES, a servant, to William PEARL, to serve additional time for being absent
C:292	10 Aug 1767	John MAHON, a servant, to Thomas LEWIS, to serve additional time for being absent. Lewis gives consent for Mahon to marry Jane Carter.
C:292	10 Aug 1767	Jane CARTER, a servant, to Thomas LEWIS, to serve additional time for being absent. Lewis gives consent for Carter to marry John Mahon.
C:299	12 Aug 1767	Charles Martin POSTON, 12 yrs old on 5 Jan 1767, to Mary MARBURY, to be a weaver
C:302	12 Aug 1767	James BRIGLAND, adjudged to be 14 yrs old, servant of Richard COOMBS
C:327	18 Sep 1767	Samuel LUCAS, adjudged to be 9 yrs old, servant of Joseph JANNEY
C:336	13 Oct 1767	Fleming WILSON, about 10 mo old, baseborn child of Mary Wilson, to Fleming PATTERSON, to be a merchant
C:336	13 Oct 1767	Margaret WILSON, 4 yrs old, baseborn child of Mary Wilson, to Fleming PATTERSON
C:336	13 Oct 1767	Jane WILSON, 3 yrs old, baseborn child of Mary Wilson, to Fleming PATTERSON
D:2	9 Nov 1767	Nancy BEARD, baseborn, 3 yrs old 23 Jan 1767, to Richard WHITE
D:23	15 Mar 1768	James HALE, 16 yrs old 25 Dec __, to Benjamin BURSON, to be a mason
D:23	15 Mar 1768	Silvester HARLEY, baseborn, 8 yrs old in May 1767, to Jonathan PIKE, to be a cooper
D:23	15 Mar 1768	John GRAY, orphan, about 15 yrs on this day, to Shadrach SAMUELS, to be a blacksmith
D:40	11 Apr 1768	James WOOD, 8 yrs old, to Thomas CARR, to be a farmer, discharged from Jacob Morris, his former master

Apprentices, Poor Children and Bastards

D:40	11 Apr 1768	Thomas ARNET, about 10 yrs old, to Samuel ARNET, to be a farmer
D:40	11 Apr 1768	Sarah ARNET, 8 yrs old, to Samuel ARNET
D:40	11 Apr 1768	Ruth ARNET, 6 yrs old, to Samuel ARNET
D:40	11 Apr 1768	Elisha JOHNSON, 16 yrs old 4 Jun 1768, to James HAMILTON, to be a shoemaker
D:41	11 Apr 1768	Cornelius HURLEY, a servant, vs John EBLIN, his master, for ill usage. Suit dismissed 12 Apr 1769 D:181
D:58	10 May 1768	Catherine WILLIAMS vs Robert FRYER, for her freedom. Her indenture deemed valid, she was ordered to return to her master's service
D:63	11 May 1768	Jesse HALL to Isaac FOUCH, to be a shoemaker. His indenture was transferred to John Evans 13 Oct 1768, D:140
D:64	11 May 1768	Leven Powell HAYS, about 6 yrs old, to Vincent LEWIS
D:64	11 May 1768	Margaret PIPER's children to be bound
D:64	11 May 1768	Anthony WHARTON's children to be bound
D:78	13 Jun 1768	Chloe REEVES, mulatto, 4 yrs old in Mar 1768, to Nathaniel GRIGSBY
D.B. F:345	13 Jun 1768	Henry GREGORY, a blacksmith, to Francis DADE for 3 yrs
D:83	15 Jun 1768	Samuel HARRIS, orphan of William Harris, deceased, 12 yrs old, to Francis WILKS, to be a farmer
D:89	11 Jul 1768	John PAINTER to Joseph COLLINS, to be a shoemaker
D:90	8 Aug 1768	Terence CURREY to Thomas GIBSON, to serve his master for time and expense as a runaway
D:92	8 Aug 1768	James MCKENSIE, about 16 yrs old, to Henry OXLEY, Jr., to be a blacksmith
D:92	8 Aug 1768	John Nisbet COLQUHOON, about 2 yrs old, to John POPKINS, to be a carpenter
D:97	9 Aug 1768	Robert MITCHELL a servant of James FRYER, to serve additional time for time and expense as a runaway
D:110	11 Aug 1768	Charles PIERPOINT, mulatto 5 yrs old, to William SUTHARD, until 21 Loose Papers: son of Charity Pierpoint, for 31 years?

D:114	12 Sep 1768	John CHILDS, baseborn child of Eleanor Childs, 5 yrs old, to William BUCKLEY
D:114	12 Sep 1768	Anna Barberry MILLER to Thomas HUMPHREY, until 18
D:114	12 Sep 1768	Patrick COLLINS a servant of Robert FRYER, to serve for being absent 2 days
D:115	12 Sep 1768	Margaret CARRIGAN vs Ferdinando O'NEALE, to return to her master and to receive better use from him
D.B. G:27	12 Sep 1768	Elizabeth BOWMAN to Thomas SIMMONDS, for 6 yrs from 1 Mar 1768
D:125	14 Sep 1768	John MILLER a servant of James LANE, to serve additional time for 26 days runaway
D:132	10 Oct 1768	Rachael BURSON, about 5 yrs old, orphan of Alice Alford, to Owen ROBERTS
D:145	15 Nov 1768	Jacob HARRIS, orphan, 4 yrs old, to Edmund SANDS, to be a farmer Loose Papers: age on 3 May 1769, son of Ann Harris
D:145	15 Nov 1768	Jesse HARRIS, 13 yrs old in Feb 1768, to Samuel COOMBS, to be a farmer
D:148	16 Nov 1768	Jesse CONNELL, 11 yrs old in Mar 1769, orphan of John Connell, deceased, to Zachariah CONNELL
D:148	16 Nov 1768	Jeremiah CONNELL, 9 yrs old 14 Apr 1769, orphan of John Connell, deceased, to Zachariah CONNELL
D:158	13 Mar 1769	James NUCOM, orphan, about 13 yrs, to Gabriel FOX, to be a carpenter
D:158	13 Mar 1769	Francis SAUNDERS, orphan, 17 yrs old on 20 Jan 1769, to Gabriel FOX, to be a carpenter
D:161	14 Mar 1769	Duncan MCDONALD a servant of Mahlon JANNEY, to serve additional time for being a runaway
D:165	14 Mar 1769	John PHILLIPS, orphan, 15 yrs old, to Jenkin PHILLIPS, to be a tight cooper. Complaint of William Dickson & Sarah, his wife D:209, D:229 & D:252. Dismissed, orphan to remain with Jenkin Phillips
D:165	14 Mar 1769	Mary PHILLIPS, about 13 yrs old, to Thomas PHILLIPS
D:165	14 Mar 1769	Isaac PHILLIPS, about 7 yrs old, to Thomas PHILLIPS, to be a cordwainer

Apprentices, Poor Children and Bastards

D:168	10 Apr 1769	Thomas DALE, orphan, 13 yrs old on 15 Sep 1768, to John OSBURN, to be a cordwainer
D:173	10 Apr 1769	William BERRY, orphan, about 11 yrs old, to Samuel LOVE, to be a cordwainer
D:204	15 Apr 1769	John EVANS a servant of Craven PEYTON, to serve additional time for being a runaway
D:205	8 May 1769	Lydia YATES, orphan, about 6 yrs, to John MARKS
D:232	14 Jun 1769	Ann PINKHAM, about 11 yrs old, to Thomas SHEPHERD
D:232	14 Jun 1769	Joseph LINN, orphan about 8 yrs old, to Thomas SHEPHERD, to be a cordwainer
D:233	14 Jun 1769	Isaac SCOTT, mulatto about 2 yrs old, to Thomas AMOS
D:245	14 Aug 1769	Arthur BRANIAN a servant of Thomas FRANCIS, to serve additional time for being a runaway
D:248	14 Aug 1769	Sinah FLOYD, 4 yrs old, daughter of Rachel Hall, to Charles HUGHLEY Loose Papers: birthday 26 Sep 1769, to serve until 18
D:249	15 Aug 1769	Christopher FIDDES a servant of Francis HAGUE, detected in gambling in a public house
D:250	15 Aug 1769	Elizabeth GRIMES, 12 yrs old 1 Nov 1769, to George HEADON, Jr.,
D:250	15 Aug 1769	Ann GRIMES, 14 yrs old 27 Jul 1769, to Samuel HEADON
D:252	15 Aug 1769	Charles SEEKREST (SEEKRIGHT) an apprentice of Joseph JANNEY, discharged from further service
D:253	15 Aug 1769	Mary TAVERNER, about 4 yrs old, to William MORLAN
D:254	16 Aug 1769	George ARNOLD a servant of Thomson MASON, to serve additional time for being a runaway
D:260	11 Sep 1769	Sidina STUBBS, 5 yrs old on 1 Jan 1769, to Rees CADWALLADER
D:264	12 Sep 1769	Elizabeth THOMAS a servant of Francis PEYTON, to serve additional time for being a runaway
D:265	12 Sep 1769	Fanney WRIGHT, formerly bound to Henry Wisheart, to William GUNNELL, Jr.

D:279	10 Oct 1769	Samuel HILL, orphan about 17 yrs old, to Henry FARNSWORTH
D:284	11 Oct 1769	Alexander MONEY, a servant of, Fleming PATTERSON, to serve additional time for being a runaway
D:292	13 Nov 1769	Christian READER, about 14 yrs old, to John SIGLER
D:292	13 Nov 1769	John READER, about 4 yrs old, to John SIGLER
D:292	13 Nov 1769	Nicholas READER, about 8 yrs old, to Jacob SIGLER
D:292	13 Nov 1769	William READER, about 2 yrs old, to William CLINE
D:294	13 Nov 1769	Ann KELLY vs Joseph POWER, for ill treatment. Suit dismissed 11 Dec 1769, see D:303
D:294	13 Nov 1769	Mary SAP, about 12 yrs old, to Griffith PEARCE
D:303	11 Dec 1769	Barbary DULAP, orphan about 13 yrs old, to James GIBSON
D:306	12 Feb 1770	Ann HILL, about 7 mo old, child of Catherine Hill, to Andrew ADAM
D:306	12 Feb 1770	Catherine HILL a servant of Andrew ADAM, to serve additional time
D:307	12 Mar 1770	Elizabeth OUTON, orphan, to Joseph THOMAS
D:307	12 Mar 1770	Joseph ALFORD, a son of Alice Alford, to Peter EBLIN
D:326	14 Mar 1770	Daniel CLENCY a servant of Shadrach SAMUELS, dismissed from any further service
D:330	9 Apr 1770	Martha MALONE a servant of James SANDERS, to serve additional time for having a baseborn child
D:332	9 Apr 1770	William WARFURD, about 10 yrs old, to James BRYANT, to be a wheelwright
D.B. H:124	10 Aug 1770	John THOMSON, 22 yrs old, a taylor, to William NEILSON, for 5 yrs 10 days, signed at Ayr before sailing for Virginia (Indenture recorded 10 Apr 1771)
D.B. H:125	11 Aug 1770	Aaron GIBSON, 21 yrs old, a taylor, to William NEILSON, for 5 yrs 10 days, signed at Ayr before sailing for Virginia (Indenture recorded 10 Apr 1771)

Apprentices, Poor Children and Bastards

E:3	13 Aug 1770	James HAMILTON, orphan, about 3 yrs old in May 1771, to Isaac NICKOLLS, Jr., to be a cooper
E:4	13 Aug 1770	Winney MELVIN, mullatto about 2 yrs old in Apr 1771, to Fielding TURNER
E:14	14 Aug 1770	Ruth JONES, baseborn, about 2 yrs old, to James NIXON
E:14	14 Aug 1770	John JONES, about 18 yrs old, to Richard STEPHENS
E:14	14 Aug 1770	Mary HORN, about 16 yrs old, to Richard STEPHENS
E:60	10 Oct 1770	Ann BRIDGMAN, a servant of Thomas FIELDS, vs Thomas FIELDS, for ill usage, complaint dismissed
E:71	12 Nov 1770	William ADAMS a servant of William BERKLEY or Sarah Berkley his wife, to serve additional time for being a runaway
E:79	14 Nov 1770	Thomas BYRD a servant of William LAUDER (LANDER), adjudged to be 14 yrs old
E:80	15 Nov 1770	Samuel JACKSON, orphan, 10 yrs old on 3 Mar 1770, to James BAST, to be a farmer
E:87	14 Jan 1771	Jesse WHARTON, orphan, to Benjamin BROWN Loose Papers: his mother Virgilia Sharp was left a widow with a charge of small children
E:90	11 Feb 1771	John Haddock MCGINNIS a servant of James SINCLAIR, to serve additional time for having him cured of a disease
D.B. H:68	6 Apr 1771	William THOMAS, son of Emet Thomas, to Joshua EVANS, to be a blacksmith, with consent of his mother, for 5 yrs 4 mos and 11 days
E:94	8 Apr 1771	Jesse WHARTON, orphan about 7 yrs old, to Benjamin BROWN, to be a farmer. See E:87
E:95	8 Apr 1771	Sarah JOHNSON, orphan about 8 yrs old, to Stephen ROZELL
E:101	9 Apr 1771	Isabella CARSON, a servant of, vs Fleming PATTERSON, complaint heard and dismissed
E:121	13 May 1771	William BALL, orphan of John Ball, dec'd, to William BAKER, to be a hat maker
E:129	14 May 1771	Richard TILTON to George MUIRHEAD, to be a house carpenter

E:153	10 Jun 1771	John GRIM, 5 yrs old in Dec 1770, to John WOLF, to be a blacksmith
E:166	13 Jun 1771	Joseph LACEY, about 14 yrs old, to Abel JANNEY, to be a hat maker
E:178	15 Jun 1771	Mary HARRIS, orphan, to John HOUGH
E:178	15 Jun 1771	John HARRIS, orphan, to John HOUGH
D.B. I:393	31 Jul 1771	Evan THOMAS, son of Elizabeth Askren, now 16 yrs 5 mos 9 days old, to Thomas DOUGHTY, of Fauquier Co., to be a blacksmith
E:183	12 Aug 1771	Valentine KERN to John GEORGE, according to terms of a former indenture
E:187	13 Aug 1771	William MASTELL a servant of Jonathan DAVIS, to serve additional time for being a runaway
E:203	16 Aug 1771	John SCOTT, about 14 yrs old in Dec 1770, to John SHEPARD, to be a farmer
E:213	9 Sep 1771	James BUTLER, mulatto, 13 yrs old in Mar 1772, to Hardage LANE
E:213	9 Sep 1771	Peter BRUMBACK, orphan, about 11 yrs old, to Peter HARMAN
E:214	10 Sep 1771	William ANSLEY to Oliver PRICE, a saddler, according to terms of a former indenture
E:214	10 Sep 1771	Reuben BIGGS a servant of John VIOLETT, to serve additional time for being a runaway. Again a runaway E:307 25 May 1772
E:222	11 Sep 1771	John PHILLIPS a servant of William ROBERTS, to serve additional time for being a runaway
E:224	12 Sep 1771	John CARLEY, alias John Arters, a servant of, Benjamin DAVIS, in re: a felony committed in Pennsylvania
E:231	12 Sep 1771	Jonathan BIDWELL a servant of Joseph STEPHENS, to serve additional time for being a runaway
E:244	11 Nov 1771	Jenkin OXLEY, 8 yrs old, to Clare OXLEY, to be a farmer Loose Papers: birthday 17 Mar 1771, son of Hannah Stevens
E:247	12 Nov 1771	Elijah MILLER, orphan, to George HEADON, Sr., to be a farmer
E:247	12 Nov 1771	John MILLER, orphan, to George HEADON, Sr., to be a farmer

Apprentices, Poor Children and Bastards 15

E:247	12 Nov 1771	Henry MILLER, orphan, to George HEADON, Sr., to be a farmer
E:247	12 Nov 1771	John LIKINS, orphan of John Likins, dec'd, to James MARTIN, to be a farmer
E:247	12 Nov 1771	William LIKINS, orphan of John Likins, dec'd, to James MARTIN, to be a farmer
E:248	12 Nov 1771	Bridget MCKNIGHT vs John WILKS, for her freedom. Petition dismissed 9 Dec 1771 E:254. (To serve for being runaway of Thomas West?, E:255)
E:279	15 Apr 1772	Daniel MATTHEWS a servant of David WILSON, discharged from further service
E:316	27 May 1772	Bryan RABBITT a servant of Hannah BROOKE, discharged from service
E:331	28 May 1772	Joseph HOMAN to Israel THOMPSON, according to terms of a former indenture
E:331	28 May 1772	Samuel HOMAN to Israel THOMPSON, according to terms of a former indenture
E:343	22 Jun 1772	Susanna TERRELL a servant of Isaac GIBSON, to serve additional time for being a runaway
E:344	23 Jun 1772	John COFFEY, orphan, to Robert HAMILTON, to be a shoemaker
E:344	23 Jun 1772	Denis MCCOLLINE, 7 yrs old on 9 Aug 1772, to Jonathan CONNARD, to be a farmer
E:363	25 Jun 1772	Thomas PARRY, a servant of Stephen ROZELL, vs Stephen ROZELL, for ill usage. Dismissed E:404 27 Aug 1772
E:369	26 Jun 1772	Jacob HEFNER, orphan, 3 yrs old in Aug 1772, to Adam SHAVER
E:370	27 Jul 1772	Nathan POTTS, orphan, about 8 yrs old, to Isaac POTTS
E:377	25 Aug 1772	Joseph NASH, orphan, 12 yrs old, to John REGOR Loose Papers: 13 Jan 1772
E:392	26 Aug 1772	Jane WEDGEWORTH, a servant, vs Fleming PATTERSON, for ill usage
E:405	27 Aug 1772	John BURNS a servant of Joshua EVANS, to serve additional time for being a runaway
E:405	27 Aug 1772	Thomas ROBINS a servant of Joshua EVANS, to serve additional time for being a runaway

E:408	27 Aug 1772	James MORGAN a servant of Alexander MCINTYRE, to serve additional time for being a runaway
E:408	27 Aug 1772	Reuben BIGGS a servant of Alexander MCINTYRE, to serve additional time for being a runaway. Same F:170
E:409	27 Aug 1772	Eleanor MCFARLANE a servant of Farling BALL, to serve additional time for being a runaway
E:423	30 Sep 1772	Mary BUCKLEY to Brooke BEALL, new indenture agreed upon
E:423	30 Sep 1772	Mary RYAN to Brooke BEALL, new indenture agreed upon
E:423	30 Sep 1772	Jane EDGSWORTH, a servant of Fleming PATTERSON, vs Fleming PATTERSON, for ill usage
E:438	26 Oct 1772	Matthew SAXTON, 14 yrs old in May 1772, to Jason THOMAS, to be a taylor
E:448	24 Nov 1772	Joseph GOING a servant of Samuel CANBY, to serve additional time to discharge a debt. See D.B. I:92 2 Oct 1772 for indenture
E:467	25 Nov 1772	Daniel HATCH a servant of Farling BALL, to serve additional time for being a runaway
E:467	25 Nov 1772	Elizabeth SMITH a servant of Alexander MCINTYRE, to serve additional time for being a runaway
E:480	27 Nov 1772	Zachariah JENKINS vs Frederick NICHOLS, for illegally detaining him as a servant. Set at liberty
E:480	27 Nov 1772	Zachariah JENKINS vs Ann GORHAM, see above
E:490	25 Jan 1773	Susanna YOUNG a servant of Stephen ROSZEL, agreed to serve additional time for having her cured of the veneral disease
E:490	25 Jan 1773	Thomas HERBERT a servant of Robert BURWELL, to serve additional time for having him cured of the veneral disease
E:493	23 Mar 1773	Nathaniel TURNER to Nathan SPENCER, to be a mason
E:505	26 Apr 1773	Lina BYRD to Thomas NICHOLLS
E:511	27 Apr 1773	John PHILLIPS, son of Ann Phillips, to Joseph STEERS, to stand bound according to the term of indenture, to be a farmer

Apprentices, Poor Children and Bastards 17

F:4	30 Apr 1773	John EGLETON's children to be bound out by CHURCHWARDENS
F:4	30 Apr 1773	Zaphaniah BRYAN to Joshua EVANS, in place of Samson Trammell who had ill treated him
F:18	1 May 1773	John BOUZIER, about 4 yrs old, son of John Ludwick Bouzier, to William DOUGLASS
F:36	11 May 1773	John MCKENSIE to John MOSS
F:36	11 May 1773	William MCKENSIE to John MOSS
F:47	11 May 1773	Francis IRWIN a servant of Thomas WEST, to serve additional time for being a runaway
F:53	12 May 1773	James Marks CLARK, baseborn child of Ann Clark, 4 yrs old in Jun 1773, to William MORLAN
F:79	14 Jun 1773	Elizabeth BALL, orphan, 10 yrs old in Oct 1773, to Jonathan MYERS
F:97	15 Jun 1773	Edward CALLIHAN, a servant of, vs William DOUGLASS, complaint of ill treatment, dismissed
F:136	9 Aug 1773	Samuel MERRIOTT, 13 yrs 1 mo 14 days, to Joseph LEWIS, to be a farmer, Robert Wright, his former master consented
F:138	9 Aug 1773	Thomas CHAPMAN, about 10 yrs old, to William MELLON, to be a farmer
F:139	9 Aug 1773	Catharine SMITH a servant of Amos DUNHAM, to serve additional time for having her cured of the venereal disease
F:139	9 Aug 1773	James MCGUIRE a servant of Isaac NICHOLS, to serve additional time for being a runaway
F:146	10 Aug 1773	Thomas CLARK a servant of William HATCHER, to serve additional time for being a runaway
F:152	10 Aug 1773	Mary GOHOGIN, 2 yrs old on 23 Mar 1773, to Daniel FEGINS
F:152	10 Aug 1773	Rose GOHOGIN, born 23 Jul 1773, to Daniel FEGINS
F:152	10 Aug 1773	William HALL, about 5 yrs old, to Nathaniel BARKER
F:152	10 Aug 1773	Eleanor COLEMAN a servant of Dempsey CARROL, to serve additional time for being a runaway
F:160	11 Aug 1773	Elizabeth SMITH vs John RIEGOR, complaint for ill usage, dismissed

Records Found in Court Order Books

F:167	12 Aug 1773	Samuel BALL, orphan of John, about 6 yrs old, to Thomas HAGUE, to be a shoemaker
F:168	12 Aug 1773	Zachariah JENKINS vs Mary GORHAM, for illegally detaining him as a servant-complaint dismissed
F:168	12 Aug 1773	Zachariah JENKINS vs John CRUPPER, for illegally detaining him as a servant-complaint dismissed
F:181	13 Sep 1773	Amos HAGUE, about 18 yrs old, to Francis HAGUE, to be a farmer
F:184	13 Sep 1773	Catharine SCANDLING a servant of James NICHOLS, to serve additional time for absence
F:186	13 Sep 1773	Darby CONNELL a servant of William HOUGH, to serve additional time for being a runaway
F:195	14 Sep 1773	Peter CRAUFORD, by his own consent, being 19 yrs old, to Charles ESKRIDGE
W.B. B:77	30 Sep 1773	John BURNS a servant of Joshua EVANS, not to pay for runaway time or expenses
W.B. B:77	30 Sep 1773	Thomas ROBINSON a servant of Joshua EVANS, not to pay for runaway time or expenses
F:231	11 Oct 1773	Evan THOMAS, son of Elizabeth Askren, to Thomas DOUGHTY, indenture of apprenticeship, to be recorded-see D.B. I:393-94, indenture dated 31 Jul 1771
F:232	11 Oct 1773	Hannah PARKER a servant of Nicholas WYCKOFF, to serve additional time for having a baseborn child
F:235	11 Oct 1773	Ruth Young HARRIS, daughter of Ann Harris, to Isaac NICKOLLS
F:236	11 Oct 1773	William FICKLIN a servant of Hannah MERRICK, to serve additional time for being a runaway
F:238	12 Oct 1773	Madlin MCGRAFF a servant of John MARK, agreed to serve one year additional time
F:239	12 Oct 1773	Samuel LUCAS to Joseph JANNEY, to be a tanner and currier
F:242	13 Oct 1773	Patrick RILEY a servant of John HERRYFORD, to serve additional time for being a runaway

Apprentices, Poor Children and Bastards

F:242	13 Oct 1773	William WILLIAMS a servant of Christopher PERFECT, to serve additional time for being a runaway
F:247	18 Nov 1773	Francis ERWIN a servant of Thomas WEST, to serve additional time for being a runaway
F:248	8 Nov 1773	Jesse CARTER, orphan, to Andrew MUIRHEAD, to be a cooper
F:251	9 Nov 1773	John THOMPSON to James BATSON
F:251	9 Nov 1773	James THOMPSON to James BATSON
F:251	9 Nov 1773	Richard HULLS a servant of Jonathan MONKHOUSE
F:271	11 Nov 1773	Abner WYATT, about 14 yrs old, to Thomas WOODFORD, to be a taylor
F:293	13 Dec 1773	Ann MCCLUSTER a servant of Thomas LEWIS, agreed to serve additional time for having her cured of the venereal disease
F:293	13 Dec 1773	An KELLY a servant of Thomas OWSLEY, agreed to serve additional time for having her cured of the venereal disease
F:297	13 Dec 1773	George CLINTON, with consent of his father, to Henry VANOVER
F:309	14 Mar 1774	John HILDROP a servant of Philip NOLAND, agreed to serve additional time for being a runaway
F:313	14 Mar 1774	Jesse WILSON to William COOK, to be a taylor
F:314	14 Mar 1774	Richard HUTSON, 13 yrs old in Sep 1774, to William FOX, Jr., to be a farmer
F:318	15 Mar 1774	Elizabeth EDWARDS a servant of George REVELY, agreed to serve additional time for having her cured of the venereal disease
F:322	15 Mar 1774	John CRADY to Christopher FLETCHER, to be a blacksmith, for 4 yrs and 5 mos
F:322	15 Mar 1774	David HINDS a servant of Robert THOMAS, to serve additional time for being a runaway
F:323	15 Mar 1774	Hanah ALFRED to Thomas MCCRACKIN Loose Papers: consent of Alcy Alford, surname given as ALFORD
F:350	11 Apr 1774	John LEWIS to Everett OXLEY, to be a weaver
F:354	11 Apr 1774	George HALL, orphan, 2 yrs old on 2 Oct 1774, to Elias ELLIS

F:356	11 Apr 1774	Thomas WILKINS a servant of Jacob RAMEY, to serve additional time for being a runaway
F:356	11 Apr 1774	Mary OXLEY, about 6 yrs old, to Jane CUMMINGS
F:369	13 Apr 1774	John MCCAFFERY, 5 yrs old 19 Feb 1774, to Benjamin WILLIAMS Loose Papers: son of Caterin McCaffery
F:399	14 Apr 1774	William PATTERSON to John Daniel MILLER, by his mother's consent
F:399	14 Apr 1774	John AUBER, a servant of, vs Thomas WEST, complaint discontinued Auber having obtained his liberty
F:444	9 May 1774	John RUSSELL, about 7 yrs old, to John GIBSON, to be a miller
F:446	9 May 1774	Margaret PASSMORE a servant of Thomas FIELDS, to serve additional time for having 2 baseborn children
F:446	9 May 1774	John KENNER a servant of John THORNTON, to serve additional time for being a runaway
F:447	9 May 1774	Isaac FLEETWOOD a servant of Samuel CANBY, to serve additional time
F:469	11 May 1774	Elizabeth SMITH a servant of John REIGER and Margaret his wife, complaint for ill usage, discontinued
W.B. B:102	27 May 1774	Jacob HARRISS, son of Ann Harriss, a servant of Edmund SANDS, to serve Joseph Sands until 21
F:481	13 Jun 1774	Christopher FISHER, 10 yrs old, to Joseph WILLIAMS
F:485	14 Jun 1774	Francis ERWIN a servant of Samuel CANBY, failed to appear in court
F:492	7 Sep 1774	James DOULING a servant of Samuel CANBY, to appear as a witness
F:492	7 Sep 1774	Mary MURPHY a servant of Samuel CANBY, to appear as a witness
F:492	7 Sep 1774	Reuben BIGGS a servant of Alexander MCINTYRE, to appear as a witness
F:495	12 Sep 1774	John STAPLETON, a servant of John HOUGH, vs John HOUGH, for illegally detaining him-discharged from further service, see F:501 re:Freedom Dues

Apprentices, Poor Children and Bastards

F:495	12 Sep 1774	John SMITH a servant of Elias JAMES, to serve additional time for being a runaway
F:496	12 Sep 1774	Daniel PURSLEY a servant of William OSBURN, to serve additional time for being a runaway
F:496	12 Sep 1774	Thomas BLACK a servant of Richard OSBURN, to serve additional time for being a runaway
F:496	12 Sep 1774	Lawrence REEDER a servant of Richard OSBURN, to serve additional time for being a runaway
F:496	12 Sep 1774	William HARRIS, with consent of his mother, to John HOUGH, Jr., to be a fuller
F:501	13 Sep 1774	James MORGAN, a servant of John Carr Jr., vs John CARR, Jr., for ill treatment. Dismissed F:506 10 Oct 1774. Another complaint F:547 8 May 1775, dismissed F:573 14 Nov 1775
F:501	13 Sep 1774	Samuel HOPEWELL, a servant of Isaac VOTAW, vs Isaac VOTAW, complaint, dismissed F:505 10 Oct 1774
F:504	10 Oct 1774	Dennis BURNS, a servant of Thomas BLINCOE, vs Thomas BLINCOE, complaint discontinued
F:505	10 Oct 1774	Eleanor MCFARLING a servant of Jonathan EWERS, to serve additional time for being a runaway
F:509	14 Nov 1774	Henry SHAW a servant of William NEILSON, to serve additional time for being a runaway
F:510	14 Nov 1774	Henry DUNCOMB, 17 yrs old in Sep 1774, to Arthur EDWARDS
F:511	14 Nov 1774	William SHUTER a servant of Charles BINNS, discharged from further service
F:512	14 Nov 1774	Michael CONNER a servant of Patrick MURRAY, to serve additional time for being a runaway
F:517	12 Dec 1774	Sally HILL, 4 yrs old on 16 Feb 1775, to John AXLINE
F:518	12 Dec 1774	Joseph SEXTON to James ROACH, to be a blacksmith, according to tenor of an indenture of Joseph and his mother
F:520	13 Dec 1774	Sarah MARTIN a servant of Henry EATON, to serve additional time for having her cured of the venereal disease

F:522	10 Jan 1775	Benjamin SCRIVENER, a servant of Samuel GUY, vs Samuel GUY, for being illegally detained
F:522	10 Jan 1775	Jesse LESTER, 5 yrs old, to Jonathan PRICE
F:529	13 Mar 1775	Thomas LAGGAX vs Jason THOMAS, Thomas to show cause why he detains Laggax in bondage
F:529	13 Mar 1775	John PRESCOAT, 9 yrs old 2 Dec 1774, to Joseph THOMAS, to be a farmer
F:537	10 Apr 1775	Hannah MISSETTS a servant of James COLEMAN, discharged from future service
F:537	10 Apr 1775	Mary HORNS a servant of Daniel BAYLES, to serve additional time for being a runaway
F:545	8 May 1775	John HUNTER, alias Retnuh, a servant of Thomson MASON, to serve additional time for being a runaway
F:545	8 May 1775	Elizabeth KELSEY a servant of Thomson MASON, to serve additional time for being a runaway
F:553	12 Jun 1775	Mary RULE a servant of James DICKEY, to serve additional time for having her cured of the venereal disease
F:555	12 Jun 1775	John William Strong TARMAN, about 12 yrs old, to John SINKLER
F:555	12 Jun 1775	William HEADON, about 14 yrs old, to Richard HEADON, until 18 yrs old
F:557	14 Aug 1775	John EDWARDS a servant of William NEILSON, to serve additional time for having him cured of the venereal disease
F:557	14 Aug 1775	Margaret LACEY a servant of William NEILSON, to serve additional time for having her cured of the venereal disease
F:557	14 Aug 1775	Tebby BEALL a servant of Rawleigh COLSEN, to serve additional time for having ? cured of the venereal disease
F:557	14 Aug 1775	Ann RUTHERFORD a servant of Rawleigh COLSON, to serve additional time for having her cured of the venereal disease
F:557	14 Aug 1775	Edward PARKER a servant of William STANHOPE, to serve additional time for being a runaway
F:558	14 Aug 1775	Samuel PETTIT, 18 yrs old, to William JONES, to be a linnin wheel maker

F:559	14 Aug 1775	James BRYANT a servant of Richard THATCHER, Jonathon PALMER, James BROWN, James NICKOLLS, John JARED, Samuel BONHAM, Elias JAMES, Robert SINCLAR, Phillip HOGLAND, George WHITECOR, to serve additional time for being a runaway, ten persons named having purchased him jointly as a schoolmaster
F:561	15 Aug 1775	Ann BRIDGMAN a servant of Thomas SELF, Self summoned to shew cause why he detains Bridgeman
F:566	11 Sep 1775	William GOODWIN to William AWBREY, to be a farmer
F:567	9 Oct 1775	Mary Ann GREEN a servant of Phillip NOLAND, Jr., to serve additional time for having a baseborn child
F:568	9 Oct 1775	John KENNY, a servant of William RASLER, vs William RASLER, for detaining him and for ill usage
F:568	13 Nov 1775	John GRAY a servant of William COCKE, to serve additional time
F:569	13 Nov 1775	Lucey BENNETT a servant of Jenkin PHILLIPS, agreed to serve additional time for having her cured of the venereal disease
F:572	14 Nov 1775	Ann BRIDGMAN to serve Josep GARDNER, Jr., her master, six months from this day
F:572	14 Nov 1775	Margaret TEMPLETON, born 9 Jan 1770, to Thomas SELF
F:572	14 Nov 1775	Ann BRIDGMAN, born 1 May 1772, to Thomas SELF
F:575	12 Feb 1776	Matthew KILLIMARE a servant of Isaac THOMPSON, to serve additional time for being a runaway
F:575	12 Feb 1776	Samuel HOPEWELL, 12 yrs old in Jun 1776, to Henry TALBERT
F:575	12 Feb 1776	Mary HOPEWELL, 14 yrs old, to Henry TALBERT
F:575	12 Feb 1776	Thomas BIRD a servant of Samuel GARNER, to serve additional time for being a runaway
F:575	12 Feb 1776	Mary PRESCOAT to Joseph THOMAS
F:575	12 Feb 1776	Isaac FLEETWOOD a servant of Samuel CANBY, to serve additional time for being a runaway

Records Found in Court Order Books

F:576	12 Feb 1776	Henry BRYANT, 8 yrs old 1 Feb 1776, to Jacob PHESIL
F:576	13 Feb 1776	Richard TILTON an apprentice of George MUIRHEAD, set at liberty
F:577	13 Feb 1776	Mary NEALE a servant of John NORTON, by mutual consent discharged from service
F:579	11 Mar 1776	Jeremiah HEATH a servant of Stephen DONALDSON, to serve additional time for being a runaway
F:584	12 Mar 1776	Elizabeth REDMOND, about 13 yrs old, to James RATTIKIN
F:586	8 Apr 1776	John CAHILL a servant of Isaac THOMPSON, agreed to serve additional time for having him cured of the venereal disease
F:586	8 Apr 1776	Michael KILLIHARE a servant of Isaac THOMPSON, to serve additional time for being a runaway
F:591	13 May 1776	Phebe SIMMS, 5 yrs old in Feb 1776, to Jonas JANNEY
F:591	13 May 1776	John SHEDD, 14 yrs old, to Thomas MILLAN, to be a taylor
F:592	13 May 1776	John PALMER, 2 yrs 9 mo old, to Elizabeth BOYD
F:593	13 May 1776	Mary MURPHEY, a servant of Samuel CANBY, vs Samuel CANBY, complaint concerning her freedom. Complaint dismissed F:596 10 Jun 1776
F:595	10 Jun 1776	Susanna YOUNG a servant of Peter HARBOUT, to serve additional time for having a base born child
F:595	10 Jun 1776	John MCCANN, about 9 yrs old in Oct 1776, to David BEATTEY
F:596	10 Jun 1776	George CLARK to George WILSON, Sr.
F:596	10 Jun 1776	Rhody MALONE, a base born child of Martha Malone, to James SAUNDERS
F:597	10 Jun 1776	Abraham GRAY, 7 yrs old in May 1776, to Daniel LEWIS
G:2	12 Aug 1776	Edward LEE a servant of Adam MITCHELL, to serve additional time, - absent - , runaway?

Apprentices, Poor Children and Bastards 25

G:2	12 Aug 1776	Elizabeth LAPPINGTON a servant of Mary EVANS, to serve additional time for having a base born child. Sep, 1777, G:55 (same order)
G:2	12 Aug 1776	Patk HOLDREN a servant of Farling BALL, agreed to serve an additional two months
G:3	12 Aug 1776	Stephen DONALDSON, orphan, son of John, 9 yrs old, to Stephen DONALDSON, to be a gold and silversmith
G:3	12 Aug 1776	James DONALDSON, 14 yrs old, to Samuel MURRAY, to be a cordwainer
G:3	12 Aug 1776	John PATTERSON a servant of Stephen DONALDSON, to serve additional time for absence
W.B. B:201	20 Aug 1776	Elizabeth PATTEN a servant of James MARTIN, to have 10 pounds current money when she comes of age
W.B. B:201	20 Aug 1776	Anthony SWICK a servant of James MARTIN, to have 20 pounds current money in addition to Freedom Dues when he comes of age
G:7	13 Jan 1777	Thomas BIRD a servant of John HANKS, to serve additional time for absence
G:12	10 Feb 1777	Mary Ann GREEN a servant of Philip NOLAND, discharged from service
G:18	10 Mar 1777	Stephen FISHER to William SMITH, to be a weaver
G:18	10 Mar 1777	William Hampton FISHER to William SMITH, to be a weaver
G:18	10 Mar 1777	John HARRIS to Oliver PRICE, to be a sadler
G:18	10 Mar 1777	Sarah HARRIS to Oliver PRICE
G:19	10 Mar 1777	Thomas KELLY, about 3 yrs old in Aug 1776, base born, to Charles ESKRIDGE
G:21	11 Mar 1777	Charles TYLER, orphan of Ann Tyler, dec'd, to be bound out
G:21	11 Mar 1777	Benjamin TYLER, orphan of Ann Tyler, dec'd, to be bound out
G:22	11 Mar 1777	Henry TAYLOR to Jason MORELAND, to be a carpenter
G:23	11 Mar 1777	Ann PURSELL a servant of Richard STEPHENS, to serve additional time for being a runaway

G:24	14 Apr 1777	Miller HOGUE, about 13 yrs old, to William HARRIS, to be a tanner
G:26	15 Apr 1777	Thomas BURSON to Samuel BUTCHER
G:27	15 Apr 1777	Thomas COPPER a servant of William OSBORNE, to serve additional time for being absent
G:27	15 Apr 1777	William NANBE a servant of John OSBORNE, to serve additional time for being absent
G:27	15 Apr 1777	Christinia STEWART a servant of Robert FRYER, to serve additional time for being absent
G:27	15 Apr 1777	Mary THORNTON, 3 yrs old, to John HAYNES
G:28	15 Apr 1777	Jane THORNTON, 5 yrs 3 mos old, to Richard GREGG
G:28	15 Apr 1777	Mordecai THORNTON, 7 yrs old, to Eneas JOHNS, to be a weaver
G:35	12 May 1777	Priscilla , an Indian child, to William ROGERS
G:36	12 May 1777	Enoch MALES to Elias COCKERILL
G:36	12 May 1777	Elisha HAZELL to William JONES, to be a maker of spinning wheels
G:36	12 May 1777	Mary RIGNEY to Henry SMITH
G:36	12 May 1777	Anne RIND a servant of Elias JAMES, to serve additional time for being a runaway and for having a base born child
G:47	11 Aug 1777	Nan THOMAS a servant of Thomas GIBSON, agreed to serve additional time for having her cured of the venereal disease
G:47	11 Aug 1777	Joshua WILSON to John MARKS, Jr., to be a Shoemaker
G:47	11 Aug 1777	Jacob PLYMEALL, orphan, 13 yrs old, to Peter GRAHAM
G:47	11 Aug 1777	Barbara PLYMEALL, orphan, 11 yrs old, to Peter GRAHAM
G:52	8 Sep 1777	Eleanor MCINERNY a servant of George SUMMERS, to serve additional time for having a baseborn child
G:55	8 Sep 1777	Madlin MCGEATH a servant of John MARKS, Sr., to serve additional time for having a baseborn child

G:55	8 Sep 1777	Barnard HOUGH to John HOUGH, Jr., to be a cloathier
G:55	8 Sep 1777	Liney WHEESE (WHUSE?), 5 yrs old 14 Aug 1777, to John SONGSTER
G:55	8 Sep 1777	__ LAPPINGTON, base born child of Elizabeth Lappington, to Mary EVANS
G:55	8 Sep 1777	William NINBY a servant of John OSBORN, Jr., to serve additional time for being absent
G:57	8 Sep 1777	John MCCARTY a servant of Thompson MASON, to serve additional time for being a runaway
G:63	13 Oct 1777	Thomas FEATHERSTONE a servant of Samuel COX, to serve additional time for being a runaway
G:63	13 Oct 1777	Henry MCKENZEY, 1 yr old on 15 Dec 1777, to Joseph LAY, to be a farmer
G:63	13 Oct 1777	Ann COLLINS, 5 yrs old, to William BUCKLEY
G:63	13 Oct 1777	William COLLINS, 4 yrs old, to William Bearnard SEARS
G:63	13 Oct 1777	Jonathan CHURCH, 12 yrs old next spring, to Charles LITTLETON, to be a farmer
G:63	13 Oct 1777	Nash NEWMAN a servant of William RIGHT, to return and serve out his full time
G:64	13 Oct 1777	Edward DYALL, 11 yrs old next spring, to William FOX, to be a farmer
G:70	8 Dec 1777	John KELLY, about 10 yrs old, to William SMITH, to be a weaver
G:77	10 Mar 1778	Christopher PROKER to Edward CAVINS
G:82	14 Apr 1778	Mary KELLY a servant of Charles ESKRIDGE, entitled to her freedom and discharged from servitude
G:90	11 May 1778	James BROHON to Samuel BOYD
G:91	12 May 1778	Thomas KELLY, alias Byrns, to Charles ESKRIDGE
G:91	12 May 1778	James CROSS to John PARRY, to be a blacksmith
G:92	12 May 1778	Margaret LEESON a servant of William NEILSON, to serve additional time for having two base born children
G:94	12 May 1778	Mary ANDERSON a servant of Nicholas WYCOFF, confessed she had four years to serve from 1 Mar 1778

G:94	12 May 1778	Thomas DOUGHERTY, base born son of Mary Dougherty, to Charles WEST
G:94	12 May 1778	Henry ANDERSON, base born child of Margaret Anderson, a servant of Nicholas Wycoff, to Nicholas WYCOFF
G:94	12 May 1778	Andrew BAILY, base born son of Sarah Baily, a servant of Joseph Lacey, to be bound
G:95	12 May 1778	Hannah BARTHOLOMEW to Samuel COX
G:99	8 Jun 1778	Thomas OLIVER to Richard HURST, to be a weaver
G:102	8 Jun 1778	Jane WILLIAMS, about 5 yrs 5 mo old, to Matthew WHITE
G:102	8 Jun 1778	Mary WINDSOR to George KILGORE
G:103	8 Jun 1778	Madlin MCGRAFF a servant of Robert MCWHARTER, to serve additional time for having a base born child
G:103	8 Jun 1778	John MORRIS a servant of Henry MCCABE, complaint of ill usage
G:109	9 Jun 1778	Bridget CONNOR a servant of Alexander MCINTYRE, to serve additional time for absence and for having a base born child. G:118, 11 Aug 1778, more time for absence
G:112	10 Aug 1778	John PROHEN to John ROGERS
G:112	10 Aug 1778	Rebecca YOUNG to William SMITH
G:113	10 Aug 1778	John THOMSON, orphan, to Henry DOWNER, to be a shoemaker
G:113	10 Aug 1778	James THOMSON to Benjamin DOWNS
G:113	10 Aug 1778	William WILLIAMSON to James WILLIAMSON
G:114	10 Aug 1778	John BATES to William LEWIS
G:114	10 Aug 1778	Mary PEEL, 7 yrs old, to Alexander DRUMGOLD
G:115	10 Aug 1778	Jonathan SHEDD, orphan, to be bound
G:115	10 Aug 1778	Sarah ATKINS a servant of William BOYD, to serve until debt discharged
G:118	11 Aug 1778	Mary HORN a servant of Alexander MCINTYRE, discharged from service being a free woman
G:119	14 Sep 1778	Abraham LAPPINGTON, 5 yrs old, 12 Mar 1778, to Mary EVANS

Apprentices, Poor Children and Bastards

G:120	14 Sep 1778	James BUTLER, mulatto orphan, a servant of Hardage LANE, to serve until 25 Dec 1779 for being a runaway, etc.
G:120	14 Sep 1778	Charles PRESLEY, 14 yrs old, 2 Aug 1778, to Thomas HARBERT
G:129	9 Nov 1778	Henry ANDERSON to Phinehas SKINNER, see G:183, 10 Aug 1779, Henry Martin alias Anderson
G:130	9 Nov 1778	Robert HENARD, 15 yrs old, to Josias MILES, to be a bricklayer
G:133	10 Nov 1778	Ann GOHAGAN a servant of Nathaniel GRIGSBY, to serve additional time for having a base born child and said child is bound to said Grigsby
G:134	10 Nov 1778	Bridget CONNER a servant of Alexander MCINTYRE, to serve additional time until debt is paid
G:134	10 Nov 1778	Ann KELLY a servant of Richard CARTER, to serve additional time for her absence
G:135	14 Dec 1778	Vincent MANLY to William MCCLELAN
G:136	14 Dec 1778	Sarah GRANGER a servant of Joseph LACEY, to serve additional time for having two base born children
G:140	8 Feb 1779	Jane BALL, mulatto, to William EVANS
G:140	8 Feb 1779	Thomas COLLENS, orphan of Thomas Collens, Sr., dec'd, 15 yrs old last Xmas, to John SIMPSON, to be a cordwainer
G:143	9 Feb 1779	John CROSS to Vincent LEWIS
G:147	8 Mar 1779	Jane THOMPSON a servant of John TODHUNTER, to serve additional time for being a runaway
G:147	8 Mar 1779	John COLLINS, by consent of his mother, to William CAVENS
G:147	8 Mar 1779	Joseph COLLINS, by consent of his mother, to John HENRY, Jr.,
G:158	13 Apr 1779	Mary HUGHS to Enoch THOMAS
G:166	10 May 1779	Ann GLIBBING to Amos DONHAM
G:166	10 May 1779	James WILLIAMS to Henry OWSLEY
G:168	10 May 1779	Sarah MARTIN a servant of William TAYLOR, to serve additional time
G:171	14 Jun 1779	Nelly TULLY taken from Thomas JENKINS
G:171	14 Jun 1779	Nelly TULLY to John LITTLEJOHN for 18 mos

Records Found in Court Order Books

G:172	14 Jun 1779	George TWEEDY a servant of Thomas FIELDS, to serve until account discharged
G:173	14 Jun 1779	George CLARK to Catherine WILSON
G:173	14 Jun 1779	Mary SMILEY to John ROGERS
G:179	9 Aug 1779	Elizabeth POLAND to Elizabeth BURTON
G:179	9 Aug 1779	Jeremiah BURNS a servant of Thomson MASON, to serve additional time for absence
G:179	9 Aug 1779	James BANNING a servant of Thomson MASON, to serve additional time for absence
G:179	9 Aug 1779	Elizabeth HUNTER a servant of Thomson MASON, to serve additional time for having a base born child
G:180	9 Aug 1779	Samuel HANRICK, a servant of Richard ANDERSON, vs Richard ANDERSON, for ill usage and for his freedom G:201, 11 Oct 1779, returned to his master & complaint contd. G:215, 9 Nov 1779, complaint discontinued
G:181	9 Aug 1779	Samuel PUGH, about 11 yrs old, to Spencer PUGH, to be a weaver
G:182	9 Aug 1779	John PHILIPS to John MCFARLING
G:182	9 Aug 1779	Thomas JEWELL to John MCFARLING
G:182	9 Aug 1779	Winifred JEWELL to John MCFARLING
G:203	11 Oct 1779	Joseph HUNTER, a servant of William BRAWNER, vs William BRAWNER, a complaint
G:204	11 Oct 1779	Ann LANE to Richard ANDERSON
G:207	12 Oct 1779	Daniel SAXON, 14 yrs old, to Jonathan PRICE
G:212	8 Nov 1779	Thomas SHIELDS, 14 yrs old, to Benjamin HUTCHISON
G:215	9 Nov 1779	Samuel HANRICK to Richard ANDERSON, to be a shoemaker
G:218	9 Nov 1779	Thomas Weldon WATSON to George HAMMETT, to be a cordwainer
G:224	14 Feb 1780	Joseph BOWLING to Jacob DEHAVEN Loose Papers: for 7 yrs, to be a blacksmith, by agreement of his mother, Elizabeth (name spelled Boling on indenture). Indenture found

Apprentices, Poor Children and Bastards 31

G:227	15 Feb 1780	Mary ANDERSON a servant of Jonathan DAVIS, to serve additional time for having a base born child
G:228	13 Mar 1780	James COHORNE to Benjamin BROWN
G:228	13 Mar 1780	Robert COHORNE to Benjamin BROWN
G:229	13 Mar 1780	Vincent MANLY to William BEAVERS
G:230	13 Mar 1780	Linny MARTIN, orphan, to John LITTLEJOHN
G:238	11 Apr 1780	John ROTH, 15 yrs old, by consent of his mother, Christian Roth, to Robert DEANE, to be a tanner or shoemaker
G:244	8 May 1780	Robert WHITAKER, 3 yrs old in Jul 1780, to John TODHUNTER
G:244	8 May 1780	Ned RATCLIFF, a servant of, vs Josias CLAPHAM, discharged from service
G:247	12 Jun 1780	James FOX, mulatto, to James ORAM Loose Papers: son of Ann Fox
G:247	12 Jun 1780	William POLING to Nathaniel PEGG
G:247	12 Jun 1780	Nathaniel POLING to Nathaniel PEGG
G:250	13 Jun 1780	John SHANNON to John RICHCREEK
G:251	13 Jun 1780	Thomas HARDIN, base born child of Catharine Hardin, to William HUTCHISON
G:251	13 Jun 1780	Mary DODSON, daughter of Thomas Dodson, Jr., to William HUTCHISON
G:251	13 Jun 1780	Elizabeth Chelton BRIDGMAN to Presly and Othania, his wife SELF
G:255	14 Aug 1780	Lewis MASSEY to Benjamin HUFFTY, to be a saddler Loose Papers: son of Ann White (wife of Thomas) and of Lewis Massey, deceased
G:256	14 Aug 1780	Mary KEMPE to Abraham LEWIS
G:256	14 Aug 1780	Dorcas MANLY to John TURLEY Loose Papers: consent of Sarah Manley (indenture of 20 Feb 1777 not agreeable to law)
G:256	14 Aug 1780	Benjamin MANLY to John TURLEY Loose Papers: consent of Sarah Manley (indenture of 20 Feb 1777 not agreeable to law)
G:257	14 Aug 1780	Amos HIBBS to Enoch THOMAS, to be a weaver Loose Papers: son of Rachel McGoughey
G:257	14 Aug 1780	Aaron FRYREAR to Isaac VANDEVANTER

Records Found in Court Order Books

G:257	14 Aug 1780	Francis FRYREAR to John HENRY, Sr.,
G:257	14 Aug 1780	Jeremiah FRYREAR to John HENRY, Jr.,
G:286	11 Sep 1780	James BANNING a servant of Thompson MASON, agreed to enlist for 18 mo in VA troops if required by T. Mason
G:286	11 Sep 1780	Daniel NEALE a servant of Thompson MASON, agreed to enlist for 18 mo in VA troops if required by T. Mason
G:286	11 Sep 1780	Miller HOGE to Israel THOMPSON, to be a tanner
G:286	11 Sep 1780	Morgan HOGE to William HOGE
G:293	9 Oct 1780	__ BURTON to be bound
G:299	13 Nov 1780	Joseph HOGUE to Israel JANNEY Loose Papers: born 10 Jul 1769, gr-son of William Hoge, son of Joseph Hoge, deceased
G:303	14 Nov 1780	Joseph SIMONS, now 12 yrs old, was bound by his father Simon Simons, vs Nathaniel SKINNER, removed from N. Skinner
G:306	15 Nov 1780	Samuel HAGUE to William SCHOOLEY, Jr., to be a blacksmith Loose Papers: 15 yrs old, son of Ann Wildman
G:307	15 Nov 1780	Edward TUGWELL to John MCCLAIN
G:314	8 Jan 1781	Bazel REAGAN to George HAGERLY, to be a taylor
G:314	8 Jan 1781	Elizabeth PATTEN to Isaac WALKER
G:318	12 Feb 1781	James BENHAM, orphan of Peter Benham, to Samuel COX
G:318	12 Feb 1781	Nathaniel BENHAM, orphan of Peter Benham, to Samuel COX
G:318	12 Feb 1781	Hannah DAVIS, 11 yrs old, to Peter MORGERT
G:318	12 Feb 1781	James DONALDSON, orphan, 18 yrs old, to Stephen DONALDSON, to be a gold and silversmith
G:319	12 Mar 1781	Mary Ann SHRIEVES to Joseph THOMAS Loose Papers: 8 yrs old, 27 Aug 1780, dau of Mary Shively
G:320	12 Mar 1781	Henny MANLY to Peter HARMON Loose Papers: dau. of Ann Manly
G:320	12 Mar 1781	Joseph SIMCOCK, 4 yrs old, to Andrew SMITH, mother gave consent

Apprentices, Poor Children and Bastards

G:333	11 Apr 1781	Bridget CONNER vs Alexander MCINTIRE, for detaining her in servitude, complaint dismissed
G:350	11 Apr 1781	Mary MACKEY a servant of Stephen DONALDSON, to serve additional time for having a base born mulatto child
G:350	11 Apr 1781	Anthony MACKEY, 2 yrs old 7 Aug 1780, mulatto child of Mary Mackey, to Stephen DONALDSON
G:356	14 May 1781	Elizabeth Gussett SIMPKINS, born 9 Mar 1777, to Jacob SLATOR
G:361	15 May 1781	Benjamin CANARY, orphan of Richard Canary, dec'd, to Henry LAFEVERS
G:361	15 May 1781	Nancy CANARY, orphan of Richard Canary, dec'd, to Henry LAFEVERS
G:367	15 May 1781	John MCDANNIEL, 10 yrs old, to James COLEMAN
G:369	11 Jun 1781	Margaret BOULTON, 1 yr old in Apr 1781, to James ORAM
G:369	11 Jun 1781	Isaac Spurr TEMPLETON to Elizabeth SELF
G:369	11 Jun 1781	Peter Pelter BRIDGMAN to Elizabeth SELF
G:369	11 Jun 1781	David MARSHALL to Joseph COX, to be a farmer
G:369	11 Jun 1781	Mary COMPTON, about 8 yrs old, to Isaac VANDEVANTER
G:370	11 Jun 1781	Wethers SMITH to Andrew SPECHT, to be a hatter
G:371	13 Aug 1781	Thomas HENDERSON, 6 yrs old in Mar 1781, to James RATTEKIN
G:372	13 Aug 1781	John SAXTON, about 15 yrs old, to Israel THOMPSON, to be a tanner and shoemaker
G:374	10 Sep 1781	John Mason WRIGHT, about 7 yrs old, base born child of Mary Wright, to Robert BEATY
G:374	10 Sep 1781	Dennis HOPEWELL, 7 yrs old, baseborn child of Ann Bursley, to John BERKINS, to be a woolcomber
G:375	8 Oct 1781	Bernard CREAMER, 5 yrs 1 mo old, to Bernard MANN
G:377	12 Nov 1781	Joseph SIMONS, son of Simon Simons and Amey Simons, to Nathaniel SKINNER, Indenture of Apprenticeship recorded D.B. N:237, to be a farmer until 21 yrs old, being now 9 yrs 15 Jul 1777

Records Found in Court Order Books

G:382	11 Feb 1782	Nathaniel GRYMES to William BARKER
G:382	11 Feb 1782	Daniel GRYMES to William BARKER
G:382	11 Feb 1782	Samuel BALL, apprentice, vs Thomas HAGUE, complaint
G:389	9 Apr 1782	John KELLEY, orphan apprentice, vs William SMITH, complaint, G:410, 8 Jul 1782, released from apprenticeship
G:390	9 Apr 1782	William PAYNE, son of Rachel Payne, to Joseph REED
G:395	13 May 1782	Mary CASTOR, orphan of Vincent Castor, to Philip NOLAND, Jr.,
G:396	13 May 1782	John AGGLETON, age 16 in Aug 1781, to Francis MCCLAIN
G:396	13 May 1782	Anne AGGLETON, 14 yrs old, to Francis MCCLAIN
G:396	13 May 1782	William AGGLETON, 8 yrs old 7 Sep 1781, to Francis MCCLAIN
G:401	14 May 1782	Zachariah JEWELL, 4 yrs old in Aug 1782, to John DALKIN Loose Papers: youngest son of Martha Jewell, also to Catherine Dalkin, wife of John
G:407	10 Jun 1782	Jemima MANLY, 3 yrs old, to Peter HARMON
G:407	10 Jun 1782	Linney COTTERIL to William DRISH, until age 18, formerly bound to John Littlejohn
G:410	8 Jul 1782	John KELLEY, orphan, to Benjamin SHRIEVES, of Alexandria, to be a hatter, formerly bound to William Smith
G:413	12 Aug 1782	Christopher PROHON, by consent of his mother and Edward Cavins, to John CAVINS Loose Papers: formerly bound to Edward Cavins, Cateron Prohorn his mother
G:414	12 Aug 1782	John HOLLAND, 10 yrs old 9 Mar 1782; to Stephen MCPHERSON, Jr., to be a blacksmith Loose Papers: Elonder Holland his mother
G:414	12 Aug 1782	Thomas PEDICOART, about 4 yrs 8 mo old, to John WALLACE
G:414	12 Aug 1782	George LAPPINGTON, near 6 yrs old, to George LOFLIN
G:416	12 Aug 1782	James DRAKE, 6 yrs old 10 Apr 1782, to William ELLIOTT
G:416	12 Aug 1782	John TRAMMELL, als Elliott, 6 yrs old, to William ELLIOTT

Apprentices, Poor Children and Bastards 35

G:416	12 Aug 1782	Samson TRAMMELL, 2 yrs old in Oct 1781, to William ELLIOTT
G:416	12 Aug 1782	Mary MCCARTY, 8 yrs old in Mar 1783, to James MARSHALL
G:429	9 Sep 1782	Elizabeth POLAND, apprentice, orphan, vs Elizabeth BURTON, petition to be discharged from service
G:430	9 Sep 1782	Joseph DYERS to William SMITH
G:457	11 Nov 1782	Hewin HETHERLIN, orphan of John Hetherlin, dec'd, to William WOLLARD
G:457	11 Nov 1782	Benjamin HETHERLIN, orphan of John Hetherlin, dec'd, to William WOLLARD
G:457	11 Nov 1782	James HETHERLIN, 12 yrs old 20 Dec 1782, to Thomas SANDERS
G:457	11 Nov 1782	Nathan HETHERLIN, 7 yrs old 15 Nov 1782, to Thomas SANDERS
G:460	11 Nov 1782	Thomas CREAMOUR to John COPREY Loose Papers: 13 yrs old, son of Elizabeth Wagner, formerly Cramer
G:460	11 Nov 1782	Jacob CREAMOUR to Henry WOLF Loose Papers: 7 yrs old, son of Elizabeth Wagner, formerly Cramer
G:476	9 Dec 1782	John SHAW, 4 yrs old in Jun 1783, to William WYCKOFF, to be a farmer Loose Papers: Mary Shaw his mother
G:476	9 Dec 1782	Charity MCCANN, 15 yrs old, to Isaac STEERE
G:477	9 Dec 1782	Christian HEMMERY to Bernard MANN
G:483	10 Feb 1783	Elisha MCFARLING, by agreement, to James MCCLANACHAN, to be a taylor, for 3 yrs from 1 Feb 1783
G:493	10 Mar 1783	William RAW (RAU) to Peter EBLIN
G:499	11 Mar 1783	Betty LANDERS, 11 yrs old in Oct 1782, orphan of George Landers, to Adam LONG, H:388, 14 Sep 1784, Roger Landers complains on behalf of daughter Elizabeth against Adam Long
G:502	11 Mar 1783	Ruth MCKNIGHT, 2 yrs old in May 1782, mulattoe, to Henry POTTON
G:502	11 Mar 1783	Thomas VIRGIN, 2 yrs old in Jan 1783, to Andrew CALOR
G:514	14 Apr 1783	Morgan HOGE, by consent of William Hoge, to James MOORE

Records Found in Court Order Books

G:515	14 Apr 1783	Chloe JOHNSTON, daughter of Sarah Stapleton, to William MILLAN
G:516	14 Apr 1783	Isaac RIGNEY, 10 yrs old in Oct 1782, to Jeremiah THOMAS
H:26	13 May 1783	Anna Muriah BARTHAST, alias Harper, about 7 yrs old, to Samuel CANBY
H:26	13 May 1783	Uriah, 6 yrs old in Dec 1783, mulatto, to Samuel CANBY
H:28	13 May 1783	William MCCANN, about 14 yrs old, to Samuel CANBY, to be a papermaker
H:64	16 May 1783	Richard to Alexander MCMAKEN, agreeable to the indentures of his father and mother
H:73	17 May 1783	Richard HARRIS, about 5 yrs old, to James KIRK
H:77	9 Jun 1783	Mary PETIT, 7 yrs old in Aug 1783, to Peter OVERFELT
H:78	9 Jun 1783	Fleming WILSON to James MCCLANINGHAM, to be a taylor
H:79	9 Jun 1783	Alexander TAVERNER, 14 yrs old on 24 Mar 1783, to Jacob WILDMAN
H:86	11 Aug 1783	Lydia BENHAM, orphan of Peter Benham, to Amariah BONHAM
H:88	11 Aug 1783	Thomas WARD, 4 yrs old 12 Dec 1783, to John SHEPHERD
H:88	11 Aug 1783	Robert SPENCER, 4 yrs old in Dec 1782, to Dempsey CARROLL
H:124	15 Aug 1783	Charles DRISH vs John WEAVER, for wrongfully detaining him as a servant
H:139	8 Sep 1783	Elizabeth HENDERSON, 6 yrs old 15 Oct 1783, to Andrew BROWN
H:140	8 Sep 1783	Sarah ENNES, 3 yrs old in Mar 1783, to Joseph WALLACE
H:141	8 Sep 1783	Levina STEPHENS, 12 yrs old in Jan 1784, to Thomas SANDERS
H:141	8 Sep 1783	Elizabeth ESSEX, 6 yrs old 29 Sep 1783, to Thomas SANDERS
H:146	13 Oct 1783	Elizabeth LACEY to John & Ruth PANCOAST
H:146	13 Oct 1783	William LACEY to John & Ruth PANCOAST
H:146	13 Oct 1783	Sarah RUSSELL, 4 yrs old in Feb 1783, to James ROACH, agreeable to a memorandum

Apprentices, Poor Children and Bastards 37

H:146	13 Oct 1783	Jonas THOMPSON, 11 yrs old 16 Jul 1783, to Elisha JANNEY
H:190	10 Nov 1783	Joseph BLINCOE to George SHIVELY
H:196	8 Dec 1783	Peter COLEMAN to Alexander MCMAKEN
H:197	8 Dec 1783	Thomas SHIELDS to Jacob MOORE, former master having agreed thereto
H:224	13 Apr 1784	John MATTHEWS to Isaac VOTAW Loose Papers: son of John & Mary Milner
H:224	13 Apr 1784	Joseph HOGUE, removed from Israel Janney, to William SMITH, to be a cooper
H:228	13 Apr 1784	Samuel EVANS to Mahlon SMITH, to be a sadler
H:231	13 Apr 1784	Keziah VIRGIN to George WILLIS
H:235	14 Apr 1784	Jeptha MOORE to Stephen DONALDSON, to be a goldsmith Loose Papers: 13 yrs old in Apr 1784, indenture found
H:268	10 May 1784	William WILLYARD to John SHORT Loose Papers: 2 yrs old, son of Catharin Wilyard of Frederick Co., MD, also to Catharin, wife of John
H:274	10 May 1784	Lucy OGDON, daughter of Cornelius Ogdon, to John STEER
H:280	10 May 1784	Samuel GRAHAM, 5 yrs old this day, to William LITTLETON
H:283	11 May 1784	Bartholomew LEESE to Conrod BITZER
H:312	14 Jun 1784	Margaret BAXTER, 10 yrs old in Feb 1784, to Joseph REED
H:312	14 Jun 1784	Elizabeth BAXTER, 8 yrs old in Dec 1783, to Joseph REED
H:325	15 Jun 1784	Sarah HOLMES, 13 yrs old 4 Jan 1784, to Henry BROWN
H:328	15 Jun 1784	John DRISH to Samuel SMITH, to be a house joiner
H:361	9 Aug 1784	Catharine FRY, 7 yrs old 21 Mar 1784, to William JONES Loose Papers: Mary Fry her mother
H:362	9 Aug 1784	John COCKRILL to Nathaniel ADAMS Loose Papers: 4 yrs old, son of Sebithery Cockreal
H:364	9 Aug 1784	Abraham ANDERSON, 8 yrs old 8 Jan 1784, to Moses CALDWELL

H:376	13 Sep 1784	John JENKINS, 8 yrs old in Jun 1784, to Henry DOWNS
H:376	13 Sep 1784	Abraham SKILLMAN to Moses HOUGH
H:378	14 Sep 1784	John SHANNON to James WILSON, to be a shoemaker Loose Papers: son of Mary Shannon
H:378	14 Sep 1784	John GOLDING, 3 yrs old this mo., to William REDWOOD
H:379	14 Sep 1784	Thomas BYRNS, 12 yrs old in Oct 1783, to George HAMMETT, to be a shoemaker
H:409	11 Oct 1784	William RIGNEY to John COFFEY
H:419	8 Nov 1784	Elijah CROSS to Capt. Joseph LEWIS
H:419	8 Nov 1784	Joseph CROSS to George LEWIS
H:420	8 Nov 1784	Aaron WILSON, 12 yrs old 6 Oct 1784, to George NIXSON
H:426	9 Nov 1784	Mary LEWIS, mulatto, daughter of a white woman, 19 yrs old, vs Robert STEPHENS, adjudged a free mulatto and discharged from service
H:443	14 Jan 1785	Alexander EVANS, 8 yrs old 9 Dec 1784, to Samuel SPENCER
H:443	14 Jan 1785	Allen SMITH, 8 yrs old 3 Apr 1784, orphan of James Smith, to Nathan SPENCER
H:443	14 Jan 1785	William ENNIS, 18 mo. old, to James RENNICK
H:445	14 Feb 1785	Reuben SQUIRES, 14 yrs old in Jan 1785, to George SQUIRES
H:445	14 Feb 1785	Barton NAILER, 15 yrs old, to James REED
H:454	15 Mar 1785	Jeremiah MCGAHEY, 9 yrs old 15 Jun 1785, to Jacob SHAVOR (SHOVER), to be a weaver
H:455	15 Mar 1785	Thomas PETERSON, 17 yrs old 1 Jan 1785, to Levi PRINCE
H:462	12 Apr 1785	Jeremiah MURPHEY a servant of Hugh STEUART, to serve additional time for being a runaway
H:469	12 Apr 1785	William ROBINSON, born 29 May 1780, to Edward ADAMS Loose Papers: son of Jane Robinson
H:469	12 Apr 1785	Henry ROBINSON, born 1 Jun 1782, to Edward ADAMS Loose Papers: son of Jane Robinson
H:475	9 May 1785	Betty SMITH, 13 yrs old, to John HOUGH

Apprentices, Poor Children and Bastards

H:475	9 May 1785	Alexander SMITH, 5 yrs old, to John HOUGH
H:476	9 May 1785	Christopher SKILLMAN, 18 yrs old in Mar 1785, to Cornelius SKINNER, to be a carpenter
H:478	9 May 1785	Samuel CHUNN, 12 yrs old 19 Mar 1785, to John WREN Loose Papers: son of Mary Chun
H:480	9 May 1785	William HOLLIDAY, 1 yr old 7 Sep 1785, to John WINDGROVE Loose Papers: surnames given as Holyday and Wingrove, son of Ann Holyday
H:480	9 May 1785	Joseph WOODFORD, 17 yrs old 9 Sep 1784, to John TRIBBY
H:483	9 May 1785	Alexander SMITH, about 14 yrs old, to William WOOLLARD Loose Papers: son of Ann Oxley
H:483	9 May 1785	Mary WEAVER, 14 yrs old 4 May 1785, to Philip FRYE
H:483	9 May 1785	Elizabeth WEAVER, 7 yrs old in Oct 1784, to Michael BOGAR
H:485	10 May 1785	Sarah WILKERSON, 8 yrs old, to John HOUGH
H:491	10 May 1785	John PUGH, born 1 Apr 1777, to John OSBORNE Loose Papers: son of Charity Boide
H:498	10 May 1785	William Gunnell SANDERS, 16 yrs old 16 Feb 1785, to Edward STEPHENS, to be a blacksmith
H:498	10 May 1785	Joel OXLEY, 13 yrs old in Feb 1785, to James STEPHENS
I:29	13 Jun 1785	Carr Wilson LANE, 15 yrs old, to John WILSON, to be a joiner
I:29	13 Jun 1785	Ebur POOL, 1 yr old 25 Jul 1784, to James DILLON, to be a farmer Loose Papers: son of Martha Pool
I:58	8 Aug 1785	James HAGUE to William ROBERTS, at request of his mother Sarah Hague
I:59	8 Aug 1785	Elizabeth Chelton BRIDGMAN, 5 yrs old 1 Jan 1782, to Presley SELF Loose Papers: dau. of Ann Bridgman
I:62	8 Aug 1785	John BODINE, 17 yrs old in Jan 1786, to Nathan COCKRANE, to be a blacksmith, indenture found

I:67	9 Aug 1785	Mary MACRO, 8 yrs this month, to George LEWIS Loose Papers: dau. of Ann Simons
I:68	9 Aug 1785	Sarah MCCRO, 6 yrs old 13 Apr 1785, to John WILLIAMS Loose Papers: dau. of Ann Simons
I:78	12 Sep 1785	Dennis HOUPT, 11 yrs old 5 Sep 1785, to John BERKIN, to be a farmer Loose Papers: step-son of Edward Bennett
I:80	12 Sep 1785	John RIELY a servant of Leven POWELL, to serve additional time for being a runaway
I:81	12 Sep 1785	John ELIAS to James MCKINZEY Loose Papers: surname given as Ellis, son of Elizabeth John
I:84	12 Sep 1785	John COOK, 12 yrs old, to James HAMILTON, to be a shoemaker
I:87	12 Sep 1785	Thomas BROWN, 18 yrs old 11 Oct 1784, to Asa MOORE, to be a sadler Loose Papers: son of Sarah Brown
I:87	12 Sep 1785	John HIRST to Asa MOORE, to be a sadler Loose Papers: 15 yrs old 3 Mar 1785, son of Martha Hirst
I:88	12 Sep 1785	William JOHN, 10 yrs old 10 Aug 1785, to Jacob SANDS
I:101	10 Oct 1785	William PURSLEY to Abner HUMPHREY, to serve 9 yrs from 10 Jul 1785
I:109	11 Oct 1785	Sally GRIMSLEY, 7 yrs old 1 Oct 1785, to Joel BEACH Loose Papers: base born, Jemimah Grimsley consents
I:111	11 Oct 1785	Jane WILLIAMS, 12 yrs 6 mo. old, to Gideon MOSS
I:117	12 Oct 1785	Elizabeth MOONEY, 9 yrs old in Jul 1785, to James HARROP
I:123	14 Nov 1785	John RUSSELL, 5 yrs old 17 Aug 1785, to Simeon HAINS
I:127	14 Nov 1785	John THOMAS, about 15 yrs old, to George FAIRHURST
I:128	14 Nov 1785	William FARREL, 5 yrs 9 mo old, to Philip SOUDER
I:134	12 Dec 1785	Thomas SHOCKNESS, 14 yrs old 20 Oct 1786, to Richard WHITE
I:134	12 Dec 1785	William ARMSTEAD to Richard ROACH, to be a blacksmith

Apprentices, Poor Children and Bastards   41

I:134	12 Dec 1785	Cuthbert MUSGROVE to Jacob STALEY, to be a blacksmith
I:138	9 Jan 1786	John EDWINS, 14 yrs old in Jul 1786, to John NORTON
I:139	9 Jan 1786	Amos WILSON, 16 yrs old 11 Nov 1785, to Samuel WILSON
I:144	13 Feb 1786	George CASSELL, 13 yrs old in Mar 1786, to Godfrey KIPHEART
I:144	13 Feb 1786	Adam COUNSE, 19 yrs old 19 Dec 1785, to Matthias SMITLEY, to be a blacksmith
I:178	10 Apr 1786	Mary HIRST, about 15 yrs old, to John PRESTON
I:178	10 Apr 1786	Sarah HIRST, 13 yrs old, to Mahlon TAYLOR
I:178	10 Apr 1786	Richard HIRST, 11 yrs old, to Stacey TAYLOR, a carpenter & joiner,
I:178	10 Apr 1786	Nancy HIRST, 9 yrs old, to John SMITH
I:178	10 Apr 1786	Martha HIRST, 7 yrs old, to John HIRST
I:254	12 Jun 1786	George GRIMES, 17 yrs old 23 Dec 1785, to Israel JANNEY, to be a bookkeeper Loose Papers: cousin of David & Mary Jurey
I:254	12 Jun 1786	Michael SHIELDS, 12 yrs 5 mo old, to John SCHOOLEY Loose Papers: son of Margret Shields
I:255	12 Jun 1786	Martha JONES, 7 yrs old 2 Apr 1786, to John EVANS
I:256	12 Jun 1786	Eliezer EVANS, 7 yrs old in Sep 1786, to Samuel RUSSELL, to be a weaver Loose Papers: indenture found
I:257	12 Jun 1786	Caleb WHITACRE, Jr., 14 yrs old 2 Jun 1787, to Caleb WHITACRE, Sr., to be a hatter
I:267	13 Jun 1786	Elisha RICHARDSON, 10 yrs old 1 Feb 1786, to Samuel HOUGH, to be a hatter
I:269	10 Jul 1786	Ralph SMITH to James MOORE
I:335	11 Sep 1786	William MUIRHEAD, alias Talbott, 15 yrs old 25 Mar 1786, to William MOXLEY, to be a sadler
I:336	11 Sep 1786	Joseph MCARTER, 9 yrs old in Apr 1786, to George MASON
I:336	11 Sep 1786	John EVANS, 15 yrs old 23 Sep 1786, to Thomas MOORE, to be a cabinet maker

I:336	11 Sep 1786	Reuben CAMP, 7 yrs old 25 Jul 1786, to Samuel MCPHERSON Loose Papers: son of Pashent Weathers
I:336	11 Sep 1786	Nathaniel PETTIT, 17 yrs old 4 May 1786, to Jonathan MYERS, to be a wheelwright
I:337	11 Sep 1786	Joseph STEERS, 13 yrs old 23 Jun 1786, to Banner BENTLEY, to be a joiner
I:337	11 Sep 1786	Nancy CAFFERTY, 15 yrs old in Apr 1787, to Peter EBLIN
I:337	11 Sep 1786	Nancy COMPTON, 14 yrs old 26 May 1786, to Amos SUTTON
I:342	12 Sep 1786	Samuel BRISCO, 10 yrs old in Dec 1786, to Gustavus ELGIN, to be a farmer, indenture found
I:342	12 Sep 1786	William MARONEY, 17 yrs old, to Thomas WARMAN, to be a bookkeeper
I:347	9 Oct 1786	John MCFARLING, 15 yrs old in Sep 1786, to Thomas DRAKE, to be a farmer Loose Papers: indenture found
K:3	8 Jan 1787	James WILSON, 7 yrs old 3 Mar 1787, to Capt. George RALLS Loose Papers: son of Elizabeth Wilson who was deserted by her husband in Aug 1786
K:3	8 Jan 1787	Samuel WILLIAMS, 14 yrs old, to William STEPHENSON, to be a blacksmith
K:4	8 Jan 1787	William KENNAN to William Harrison POWELL
K:5	12 Feb 1787	Elizabeth KELLY to Matthew WEATHERBY Loose Papers: daughter of Mary Kelly, 10 yrs old Oct 1787, indenture found
K:5	12 Feb 1787	John DAVIS, 8 yrs old 1 Jan 1787, to John HANBY
K:5	12 Feb 1787	Sally JOHN, 14 yrs old 10 Apr 1787, to John HANBY
K:5	12 Feb 1787	Elizabeth JOHN, 6 yrs old 16 Jan 1787, to John HANBY
K:5	12 Feb 1787	Elizabeth CLARK, 5 yrs old 27 Sep 1786, to Philip LONG
K:7	12 Feb 1787	Francis MANLY, 14 yrs old, to Jemima FIELDS Loose Papers: orphan, indenture found
K:8	12 Feb 1787	Martha JONES, 8 yrs old 1 Mar 1787, to James ROACH

Apprentices, Poor Children and Bastards 43

K:8	12 Feb 1787	Samuel FERGUSON, 18 yrs old, to Thomas WHITE Loose Papers: surname Forgison, to be a taylor, indenture found
K:9	12 Feb 1787	Sarah TURNER, 8 yrs old 29 Sep 1786, to John HARRIS Loose Papers: child of Ann Turner
K:9	12 Feb 1787	John TURNER, ? yrs old 22 Nov 1786, to John HARRIS Loose Papers: 7 yrs old, child of Ann Turner
K:88	10 Apr 1787	Israel WILKERSON, 6 yrs old 17 May 1785, to Arthur ROGERS
K:89	10 Apr 1787	Christopher MATTERSHARD, 12 yrs old 1 Jan 1787, to William WOODFORD, a farmer Loose Papers: son of Sarah Rivers, gr-son of Sarah Mattershard, nephew of Charles Mattershard, indenture found
K:89	10 Apr 1787	Samuel BRADFIELD, 5 yrs old 23 Apr 1786, to William WOODFORD Loose Papers: indenture found
K:90	10 Apr 1787	Charles MATTERSHARD, 17 yrs old 25 Dec 1786, to William WOODFORD Loose Papers: indenture found
K:166	11 Jun 1787	Elijah SMALLWOOD, 15 yrs old 7 Jan 1787, to Jasper SEYBOLD, to be a blacksmith Loose Papers: son of Jemima Smallwood
K:167	11 Jun 1787	Moses RACE, 6 yrs old, to Thomas SANDERS Loose Papers: age in Apr 1787, son of Phebe Race
K:168	11 Jun 1787	John KID, 2 yrs old 25 Jan 1787, to Thomas SIMMS
K:168	11 Jun 1787	Nicholas COONTS, 18 yrs old 20 Sep 1786, to Simon RICKETT, to be a taylor
K:168	11 Jun 1787	Job MORGAN, 16 yrs old 20 Apr 1787, to Matthias SMITLEY, to be a blacksmith. K:261, 10 Sep 1787, discharged from apprenticeship
K:169	11 Jun 1787	John YOUNG to Nathan HUDDLESTONE
K:170	11 Jun 1787	Alice CLARK, 7 yrs old next spring, to David KING
K:175	12 Jun 1787	Catharine CAGIER, 3 yrs old, to John PERRY Loose Papers: daughter of Rachell Cagier, John's name given as John & Ann Perryman

Records Found in Court Order Books

K:176	12 Jun 1787	Chloe COOK, rising 12 yrs old, to William MILLAN Loose Papers: surname-Crook, dau of Sarah Crook (has lived with Millan 10 yrs already)
K:181	12 Jun 1787	Lott TOON, 5 yrs old in Nov 1787, to Charles SHEPHERD
K:188	13 Jun 1787	Abraham LAPPINGTON, 14 yrs old, to Samuel CANBY, formerly bound to Mary Evans
K:256	10 Sep 1787	Jeremiah MCGAHEY, 12 yrs old, to William THOMAS, until 16 yrs old
K:261	10 Sep 1787	Joseph FEGG, 10 yrs old, to Thomas GIST
K:262	10 Sep 1787	Samuel GRAHAM, 7 yrs old 15 Jan 1787, to William LITTLETON
K:262	10 Sep 1787	Elizabeth COCKRILL, 8 yrs old 27 Mar 1787, to John MAHUE
K:262	10 Sep 1787	Jemes SHORT, 12 yrs old 29 Aug 1787, to Elisha SCHOOLEY, to be a blacksmith
K:262	11 Sep 1787	Nancy MCMULLEN, 6 yrs old 20 Jan 1787, to Samuel ERVIN
K:262	11 Sep 1787	Samuel MCMULLEN, 4 yrs old 10 Apr 1787, to Samuel ERVIN
K:267	11 Sep 1787	Henry DAVIS, born 1 Dec 1773, to James SINCLAIR
K:305	9 Oct 1787	Margaret BROOKHEAD, 8 yrs old 25 Feb 1788, to Thomas GIBSON Loose Papers: indenture found (Bruchart)
K:305	9 Oct 1787	William INGELDUE, 17 yrs old, to Stacey TAYLOR, to be a carpenter
K:305	9 Oct 1787	Ebener INGELDUE, 10 yrs old, to Richard BROWN
K:305	9 Oct 1787	William JACOBS, 16 yrs old 13 Sep 1787, to William MCPHERSON
K:335	10 Dec 1787	Nelly GREEN, 10 yrs old 1 Mar 1788, to Jesse DEHAVEN
K:336	10 Dec 1787	John HOCKLEY, 14 yrs old 6 Mar 1788, to Samuel MARSHALL
K:338	11 Dec 1787	Joshua MOXLEY, 4 yrs old, to John DREANE, to be a cooper, indenture found
K:340	14 Jan 1788	Susanna BURNES, 15 yrs old 30 Sep 1787, to Thomas MATTHEWS
K:342	14 Jan 1788	Martha WHITACRE, 12 yrs old 24 May 1788, to Caleb WHITACRE

Apprentices, Poor Children and Bastards 45

K:342	14 Jan 1788	George WHITACRE, 11 yrs old 7 Nov 1788, to Caleb WHITACRE, to be a hatter
K:345	11 Feb 1788	Mary MCDONALD, 10 yrs old in Nov 1787, to John BERKLY
K:348	11 Feb 1788	Molly PEARCE, 12 yrs old, to Isaac HUMPHREY Loose Papers: indenture found
K:348	11 Feb 1788	James FOX to John GUNNELL
K:348	11 Feb 1788	Mary BATSON to John STANHOPE
K:348	11 Feb 1788	Richard BATSON, 13 yrs old in Jun 1788, to John SWART, to be a wheelwright
K:385	14 Apr 1788	Isabella MCGUIRE a servant of Samuel CLANDENING, discharged from further service
K:385	14 Apr 1788	Ann SEAGER, 4 yrs old, to Samuel ARNOTT
K:385	14 Apr 1788	Charles SEAGER, 2 yrs old, to Samuel ARNOTT Loose Papers: 2 yrs old 15 Jul 1788, to be a farmer, surname given as Singer, indenture found
K:395	15 Apr 1788	David THARP, 7 yrs old 7 Sep ____, to Jacob MUCKLER, to be a waggon maker
K:395	15 Apr 1788	Benjamin PEEMY, 10 yrs old 10 Feb 1788, to Jacob MUCKLER, to be a waggon maker
K:395	15 Apr 1788	Azariah PEEMY, 16 yrs old, to Adam BOOS, to be a tanner
K:395	15 Apr 1788	Ann GLIBREY, 11 yrs old last Xmas, to John SWART Loose Papers: dau of Elizabeth Glibrey
K:396	15 Apr 1788	Robert INGMYER, 17 yrs old, to Dominick MCNEIL
K:396	15 Apr 1788	William NORRIS, 12 yrs old 15 Jan 1787, to Nathaniel FORLER, to be a sadler
K:399	15 Apr 1788	George MURPHEY, born 25 Jul 1774, to John ELLZEY
K:399	15 Apr 1788	Charles MURPHEY, born 20 Jan 1779, to John ELLZEY
K:405	15 Apr 1788	John ANDERSON, 17 yrs old 19 Jul 1788, to Joseph PIERPOINT, to be a blacksmith
K:410	16 Apr 1788	John MOXLEY, 13 yrs old in Jan 1788, to Francis HAGUE, to be a tanner Loose Papers: indenture found

DPP I:307	25 Apr 1788	Rose BROOKE, 4 yrs old 1 May 1787, dau of Affee, a free negro woman, to Samuel HOUGH
K:457	9 Jun 1788	Letty DALIHON (DILLAHON) to Charles BINNS, Jr., D.P.P. I:635, Letty Dalihan, until 18 yrs old Loose Papers: 10 yrs old 16 Jan 1789, dau of Mary Dalihan
K:462	9 Jun 1788	David NEWMAN to Joseph WHITE Loose Papers: 11 yrs old 1 Jan 1788, son of Sarah Martin, surname given as Newhouse
K:463	9 Jun 1788	Sally PILLER to Robert SMARR, K:476, 14 Jul 1788, order of June 9, 1788 set aside and children permitted to stay with their mother, Lettice Piller
K:463	9 Jun 1788	Ellsey PILLER to Robert SMARR, K:476, 14 Jul 1788, order of June 9, 1788 set aside and children permitted to stay with their mother, Lettice Piller
K:473	10 Jun 1788	Thomas CAMERON, about 12 yrs old, to Cornelius SKINNER
K:475	11 Jul 1788	Elizabeth TARR to Mahlon HOUGH
K:478	14 Jul 1788	Rose BROOKE, 4 yrs old 1 May 1788, to ___ HOUGH
K:478	14 Jul 1788	Caleb WADE a servant of Abraham Barnes Thomson MASON, to serve additional time for absence
K:491	8 Sep 1788	Peter HIRKLY, 14 yrs old, to Elisha MARKS Loose Papers: surname Hockley
K:503	9 Sep 1788	William PATTERSON, 17 yrs old 13 Sep 1788, to Jacob HOWDERSHELL, to be a blacksmith
L:22	10 Sep 1788	Richard COLEMAN, son of Peter and Hagar Coleman, apprentice of Alexander MCMAKIN, delivered to him from Patrick Cavan, Exor. Of Jacob Coutsman. Case appealed to District Court in Dumfries
L:26	13 Oct 1788	John SHIELDS, 17 yrs old 14 Jan 1789, to Benjamin MEAD, to be a tanner and currier
L:28	13 Oct 1788	William EVANS, 14 yrs old, to Andrew REDMON, to be a tanner
L:29	13 Oct 1788	Samuel FERGUSON, 9 yrs old 31 May 1788, to Richard RICHARDS Loose Papers: to be a farmer, indenture found

Apprentices, Poor Children and Bastards   47

L:29	13 Oct 1788	Joseph MONTAWNEY, 8 yrs old, to David REESE, to be a millwright
L:29	13 Oct 1788	Burgois MONTAWNEY to Nicholas MERRILL
L:29	13 Oct 1788	Reuben CAMP to Daniel MCPHERSON
L:30	13 Oct 1788	William ANNASON, 5 yrs old in Jul 1788, to Isaac NICHOLS Loose Papers: alias Smith, son of Margaret Annason, left by his mother when 2 yrs old to have him bound
L:30	13 Oct 1788	Abijah PEARCE, 15 yrs old 22 Feb 1789, to Robert MCCULLA, to be a tanner and currier
L:31	13 Oct 1788	Sarah PEARCE, 10 yrs old 10 Sep 1788, to Robert MCCULLA
L:31	13 Oct 1788	Ann PEARCE, 8 yrs old 7 Mar 1789, to James BEST Loose Papers: indenture found
L:31	13 Oct 1788	Daniel BRICKELL, 5 yrs old 1 Dec 1788, to Josiah HERBERT
L:31	13 Oct 1788	Mary ROBERTS, 12 yrs old 10 Oct 1788, to Jonathan CONNARD
L:37	14 Oct 1788	Thomas COLLINS a servant of Joseph REED, to serve for absent time
L:43	14 Oct 1788	John BLINSTONE, 16 yrs old, to Thomas EDWARDS, to be a tanner and currier
L:78	8 Dec 1788	Thomas LAPPINGTON, alias Pickeley, 8 yrs old in Feb 1789, to James GREENLEES
L:81	8 Dec 1788	Charles HOWARD, 9 yrs old 1 May 1789, to Osborn KING
L:82	8 Dec 1788	Caty HOWARD, 7 yrs old 1 Feb 1789, to Conrade HICKMAN
L:82	8 Dec 1788	Michael HOWARD, 5 yrs old 25 Feb 1789, to John VINCELL
L:86	9 Dec 1788	John BARTLETT, 10 yrs old in Feb 1789, to Peter DOW Loose Papers: surname Barthart, 7 yrs old, son of Jean Barthart. Mother in bad state of health. She and son have been at Mr. Dow's for some time
L:89	12 Jan 1789	Robert COLCLOUGH, 14 yrs old in Jul 1788, to Benjamin MASON
L:98	9 Feb 1789	Benjamin WHITACRE, 14 yrs old 2 Jul 1788, to Robert WHITACRE Loose Papers: son of Ruth Whitacre

L:98	9 Feb 1789	Fanny HURST, 6 yrs old 1 Oct 1788, to Thomas TRIBBE
L:100	10 Feb 1789	John HOCKLEY, 17 yrs old 18 Mar 1789, to James NICHOLS Loose Papers: orphan
L:100	10 Feb 1789	Moses HUTCHISON, 13 yrs old 3 Apr 1789, to James NICHOLS Loose Papers: orphan
L:166	15 Apr 1789	John JACOBS to Samuel HOUGH, to be a hatter
L:166	15 Apr 1789	Walter DAVIS, 11 yrs old 14 Dec 1788, to Peter DOW Loose Papers: son of Martha (Patty) Davis
L:166	15 Apr 1789	Robert HANNAH, 19 yrs old, to Peter DOW, until 21 yrs old
L:166	15 Apr 1789	Dennis KELLYHAM, 18 yrs old this day, to Samuel MCCUTCHEN
L:195	8 Jun 1789	Sarah JAMES, born 26 Dec 1778, to Thomas SMITH Loose Papers: to Thomas & Martha Smith
L:194-195	8 Jun 1789	Elizabeth ESSEX, returned to her mother (formerly bound to Thomas Sanders)
L:196	8 Jun 1789	Elizabeth ROBINSON, 8 yrs old 15 Jun 1789, to William SMITH
L:198	9 Jun 1789	Elizabeth GREEN, 14 yrs old 18 Jan 1790, to Richard BROWN, by consent of her mother
L:201	9 Jun 1789	Mary PETTIT, 13 yrs old, to Peter OVERFIELD
L:270	14 Sep 1789	James WILSON, 10 yrs old 26 Sep 1789, to William PAXON, to be a house carpenter and fanmaker
L:271	14 Sep 1789	Job MCPHEARSON, born 22 May 1785, to Richards RICHARDS Loose Papers: consent of Ruth Merrill, indenture found
L:271	14 Sep 1789	Hannah THARP, born 6 May 1783, to Joseph WEST
L:271	14 Sep 1789	Ann THARP, 2 yrs old 7 Aug 1789, to Thomas SEALOCK
L:271	14 Sep 1789	John BUCKLEY, 10 yrs old 10 Jan 1790, to Daniel JOHN
L:271	14 Sep 1789	John EDDINGS to Dennis MCNAMARE, to be a taylor

Apprentices, Poor Children and Bastards   49

L:271	14 Sep 1789	Jonas GORE, 16 yrs old 16 Jul 1789, to John IREY, to be a blacksmith
L:271	14 Sep 1789	Abner FERGUSON, 16 yrs old in Mar 1789, to Simion PANCOAST, to be a joyner and house carpenter
L:271	14 Sep 1789	Eaton MOORE, 9 yrs old, to John MOORE
L:271	14 Sep 1789	John MOORE, 5 yrs old, to John MOORE
L:271	14 Sep 1789	Samuel WILSON, 5 yrs old, to John MOORE
L:271	14 Sep 1789	Ezekiel COMPTON, 10 yrs old in Aug 1789, to Samuel GREGG
L:271	14 Sep 1789	Sarah MILLETT, 6 yrs old 26 Feb 1789, to Samuel GREGG
L:275	15 Sep 1789	Priscilla , a free negro, 5 yrs old, to William STABLER
L:292	12 Oct 1789	Nancy MOORE servant of James WILEY, to serve additional time for being a runaway and having a base born child
L:293	12 Oct 1789	Elizabeth WHITACRE, 9 yr old 7 Jun 1789, to Robert WHITACRE Loose Papers: dau of Ruth Whitacre
L:320	14 Dec 1789	Jesse SCHOOLEY, 17 yrs old, to Aaron SCATTERDAY Loose Papers: son of Dority Schooley
L:323	14 Dec 1789	David EVANS, 7 yrs old 7 Jun 1789, to Israel WILLIAMS, to be a blacksmith
L:325	11 Jan 1790	Edwart DEMSEY a servant of Robert POWER, released from his indenture
L:327	11 Jan 1790	Abner FERGUSON, 17 yrs old, to Thomas HUMPHRIES, Jr., to be a blacksmith
L:338	8 Feb 1790	Nathan WILCOX, 9 yrs old 25 Sep 1789, to George MOUL, to be a blacksmith Loose Papers: called "our son" by Lenard and Elenor Pumcrats
L:339	8 Feb 1790	Elijah COKELY, 14 yrs old 1 May 1790, to William KELLY
L:339	8 Feb 1790	Mahlon COMBS, 8 yrs old 18 Aug 1789, to Mahlon COMBS Loose Papers: to be a farmer, indenture found
L:339	8 Feb 1790	Jonas SANDS, 14 yrs old 17 Dec 1789, to William PAXTON, to be a wheelwright and fanmaker

Records Found in Court Order Books

L:339	8 Feb 1790	Amos PYOTT, 18 yrs old 14 Aug 1789, to William PAXTON, to be a wheelwright and fanmaker
M:7	13 Apr 1790	Hannah POLAND, 7 yrs old in Oct 1790, to Nicholas WYCOFF
M:8	13 Apr 1790	John DUNLOP, 8 yrs old, to George WALENTINE, to be a blacksmith
M:9	13 Apr 1790	Charles JENKINS to Henry STOTTS
M:9	13 Apr 1790	Hamilton JENKINS to Henry STOTTS
M:100	10 May 1790	Absolem BRADY, 2 yrs old in Feb 1790. Son of James Brady (Rough Minute Book says Jane Brady servant of Joseph Lacey), to Israel LACEY
M:105	10 May 1790	William HORTON, 18 yrs old, to James ROBINSON, to be a tanner and currier
M:203	12 Jul 1790	Alexander TURNER to Thomas REESE, to be a stone mason
M:204	12 Jul 1790	Ann FERGUSON, 7 yrs old 3 May 1790, to Edward REESE
M:206	12 Jul 1790	Richard DONIPHAN (DONIVAN) a servant of Patrick CAVAN, discharged from indenture, it having expired
M:206	12 Jul 1790	Richard DONIPHAN (DONIVAN), 17 yrs old, to Charles SWANN, to be a saddle tree maker
M:314	13 Sep 1790	Uphama DIVINE, 3 yrs old in May 1790, to Andrew BROWN Loose Papers: dau of Sarah Divine
M:320	13 Aug 1790	Daniel JAMES, 16 yrs old 20 Jun 1790, to Davis STONE
M:323	13 Sep 1790	Daniel LOVETT, 14 yrs old 18 Dec 1789, to Thomas MOORE, to be a joiner
M:323	13 Sep 1790	David LOVETT, 12 yrs old 5 Oct 1789, to Asa MOORE, to be a saddler
M:323	13 Sep 1790	Elias LOVETT, 10 yrs old 29 Jun 1790, to James MOORE, to be a tanner
M:324	13 Sep 1790	William MURRAY to Aron BORAM Loose Papers: son of Susannah Murray then a widow (6 years ago)
M:324	13 Sep 1790	Peggy MURRY to Aron BORAM Loose Papers: son of Susannah Murray then a widow (6 years ago)
M:331	13 Sep 1790	Sarah RUSSELL, 2 yrs old 20 Mar 1790, to Joseph TREBBE

Apprentices, Poor Children and Bastards 51

M:345	14 Sep 1790	Nathaniel GRIMES, (formerly ordered to be bound to William Barker), to John GUNNELL
M:364	14 Sep 1790	George CAMMELL, with consent of his father, Alexander Cammell, to Hugh DOUGLASS
M:385	15 Sep 1790	Thomas MATTHEWS, 10 yrs old, child of Rachel Matthews a free mulatto, to be bound at discretion of O.P. and their mother
M:385	15 Sep 1790	Samuel MATTHEWS, 6 yrs old, child of Rachel Matthews a free mulatto, to be bound at discretion of O.P. and their mother
M:385	15 Sep 1790	William MATTHEWS, 4 yrs old, child of Rachel Matthews a free mulatto, to be bound at discretion of O.P. and their mother
N:4	11 Oct 1790	Daniel THOMPSON, 16 yrs old 9 Sep 1790, to Francis DAVIS, to be a blacksmith
N:4	11 Oct 1790	Meca KIRK, 2 yrs old 8 Jun 1790, to Aaron GREGG Loose Papers: (Maca), dau of Mary Kirk
N:4	11 Oct 1790	Thomas JAMES to Thomas SMITH Loose Papers: born 25 Jan 1783, son of Jane James
N:7	11 Oct 1790	Elizabeth CAMMELL, 14 yrs old 1 Oct 1790, to Israel THOMPSON
N:7	11 Oct 1790	Mary JONES, 10 yrs old in Sep 1790, to Israel THOMPSON
N:8	11 Oct 1790	Isaac WELLS, 8 yrs old 6 Feb 1790, to Joseph WOOLLARD
N:53	13 Dec 1790	William HUTCHISON to William LANE, 3rd, to be a blacksmith
N:58	13 Dec 1790	Nancy DIAL, 2 yrs 9 mo old, to Samuel HOLLUM Loose Papers: dau of Elizabeth Diall
N:65	10 Jan 1791	William BINSTON (BENTSON), 16 yrs old in Feb 1791, to John BROWN, to be a millwright
N:65	10 Jan 1791	Violinda KNOTT to John CARNICKLE
N:74	14 Feb 1791	Abijah PIERCE, 17 yrs old 14 Feb 1791, to John DICKS, to be a tanner
N:75	14 Feb 1791	John PEYTON to Robert DAGG, to be a saddler
N:75	14 Feb 1791	Thomas THORNTON, 17 yrs old 18 Feb 1791, to Samuel EVANS, to be a sadler

Records Found in Court Order Books

N:77	14 Feb 1791	John EADES, 11 yrs old 18 Jan 1792, to William FOX
N:77	14 Feb 1791	Ann HANY, 3 yrs old 28 Dec 1790, to John YOUNG
N:77	14 Feb 1791	Thomas JACOBS, 18 yrs old 4 Jul 1791, to John TREBBE, to be a cordwainer
N:85	15 Feb 1791	William RACE, 14 yrs old, to Joseph BRADEN, for the benefit of Elizabeth Eblin, widow of Peter Eblin
N:85	15 Feb 1791	William CASTOR, 4 yrs old 10 Mar 1790 (Rough Min. Bk. - 1791), to John HEATOR
N:85	15 Feb 1791	George RHODES, 14 yrs old 12 Jul 1791, to John LITTLEJOHN, to be a blacksmith
N:152	12 Apr 1791	Ellender HERBERT, 15 yrs old 20 Mar 1791, to William HOUGH
N:154	12 Apr 1791	John VOWELLS, 6 yrs old 8 Mar 1791, to Joseph CAVENS Loose Papers: age given as of 8 Mar 1790, son of Phebe Vowells
N:154	12 Apr 1791	Susanna BYRNE (BYRNS), 3 yrs old 17 Sep 1790, to Mary Ann GRAVES
N:154	12 Apr 1791	Benjamin LACEY, 16 yrs old 27 Jul 1791, to William PAXON, to be a carpenter, wheelwright and fann maker Loose Papers: son of Elizabeth Lacey, William's surname spelled Paxson
N:157	12 Apr 1791	John KIBBY, 11 yrs old 13 Oct 1790, to John DUNHAM
N:158	12 Apr 1791	David LOVETT to Asa MOORE, to be a tanner and sadler
N:158	12 Apr 1791	Zachariah GOWING (GOING), 16 yrs & 6 mo old, to John HOUGH, to be a blacksmith
N:163	13 Apr 1791	Thomas BURNS (BYRNS), 16 yrs old, to John TRIBBE, to be a shoemaker (with consent of his former master)
N:165	13 Apr 1791	George LUCAS, 6 yrs old, to Charles SWANN, to be a saddletree maker
N:169	13 Apr 1791	William KIBBE, 13 yrs old 6 Jun 1791, to James MCCLAIN, to be taught bookkeeping (in addition to reading, writing and arithmetic)
N:172	13 Apr 1791	Rachel BORDLEY to Sarah PRITCHARD
N:174	9 May 1791	Nancy O'NEAL, 11 yrs old 1 Nov 1791, to John MUIR

Apprentices, Poor Children and Bastards 53

N:174	9 May 1791	William WILLIARD, 8 yrs old, to John DORST
N:174	9 May 1791	Jonathan PALMER, 16 yrs old 26 Jun 1791, to Thomas HUMPHREYS, to be a blacksmith
N:175	9 May 1791	Hannah BIRCHETT to Jonah NIXON, according to the former indenture
N:176	9 May 1791	Mary KENNEDAY a servant of William LANE, to serve additional time for being a runaway and for having two base born children
N:245	11 Jul 1791	Susanna WILSON, 5 yrs old 11 Feb 1791, to George and Ann ROBINSON
N:245	11 Jul 1791	Jesse JAMES, 15 yrs old 7 Aug 1790, to Thomas MOORE, to be a cabinet maker Loose Papers: son of Jane James to Thomas Moore Jr.
N:245	11 Jul 1791	Levi JAMES, 14 yrs old 14 Dec 1790, to Asa MOORE, to be a sadler Loose Papers: son of Jane James
N:255	11 Jul 1791	Judah BOARDLY to Thomas PRITCHARD
O:1	12 Sep 1791	George BIMER, 4 yrs 1 mo 12 days old, to Laurence AMAND Loose Papers: son of Ann Bimer
O:1	12 Sep 1791	Abraham LAPPINGTON, 17 yrs 12 May 1791, to Elijah MOUNT
O:3	12 Sep 1791	William POLAND, 4 yrs old 10 Apr 1792, to John HOUGHMAN, Jr. Loose Papers: son of Elizabeth Polen
O:3	12 Sep 1791	Amasa POOL to Samuel GREGG Loose Papers: son of Elizabeth Pool, indenture found
O:10	12 Sep 1791	John CORRY to Levin POWELL, to be a blacksmith
O:15	12 Sep 1791	Elijah FERGUSON, 12 yrs old 14 Jul 1791, to Thomas MCCABE, to be a taylor, indenture found
O:15	12 Sep 1791	Jeremiah HAMILTON, 15 yrs old, to Amos SINCLAIR
O:43	10 Oct 1791	Samuel HENDERSON, 17 yrs old 26 Feb 1791, to David CRIDER, to be a tanner
O:48	10 Oct 1791	Samuel DILLON, 14 yrs old 23 Jun 1791, to Josiah DILLON, to be a house joiner and cabinett maker

Records Found in Court Order Books

O:48	10 Oct 1791	William ADAMS, 18 yrs old 1 Aug 1791, to Josiah DILLON, to be a joiner and cabinett maker
O:48	10 Oct 1791	David POPKINS, 17 yrs old 15 Apr 1791, to James DILLON, to be a joiner
D.B. T:122	10 Oct 1791	Zacheriah CHAPPELIER to Samuel THATCHER, to be a wheelwright, for 3 yrs with consent of his father Elias Chappelier
O:50	10 Oct 1791	George H. CLEMMONS, 2 yrs old 10 Aug 1791, to Presley SELF
O:50	10 Oct 1791	Henry BODINE, 8 yrs old 1 Oct 1791, to Robert MCCULLA, to be a tanner
O:123	12 Dec 1791	Zacheriah GOING, 6 1/2 yrs old, to Moses HOUGH, to be a blacksmith
O:124	12 Dec 1791	Mary , a Negro (margin says free negro), to James MOORE
O:128	12 Dec 1791	Charles , free mulatto, 8 yrs old, to Thomas MOORE, to be a joiner
O:128	12 Dec 1791	Stephen , free negro 6 yrs old, to James MCCORMICK, to be a miller
O:134	13 Dec 1791	Charles MCINTYRE, 14 yrs old in Aug 1791, orphan of Alexander McIntyre, to John RICHARDSON, to be a shoemaker
O:138	13 Dec 1791	Jonathan , mulatto, 17 mo old, to John YOUNG
O:150	9 Jan 1792	William SHARO, 14 yrs old, to Jacob WILDING
O:155	9 Jan 1792	Hesther SHIVERS, 5 yrs old 1 Dec 1792, to William WOODFORD Loose Papers: dau of Mary Shivers, age given as of 1 Dec 1790, spelling Hester
O:155	9 Jan 1792	Elizabeth CAMPBELL to Samuel GREGG, per agreement with Israel Thompson Loose Papers: formerly bound to Israel Thompson
O:155	9 Jan 1792	Sarah BOARDLY, 8 yrs old, to Thomas PRITCHARD Loose Papers: dau of Mary Boardly
O:155	9 Jan 1792	Jacob BOARDLY, 6 mo old, to Thomas PRITCHARD Loose Papers: son of Mary Boardly
O:156	9 Jan 1792	Elizabeth CARTRIGHT, born 19 Dec 1783, to William and Ann, his wife ANSLEY
O:158	13 Feb 1792	Hannah HAGUE to William ROBERTS

Apprentices, Poor Children and Bastards 55

O:246	9 Apr 1792	Thomas SLOACOMB, 16 yrs old 22 Sep 1791, to Charles BENNETT, Jr., to be a blacksmith
O:248	10 Apr 1792	William MCFARLING, 7 yrs old 27 Apr 1792, to Thomas ADAMS Loose Papers: son of Mary McFarling
O:248	10 Apr 1792	Richard WATSON, 7 yrs old 26 Jan 1792, to John ROADS, to be a house joiner
O:248	10 Apr 1792	Nancy MURRAY, 7 yrs old 20 Jul 1792, to Edward and Dorinda, his wife LOYD
O:252	10 Apr 1792	Jeremiah MCGAHEY, 15 yrs old 3 Sep 1791, to Francis TYTUS
O:252	10 Apr 1792	Daniel MCGAHEY, 12 yrs old 30 Sep 1791, to Francis TYTUS
O:252	10 Apr 1792	Leven MCFARLING, 15 yrs old 14 Sep 1791, to David FULTON, to be a waggon maker
O:253	10 Apr 1792	Catherine QUEEN to John Daniel MILLER
O:255	10 Apr 1792	Sarah ENGLISH, 8 yrs old 25 May 1792, to John DAVIS Loose Papers: dau of Susana English
O:255	10 Apr 1792	Jeremiah OXLEY, alias McGahey, to Jeremiah MCGAHEY, to be a weaver
O:266	14 May 1792	Richard FLING, 9 yrs old in Dec 1792, to John MORRISON
O:282	9 Jul 1792	Sarah BUTLER, 11 yrs old 25 Sep 1792, to William and Rebekah, his wife GREGG
O:286	9 Sep 1792	William DAVIS, 18 yrs old 1 Sep 1793, to Samuel SINCLAIR
O:321	17 Aug 1792	Francis MANLY, negro claiming to be of lawful age, a servant, vs Jemimah FIELDS, for neglect of his education
O:330	10 Sep 1792	William BRYAN, 4 yrs old 13 Jan 1792, to Alexander HARRISON, to be a weaver Loose Papers: son of Charles & Sarah Ann Brian, spelling Brian
O:330	10 Sep 1792	James WHITACRE, 14 yrs old 12 Mar 1792, to Joseph WHITACRE, to be a hatter Loose Papers: son of Esther Whitacre
O:330	10 Sep 1792	Ann BUTLER, 13 yrs old 25 Dec 1792, to Joseph WILKERSON

O:331	19 Sep 1792	Henry MUNKS, 2 yrs old 15 Jul 1792, to Daniel STUART Loose Papers: son of Mary Munks, Daniel Steward (spelling)
O:332	10 Sep 1792	John PRINCE, 11 yrs old 8 Aug 1792, to Jacob CORDALL
O:334	10 Sep 1792	Daniel HUTCHISON, 8 yrs old in Nov 1792, to Edward PAUL
O:341	10 Sep 1792	John MYERS, 9 yrs old, to Robert WHITE Loose Papers: age as of 8 Aug 1792
O:342	10 Sep 1792	William COLLINS, 11 yrs old 14 Jun 1792, to Peter BETTS (BELTS)
O:361	12 Sep 1792	Salathiel, an orphan 5 mo old 22 Aug 1792, to James MCNAB, the reputed father,
O:374	8 Oct 1792	Jonathan KENNEDY, son of Mary Kennedy, to Daniel LOSH, former order not being complied with
P:2	10 Dec 1792	Asa METCALF to William DAVIS
P:2	10 Dec 1792	Ezekiel MCFARLING, 11 yrs old 10 Nov 1792, to Jonah NIXON
P:2	10 Dec 1792	John MCFARLING, 14 yrs old 10 Sep 1792, to George NIXON, Jr.,
P:3	10 Dec 1792	Susannah MANLY to John HOUGH, of Broad Run,
P:3	10 Dec 1792	Edy MANLY to John HOUGH, of Broad Run,
P:21	11 Dec 1792	Jonathan VOWELS, 4 yrs 3 mo old, to Isaac EBLIN Loose Papers: son of Febey Vowels (about to move out of this county - dated 29 Oct 1790)
P:23	11 Dec 1792	Elizabeth BURN, 16 yrs old, to William REED
P:26	14 Jan 1793	Ezekiel COMPTON, 10 yrs old 14 Mar 1789, to Samuel GREGG
P:26	14 Jan 1793	Sarah MILETT, 6 yrs old 26 Feb 1789, to Samuel GREGG
P:28	14 Jan 1793	James WILSON to Timothy HIXON
P:35	11 Feb 1793	Mary MICAL to Moses HOUGH
P:35	11 Feb 1793	Hannah MICAL, O.P. to bind her out
P:36	11 Feb 1793	Charles MCGEE to Thomas NOLAND
P:36	11 Feb 1793	George WAGLEY, 16 yrs old 3 Mar 1793, to John BOARD, to be a blacksmith

Apprentices, Poor Children and Bastards 57

P:96	9 Apr 1793	Margarett PALMER, 8 yrs old 15 Aug 1793, to William SMITH Loose Papers: dau of Mary Palmer
P:99	9 Apr 1793	George, free negro, 10 yrs old, to Josias CLAPHAM
P:99	9 Apr 1793	Dilley, free negro, 5 yrs 10 mo old, to Josias CLAPHAM
P:99	9 Apr 1793	Hannah, free negro, 3 yrs 10 mo old, to Josias CLAPHAM
P:99	9 Apr 1793	Andrew, free negro, 11 mo old, to Josias CLAPHAM
P:100	9 Apr 1793	Eliza DARR, 12 yrs old 1 Mar 1793, to Nathaniel PEGG
P:100	9 Apr 1793	John DARR, 7 yrs old 1 Mar 1793, to Nathaniel PEGG
P:100	9 Apr 1793	Sally DARR, 4 yrs old 1 Dec 1792, to Nathaniel PEGG Loose Papers: Sarah, indenture found
P:100	9 Apr 1793	Bazill MUSCHETT, 12 yrs old 1 Sep 1792, to Abraham WARFORD
P:101	9 Apr 1793	John BEAVERS, 18 yrs old 13 Dec 1792, to Silas REESE, to be a blacksmith Loose Papers: son of Mary Philips
P:104	9 Apr 1793	Nancy REED, 8 yrs old, to John JACOBS Loose Papers: Ann, daughter of Mary Reed
P:111	13 May 1793	Daniel BRICKLE, 10 yrs old 1 Dec 1793, to Peter HESSER, (formerly ordered to be bound to Josiah Herbert)
P:111	13 May 1793	Elizabeth PAGE to Joseph ALLEN
P:111	13 May 1793	Robert PAGE to Joseph ALLEN
P:113	13 May 1793	Ann INGLEDOE, 13 yrs old 4 Dec 1793, to William HATCHER Loose Papers: dau of Ann Ingledew, widow of Blackstone Ingledew, to William & Mary Hatcher
P:116	14 May 1793	Samuel GOING, 10 yrs old, to John Alexander BINNS
P:116	14 May 1793	Jacob BOARDLEY to Thomas PRITCHARD, Jr. Loose Papers: son of Mary Boardley
P:169	8 Jul 1793	Mary KYE to William STEPHENS, (indexed Key, Rough Minute Book Kye)

P:202	16 Aug 1793	John HILLIARD, John Hilliard his father, an apprentice of William CARR, complains of ill treatment
P:215	9 Sep 1793	Sarah HOWELL to Elizha EDWARDS, order of 9 Sep 1793 recinded P:235, 10 Sep 1793. P:281, 14 Oct 1793, Hannah Howell, mother of Sarah to bind out her dau to whom she pleases with approval of the Court
P:223	9 Sep 1793	Jesse JAMES to Henry BERKETT, (formerly ordered to be bound to Thomas Moore)
P:224	9 Sep 1793	James TILLETT, 5 yrs old 25 Mar 1793, to William ROBERTS
P:229	9 Sep 1793	Edward HINDS vs John WINGROVE, for detaining him in servitude
P:240	10 Sep 1793	Alexander KIBBY to Alexander MCMAKEN
P:278	14 Oct 1793	Nancy MAHUE, born 29 May 1783, to John MAHUE
P:281	14 Oct 1793	Michael BEST to Anthony AMAND
P:317	9 Dec 1793	Benjamin DAVIS, 18 yrs old 16 Sep 1793, to Garret STANDEY, to be a joyner Loose Papers: son of William Davis, consent of Casander Davis
P:319	9 Dec 1793	William LANE, son of Rachel Lane, , now in possession of Richard Davis - to be released to his mother, Rachel Lane (previously ordered to be bound to William Hamilton)
P:321	9 Dec 1793	Daniel LOVETT to Henry BIRKITT, to be a joiner (with consent of Thomas Moore to whom he was formerly bound)
P:323	10 Dec 1793	Betsey CANTER, 6 yrs old 14 Dec 1793, to William MEANS Loose Papers: dau of Ada Canter, to William Mains & wife
P:328	13 Jan 1794	Jacob WEISNER, 8 yrs old 1 Oct 1793, to Peter WARNER
P:328	13 Jan 1794	Constant HUGHES, born 10 Jan 1783, to Joseph FREDD Loose Papers: orphan son of George Hughes
P:328	13 Jan 1794	Hannah MANLY, 17 mo old 14 Jan 1794, to Peter HARMAN
P:333	10 Feb 1794	Patrick WARD a servant of Philip NOLAND, to serve additional time for being a runaway

Apprentices, Poor Children and Bastards

P:336	10 Feb 1794	Thomas HUTCHISON, 12 yrs old, to George ROBISON
P:336	10 Feb 1794	Rachel MARR, 13 yrs old 12 Jun 1793, to Charles HUFFMAN
P:383	15 Apr 1794	Samuel , 13 yrs old 1 Nov 1793, to be bound out Loose Papers: Negro Sam to William Hough
P:386	15 Apr 1794	Elihu GOING, 9 yrs old in Apr 1794, to Samuel DONOHOE
P:340	10 Feb 1794	William MATTHEWS to be delivered up by Rachel Lane to William HAMILTON, P:428, 17 Apr 1794, complaint of Wm & Samuel Lane against their master William Hamilton, dismissed
P:340	10 Feb 1794	Samuel MATTHEWS to be delivered up by Rachel Lane to William HAMILTON, P:428, 17 Apr 1794, complaint of Wm & Samuel Lane against their master William Hamilton, dismissed
P:379	14 Apr 1794	Tracey SMALLWOOD, 10 yrs old, to Edward POTTS
P:383	15 Apr 1794	James CASTER, 4 yrs old 26 Dec 1793, to James PAXON Loose Papers: son of Mary Caster, to James Paxson
P:389	15 Apr 1794	Thomas GOING, 5 yrs old 1 Dec 1793, to Luke GOING
P:389	15 Apr 1794	Mary GOING, 7 yrs old 25 Feb 1795, to Luke GOING
P:389	15 Apr 1794	Levi GOING, 14 yrs old 3 Jun 1794, to Joseph GARNER
P:389	15 Apr 1794	Leitha GOING, 11 yrs old 22 Feb 1795, to Mary BAKER
P:394	15 Apr 1794	Jeremiah MCGAHEY, 16 yrs old in Feb 1794, to Francis TYTUS
P:433	12 May 1794	Leven MCFARLAND, 15 yrs old 14 Sep 1791, to David FULTON, to be a farmer Loose Papers: son of Mary Leaich, surname McFarling
P:435	12 May 1794	Janett LISHMAN to George BROWN Loose Papers: 9 yrs old 4 Jun 1793, dau of Jane Lishman

Records Found in Court Order Books

P:437	12 May 1794	Benjamin LACEY, 16 yrs old 27 Jul 1793, to Samuel BARBER, to be a stone mason (formerly ordered to be bound to William Paxon)
P:477	14 Jul 1794	William GIBBS to Bartleson FOX, by consent of his father Joseph Gibbs
Q:8	8 Sep 1794	Benjamin BAZILL, 15 yrs old 1 Sep 1794, to Ann PERRY
Q:9	8 Sep 1794	Mary DORNING, 4 yrs old 12 Jul 1794, to David JURY
Q:9	8 Sep 1794	Andrew DORNING, 6 yrs old 2 May 1794, to William CARTER
Q:9	8 Sep 1794	Rebekah PLUMMER to John CONNELLY
Q:9	8 Sep 1794	John PUGH, 4 yrs old in Dec 1794, to Isaac HUMFREY
Q:10	8 Sep 1794	Leviston MAHUE to Alexander TRACEY
Q:11	8 Sep 1794	Jane JAMES, 10 yrs old in Mar 1795, to Jonathan TAYLOR
Q:11	8 Sep 1794	Walter Bear SMALLWOOD to Aaron SCATTERDAY, to be a blacksmith
Q:11	8 Sep 1794	William SMITH to John ROBERTS, to be a blacksmith
Q:37	13 Oct 1794	Jonah TOMKINS, 8 yrs old 26 Nov 1794, to William CARR Loose Papers: surname Tompkins
Q:37	13 Oct 1794	Ellzey ROE, 11 yrs old 31 Jan 1795, to John WOLF Loose Papers: name Eliz., dau of Mary Roe
Q:39	13 Oct 1794	Linney SINCLAIR, 7 yrs old 11 May 1795, to Archibald ROGERS Loose Papers: to Arthur Rogers, indenture found
Q:39	13 Oct 1794	Amy SINCLAIR, 4 yrs old 10 Nov 1794, to Hamilton ROGERS
Q:39	13 Oct 1794	Jacob SMITH, 13 yrs old 20 Jun 1795, to John EDMONDS Loose Papers: son of Meraia Smith
Q:40	13 Oct 1794	George FRYER, 14 yrs old 16 Mar 1794, to Francis TITUS
Q:40	13 Oct 1794	Jesse FRYER, 5 yrs old 3 Apr 1795, to Francis TITUS

Apprentices, Poor Children and Bastards

Q:40	13 Oct 1794	Erasmus SMITH, 16 yrs old 29 Mar 1795, to John SMITH Loose Papers: age given as of 29 Mar 1794, son of Mary Smith, John Smith his grandfather
Q:40	13 Oct 1794	John SMITH, 6 yrs old 25 Jun 1795, to John SMITH Loose Papers: age given as of 25 Jun 1794, son of Mary Smith, John Smith his grandfather
Q:40	13 Oct 1794	Mary WARRENBURG, born Jun 1780, to William DAVIDSON
Q:41	13 Oct 1794	Sarah WINDSOR, 5 yrs old 12 May 1794, to William REDWOOD, and Elizabeth, his wife,
Q:63	8 Dec 1794	William SMITH, 2 yrs 3 mo 10 das old, to Benjamin WHITE
Q:64	8 Dec 1794	Asahel PHILIPS to Richard MATTHEWS, to be a sadler
Q:64	8 Dec 1794	Thomas BATSON, 17 yrs old 17 Dec 1794, to James BATSON Loose Papers: to be a wheelwright, indenture found
Q:70	12 Jan 1795	Thomas EDI, 9 yrs old 1 Jan 1795, to Anthony CONNARD Loose Papers: to be a stonecutter, indenture found
Q:71	12 Jan 1795	John WEBB, 15 yrs old 9 May 1795, to James BLINCO, to be a house carpenter
Q:71	12 Jan 1795	James WHITECOTTEN, 16 yrs old 15 Apr 1795, to Asa WILKERSON, to be a hatter
Q:71	12 Jan 1795	William LACEY, 16 yrs old 20 Sep 1794, to Ephraim LACEY
Q:71	12 Jan 1795	Ann MCFARLING, 11 yrs old 23 Jul 1794, to Ephraim LACEY
Q:81	13 Jan 1795	Eleanor CHAPMAN, 12 yrs old 5 Apr 1795, to David POTTS
Q:83	9 Feb 1795	James JAMES, 17 yrs old 26 Oct 1794, to Asa MOORE, to be a tanner and currier
Q:89	10 Feb 1795	John SHIRLOCK to Richard RUTLEDGE, to be a taylor
Q:121	13 Apr 1795	Ambrose POLTON, 16 yrs old 5 Mar 1795, to John TREBBEE
Q:123	14 Apr 1795	Joseph HAWKINS, 9 yrs old in Aug 1795, to Thomas FRANCIS, to be a blacksmith

Q:124	14 Apr 1795	Alexander TURNER to John DIVERS, to be a blacksmith (formerly bound to Thomas Reece)
Q:142	14 Apr 1795	Soury BEAMER, 4 yrs 4 mo & 15 das old, to John DAVIS Loose Papers: Sarey, dau of Ann Beamer
Q:144	14 Apr 1795	4 children MCGAHEY, Jeremiah McGahey's children, to be bound out
Q:153	11 May 1795	John MOXLEY to John WRIGHT, to be a blacksmith
Q:153	11 May 1795	Thomas POLTON, 12 yrs old 18 May 1795, to Joseph WOOD Loose Papers: Poulton, son of Martha Poulton
Q:194	13 Jul 1795	George WHITACRE to Jonah HAGUE, to be a hatter (bound to Caleb Whitacre in Jan 1788)
Q:196	13 Jul 1795	John SMITH, 15 yrs old 1 Apr 1795, to Enoch FRANCIS, to be a millwright
Q:206	10 Aug 1795	Daniel LOVETT, a servant, vs Henry BERKETT, for ill treatment. Q:213 - 11 Aug 1795 - Berkett to employ medical aid to Lovett
Q:212	11 Aug 1795	Charles SMITH to James BLINCO, to be a carpenter Loose Papers: son of Winnifred Smith, to James Blincoe, for 3 yr 6 mo, to be a house carpenter & joiner
Q:239	14 Sep 1795	Rebekah MCFARLING, 8 yrs old in Mar 1795, to Robert WADE
Q:239	14 Sep 1795	Joseph SIMCOCKE to William PAXON, formerly bound to Andrew Smith
Q:239	14 Sep 1795	James CANARY, 7 yrs old 15 Feb 1796, to Robert WILSON
Q:239	14 Sep 1795	Samuel HARVEY to Nero LAWSON
Q:239	14 Sep 1795	Nathan HARVEY to Nero LAWSON
Q:239	14 Sep 1795	John PEW, 5 yrs old at Christmas 1795, to Isaac HUMFREY Loose Papers: indenture found
Q:241	14 Sep 1795	Jonathan KENNEDY, 5 yrs 1 mo old, to John YOUNG
Q:243	14 Sep 1795	William BEAVERS, 3 yrs old 12 May 1795, to Thomas FLOOD, (book incorrectly shows 1796 on this page)

Apprentices, Poor Children and Bastards

Q:243	14 Sep 1795	Christopher DARNAL, 3 yrs old 25 Jun 1795, to William PALMER, (book incorrectly shows 1796 on this page) Loose Papers: to be a farmer, indenture found
Q:244	14 Sep 1795	Owen FLING to Sebastian MCPHERSON
Q:252	15 Sep 1795	George FRYER, 14 yrs old 16 Mar 1795, to Francis TITUS
Q:252	15 Sep 1795	Jesse FRYER, 6 yrs old 3 Apr 1795, to Francis TITUS
Q:253	16 Sep 1795	John GARNER to John DRISH, to be a joyner
Q:276	12 Oct 1795	Bayly DONALDSON to Jacob BAUGH, until 21 yrs old
Q:276	12 Oct 1795	William LACEY, 8 yrs old 1 Jul 1795, to Jonathan EWERS
Q:276	12 Oct 1795	Ann MCVICKERS, 7 yrs old, to Sarah TRAYHORN Loose Papers: indenture found
Q:279	9 Nov 1795	Robert BELLAMY, 14 yrs old 13 Jan 1796, to David MILLER
Q:307	14 Dec 1795	Samuel HAWKINS, 5 yrs old 10 Sep 1795, to Giles CRAVEN
Q:307	14 Dec 1795	George RUSSELL, 5 yrs old, to John GUNN Loose Papers: 5 yrs 8 mo old, mother moves from place to place
Q:307	14 Dec 1795	Peter MANLY, 8 yrs old, son of Hannah Manly, to Joseph LACEY Loose Papers: to Joseph Lay, to be a farmer, indenture found
Q:307	14 Dec 1795	Thomas MANLY, 3 yrs old, son of Hannah Manly, to Joseph LACEY Loose Papers: to Joseph Lay, to be a farmer, indenture found
Q:308	14 Dec 1795	Peter MASH, 8 yrs old, son of Nanny Mash, to Nicholas GRIMES, Jr.,
Q:308	14 Dec 1795	Lewis JONES, 4 yrs old in Sep 1795, to John BARROTT
Q:309	14 Dec 1795	Leven MCFARLING to James LEECH, (formerly bound) Loose Papers: Mary Leech requested change of masters
Q:309	14 Dec 1795	Eli CARTER, 7 yrs old 25 Nov 1795, to George LEWIS

Q:313	14 Dec 1795	Elizabeth CHRIESMAN to Isaac GIBSON, Sr. Loose Papers: surname Chisman, dau of Elizabeth Chrisman
Q:319	11 Jan 1796	Benjamin THOMKINS to Jacob MYERS, for 7 yrs
Q:322	8 Feb 1796	Mary SHIVERS, 9 yrs old 25 Nov 1796, to William WOODFORD Loose Papers: dau of Mary Shivers
Q:322	8 Feb 1796	William SUTHARD, 18 yrs old, to James COONEY
Q:322	8 Feb 1796	Robert WHITACRE, 14 yrs old, to Jesse MCVAY, to be a taylor Loose Papers: a cripple, to Jesse McVeigh
Q:322	8 Feb 1796	Jonathan RUSSELL, 5 yrs old 6 Jul 1795, to John CARNELL, stonemason,
Q:337	9 Feb 1796	Mary REED to John BROWN
Q:352	11 Apr 1796	William URTON, 10 yrs old 9 Feb 1796, to Thomas RUSSELL Loose Papers: consent of Mary Triplet
Q:354	11 Apr 1796	Sarah CROSS, 7 yrs old 21 Dec 1796, to William DANIEL Loose Papers: dau of Joseph & Maryan Cross, indenture found
Q:354	11 Apr 1796	Nancy CROSS, 5 yrs old 5 Aug 1796, to David THOMAS Loose Papers: dau of Joseph & Maryan Cross
Q:355	11 Apr 1796	Patty RACE to Phillip LONG Loose Papers: dau of Pheby Race, to Phillip & wife
Q:357	12 Apr 1796	William FERGUSSON, 10 yrs old 27 Dec 1795, to James BROWN, Sr. Loose Papers: Ferguson, to his gr-father, indenture found
Q:370	12 Apr 1796	Abigail MOXLEY, 10 yrs old, to John DONOHOE
Q:391	9 May 1796	Lewis JONES, 4 yrs old 10 Sep 1795, to Samuel RICHARDS, (previously ordered to be bound to John Barrett) Loose Papers: son of Sarah Lewis
Q:391	9 May 1796	Mary WHITLEY, 6 yrs old 15 Jul 1796, to James SINKLER
Q:408	14 Jun 1796	George WAIGLY, servant, vs John BORD, for misusage

Apprentices, Poor Children and Bastards

Q:442	11 Jul 1796	John WEAVER, 17 yrs old 10 May 1796, to Thomas FRANCIS, to be a blacksmith
Q:443	11 Jul 1796	William STUART, 4 yrs old 28 Aug 1796, to John BROWN
Q:445	11 Jul 1796	Rachel MARR, (alias Huet), 16 yrs old 12 Jun 1796, to Anthony LAMBAG
Q:446	11 Jul 1796	Rebekah HAWKINGS, 3 yrs old 15 Mar 1796, to Thomas FOUCH
Q:475	12 Sep 1796	Suckey, 6 yrs old 1 Jun 1796, a free negro, to Susanna Pearson BINNS
Q:476	12 Sep 1796	Charles, 3 yrs old 1 Apr 1796, a free negro, to Simon A. BINNS
Q:476	12 Sep 1796	Sarah HAWKINS, 7 yrs old 21 Jan 1796, to Simon A. BINNS
Q:478	12 Sep 1796	Robert HUTCHISON, 14 yrs old 18 Apr 1796, to Robert LATHAM Loose Papers: surname Hutchinson, son of Ann Hutchinson
Q:478	12 Sep 1796	Edmond LOVETT to Abner WILLIAMS
Q:479	12 Sep 1796	Walter Bayne SMALLWOOD to Abner WILLIAMS
Q:482	12 Sep 1796	Polly HOWELL, 7 yrs old 20 Mar 1796, to James BRADY
Q:482	12 Sep 1796	Amasa POOL, 14 yrs old 3 Dec 1795, to Noah JOHNSTON, to be a blacksmith
Q:482	12 Sep 1796	Eleanor MCDEVIT, 11 yrs old, to Robert GRAHAM, indenture found
Q:491	13 Sep 1796	Casper LYNIMYER to William MAINS
Q:503	10 Oct 1796	Nathan SELF, 1 yr old 8 Feb 1797, to Emanuel LAY Loose Papers: son of Ann Self
Q:505	10 Oct 1796	Daniel, 12 yrs old in Dec 1796, a Black, to John SCHOOLEY
Q:508	11 Oct 1796	John PHILIPS to Andrew REDMOND, to be a tanner and currier
R:10	15 Nov 1796	Polly HESSE to John GREEN
R:31	12 Dec 1796	John MCCANN, 3 yrs old 28 Apr 1796, to William WOODFORD Loose Papers: son of Rebeckah Eaton, indenture found
R:55	13 Feb 1797	James WILLSON, 15 yrs old 20 Apr 1797, to Samuel LOVE, to be a miller

R:55	13 Feb 1797	Peggy CONNELLY, 5 yrs old 1 Sep 1796, to Thomas GIBSON
R:56	13 Feb 1797	Lavitha VIOLETT, 8 yrs old 4 Apr 1797, to Thomas WILSON Loose Papers: a baseborn child sworn to Enoch Triplett by Jemimah Violett who has left these parts and left the child with him
R:56	13 Feb 1797	Mahlon HOWELL, 19 yrs old in Mar 1797, to John GARNER, to be a taylor Loose Papers: son of Rebekah Howell
R:58	13 Feb 1797	J__ RALPH to John GARNER, to be a taylor
R:58	13 Feb 1797	Delilah HEPBURNE, 7 yrs old 6 Sep 1797, to John CAMMELL, (stonemason),
R:58	13 Feb 1797	Simpson DUTY, 5 yrs old, to Charles LITTLETON
R:58	13 Feb 1797	William KENT, 16 yrs old 1 Mar 1797, to Joseph NEWMAN, to be a carpenter Loose Papers: consent of June (Jane or Jean) Kent, mother
R:63	14 Feb 1797	Hannah HUNT, 11 yrs old 15 Jun 1796, to Thomas GREGG
R:63	14 Feb 1797	William HUNT, 6 yrs old 14 Mar 1796, to Thomas GREGG
R:63	14 Feb 1797	Lewis HUNT, 9 yrs old 15 Apr 1796, to William SMITH
R:68	14 Feb 1797	Elizabeth BEEZELY, 5 yrs old 14 Feb 1797, to John SUTHARD Loose Papers: indenture signed by William Suddith, indenture found
R:68	14 Feb 1797	GOING, 5 yrs old in Jul 1796, a black boy, to Stacey TAYLOR
R:71	14 Feb 1797	Casper LYNIMIER to John STOUTSENBARGER, to be a shoemaker (formerly bound to William Mains)
R:104	11 Apr 1797	John DAVIS, 14 yrs old 22 Sep 1796, to John BEEZER, to be a plaisterer
R:107	8 May 1797	Nancy ABBOTT to Richard & Hannah ROACH Loose Papers: dau of Mary Abbott
R:107	8 May 1797	Mary ACRES, dau of James Acres, to William JAMES, until she becomes of age
R:108	8 May 1797	Elijah FERGUSSON to Josiah WHITE, to be a taylor (formerly bound to Thomas McCabe)

Apprentices, Poor Children and Bastards

R:120	9 May 1797	Thomas HUTCHISON, apprentice, vs George ROBISON, for ill treatmen
R:155	10 Jul 1797	Sophia, 4 yrs old 1 Feb 1797, a free negro, to Casper ECKHART
R:159	14 Aug 1797	Sarah BUCKLEY, 9 yrs old 22 Nov 1797, to John JOHNSTON Loose Papers: surname Berkely, on request of Nicholas & Mary Kile - orphan brought from MD - dau of Mary Kile's dec'd sister, to John Johnston (son of George), indenture found
R:187	11 Sep 1797	John POLING, 9 yrs 9 mos old 12 Aug 1797, to Theophilus HUGHS Loose Papers: step-son of William Cross (or Crows)
R:190	11 Sep 1797	John MAHONEY, 4 yrs old, to John HOLDING Loose Papers: to be a planter & farmer, son of Riner Mahoney
R:190	11 Sep 1797	Thomas MAHONEY, 2 yrs 9 mos old, to John HOLDING Loose Papers: to be a planter & farmer, son of Riner Mahoney
R:190	11 Sep 1797	Ambrose POULTON to Price JACOBS, to be a stone mason (formerly bound to John Trebbe - indenture assigned to Jacobs)
R:191	11 Sep 1797	Amos PEARCE, 12 yrs old 1 Apr 1797, to Richard MATTHEWS, to be a sadler
R:193	11 Sep 1797	Sally TRIP, 7 yrs old, to Thomas GIBSON
R:193	11 Sep 1797	Joshua TRIP, 3 yrs old, to Hugh ROGERS
R:193	11 Sep 1797	James BURCH to Harrison BRADSHAW, for 10 yrs from 1 Dec 1797 Loose Papers: son of Linny Burch, to be a farmer, until 21
R:194	11 Sep 1797	John HOWELL, 6 yrs old 10 May 1798, to John OXLEY
R:194	11 Sep 1797	Thomas RIDER, 16 yrs old 23 Jul 1797, to Jacob FRYE, to be a blacksmith Loose Papers: son of Catharin Cusine(?)
R:198	12 Sep 1797	Thomas COLLINS to Samuel THATCHER, to be a waggonmaker
R:203	13 Sep 1797	Daniel SPECHT, 12 yrs old 10 Jan 1797, to James REVELLS, to be a taylor Loose Papers: son of Catherine Callihan

R:213	9 Oct 1797	Mahlon COCKERILL, 8 yrs old 27 Jan 1797, to Theophilus HUGHS
R:216	9 Oct 1797	Charlotte PARKER, 3 yrs old, to Thomas HATCHER Loose Papers: indenture found
R:216	9 Oct 1797	Hannah SMITH, 7 yrs old, to Benjamin BARTON
R:216	9 Oct 1797	Daniel SMITH, 5 yrs old, to Thomas EWERS Loose Papers: to be a farmer, 8 yrs old in Mar 1798, indenture found
R:260	11 Dec 1797	John TAPIN, 7 yrs old 12 Dec 1797, to D. HURST Loose Papers: age as of 12 Nov 1797, to David Hurst
R:260	11 Dec 1797	John PUE to Edward POTTS, (formerly bound to Isaac Humphrey who is now dead) Loose Papers: surname Pew
R:265	12 Dec 1797	Catherine VANPELT vs Thomas CHAPMAN, for ill treatment. R:278, 9 Jan 1798, removed from Chapman's possession
R:266	12 Dec 1797	Rachel MARR, alias Huet, to Thomas FRANCIS Loose Papers: 16 yrs old 12 Jun 1797
R:266	12 Dec 1797	John MCGAHEY, child of Jeremiah McGahey, to be bound
R:266	12 Dec 1797	David MCGAHEY, child of Jeremiah McGahey, to be bound
R:266	12 Dec 1797	Curtis MCGAHEY, child of Jeremiah McGahey, to be bound
R:266	12 Dec 1797	Venus, 11 yrs old, a free negro, to George BROWN
R:268	12 Dec 1797	Betty KNIGHTING, dau of Betty Knighting, to be bound
R:268	12 Dec 1797	Jane CAMPBELL, 8 yrs old 14 May 1797, to John PERRY Loose Papers: dau of Clary Jones
R:268	12 Dec 1797	Edmond PERRY, 3 yrs old 3 Aug 1797, to John PERRY Loose Papers: son of Clary Jones
R:273	8 Jan 1798	Jacob JENKINS, 16 yrs old 16 Dec 1797, to Asa MOORE Loose Papers: son of Anne Taylor, stepson of Ambrose Taylor

Apprentices, Poor Children and Bastards 69

R:275	8 Jan 1798	James HARDING to Jonah THOMPSON, et al.,owners of the Potowmack Chief,
R:283	12 Feb 1798	Andrew , a free negro, to James MOORE, formerly bound to Josias Clapham
R:284	12 Feb 1798	Betsey , 3 yrs old, a free mulatto, to John ASKIN
R:284	12 Feb 1798	Clarissa JONES, 4 yrs old 4 May 1798, to Gideon CUMMINGS, (weaver),
R:285	12 Feb 1798	William MURPHEY, 17 yrs old 20 Mar 1798, to Jacob SILCOAT, to be a blacksmith Loose Papers: son of Mary Murphey, to Jacob Silcott, indenture found
R:285	13 Feb 1798	Jeremiah SLACK, 16 yrs old 28 Sep 1797, to Jacob DAMEWOOD, to be a joyner and house carpenter
R:287	13 Feb 1798	Mason TILLET, 10 yrs old 12 Jun 1798, to Amos DONHAM
R:289	14 Feb 1798	William ELLIOT, 17 yrs old 1 Dec 1797, to John DRISH, to be a joyner and house carpenter
R:290	14 Feb 1798	Catherine VANPELT to Thomas TORBERT
R:348	9 Apr 1798	Samuel MURPHEY, 16 yrs old 31 Jan 1798, to Theophilus HOUGH, to be a house carpenter Loose Papers: indenture found
S:17	15 May 1798	John POULTON, 13 yrs old 18 Apr 1798, to Samuel HOUGH, to be a hatter Loose Papers: son of Martha Poulton
S:88	9 Jul 1798	Maria BAGLEY, 7 yrs old in Sep 1798, to Abraham WARFORD
S:89	9 Jul 1798	William HALBERT to Joseph NEWMAN, to be a joiner
S:89	9 Jul 1798	Thomas HALBERT to Joseph NEWMAN, to be a joiner
S:89	9 Jul 1798	Michael HALBERT to Henry STORTS, to be a millwright
S:89	9 Jul 1798	James HALBERT to Henry STORTS, to be a millwright
S:176	10 Sep 1798	Polly , 2 yrs 9 mo old, a free negro, to Mahlon HOUGH
S:178	10 Sep 1798	Linna SINCLAIR to Jesse MCVEIGH, (formerly bound to Arthur Rogers)
S:179	10 Sep 1798	Thomas JONES, 16 yrs old 1 Sep 1798, to Griffith THOMAS, to be a carpenter

S:179	10 Sep 1798	Thomas RIDER to Abraham BROWN, to be a blacksmith (formerly bound to Jacob Frye)
S:183	11 Sep 1798	Beninah RICE, 3 yrs old 10 Sep 1798, to William ROBERTS Loose Papers: to be a farmer, indenture found
S:190	11 Sep 1798	Luke GOING to George RHODES, to be a blacksmith (formerly bound to John Littlejohn)
S:190	11 Sep 1798	Peter COLEMAN vs Alexander MCMAKEN, for detaining him in servitude - complaint dismissed
S:201	13 Sep 1798	Elizabeth CARTWRIGHT to Mrs. Ann ANSLEY
S:208	8 Oct 1798	Milley BEEZELY, 15 yrs old 8 Feb 1799, to Elizabeth SWARTS
S:210	8 Oct 1798	James WOOLCARD, 12 yrs old 15 Nov 1798, to George SHIVELY Loose Papers: requested by William Wolcard
S:212	8 Oct 1798	Susanna WILT, 10 yrs old 17 Dec 1798, to Jacob WALTMAN
S:212	8 Oct 1798	John TALBOTT, 12 yrs old 23 Dec 1798, to Henry TAYLOR, to be a miller
S:257	10 Dec 1798	William BUFFINGTON, 6 yrs old 5 Oct 1798, to Thomas TREBBE Loose Papers: son of Ester Phillips, to Thomas Trebbe Sr., indenture found
S:257	10 Dec 1798	John HAWKINS, 14 yrs old 25 Dec 1798, to Thomas TREBBE
S:258	10 Dec 1798	James EATON, 16 yrs old 27 May 1798, to John DODD, Jr., to be a stonemason Loose Papers: son of Lydia O'Neal
S:259	10 Dec 1798	Joseph HOGUE to Samuel GREGG, Jr., to be a miller
S:278	11 Dec 1798	Lydia MCKNIGHT, 8 yrs old 28 Oct 1798, to Griffith PIERCE Loose Papers: dau of Mary Alexander, indenture found
S:284	14 Jan 1799	Joseph LACEY, 12 yrs old 23 Jan 1799, to Asa MOORE, to be a sadler Loose Papers: son of Margaret Lacey
S:284	14 Jan 1799	Amos BEALE to William SMITH, to be a stone mason

Apprentices, Poor Children and Bastards

S:285	14 Jan 1799	Henry NICHOLS to John HEAD Loose Papers: son of Elizabeth Meredith
S:289	15 Jan 1799	John PIERCE, 17 yrs old 17 Mar 1798, to James COCKRANE Loose Papers: to be a blacksmith, son of Nancy Vickers, indenture found
S:289	15 Jan 1799	Polly JACOBS, 14 yrs old 31 Jan 1799, to William HOUGH Loose Papers: (Patty)
S:295	11 Feb 1799	Constan HUGHES, 16 yrs old 10 Jan 1799, to Jacob STATER, to be a tanner
S:297	11 Feb 1799	Daniel FARNSWORTH, 12 yrs old 30 Jan 1799, to James CAMELL, to be a waver and farmer Loose Papers: son of Hannah Farnsworth, to James Campbell
S:305	12 Feb 1799	Betty CARTWRIGHT to Jehu MILLER, (formerly bound to Ann Ansley)
S:366	8 Apr 1799	James SHERVIN, 12 yrs old, to James N. FISHBACK Loose Papers: no parents to his (Shervin's) knowledge
S:368	8 Apr 1799	Alexander WILSON, 17 yrs old 16 Nov 1798, to John WRIGHT, to be a hatter
S:370	8 Apr 1799	Jesse JONES, 15 yrs old 2 Aug 1799, to James COCKRANE, to be a blacksmith Loose Papers: son of Ellender Jones
S:371	8 Apr 1799	El___ MILBURNE, 3 yrs old 25 Oct 1798, to Jonathan EWERS, Jr. Loose Papers: son of Rebecah Milburne
S:371	8 Apr 1799	Thomas LYNN, 2 yrs old 14 Jan 1799, to William RACE Loose Papers: son of Jane Lynn
S:371	8 Apr 1799	Lydia CATLETT, 5 yrs old 12 Feb 1799, to William RACE Loose Papers: consent of Jemima Catlett
S:371	9 Apr 1799	Mahala JONES, 5 yrs old 4 May 1799, to Gideon CUMMINGS, (a weaver) Loose Papers: child of Cleareny Jones, raised by Ann Derrey, correction of name
S:371	9 Apr 1799	Joseph COCKERILL to John BEATTY
S:372	9 Apr 1799	William LEWIS, 17 yrs old, to Charles JOHNSTON, to be a house carpenter

S:379	10 Apr 1799	Abijah SANDS, 16 yrs old 17 Feb 1799, to Reuben HIXON, to be a blacksmith Loose Papers: son of Mary Dunsmore
T:1	13 May 1799	Fanny MANLY, 3 yrs old, negro, to Bazel STONESTREET
T:1	13 May 1799	Susanna MANLY, 1 yr old in Oct 1798, free negro, to Robert JACKSON
T:2	13 May 1799	Charles POULTON, 12 yrs old 2 Jan 1799, to James BEST, to be a farmer Loose Papers: son of Martha Poulton
T:5	13 May 1799	Betsey ROOF, 13 yrs old 18 Dec 1799, to Philip EVERHEART
T:5	13 May 1799	Catey ROOF, 10 yrs old 29 Aug 1799, to David AXLINE
T:8	14 May 1799	John JAMES, 15 yrs old 23 Jan 1799, to William CANN, (Caun?),
T:9	14 May 1799	Joseph COMBS, 18 yrs 5 mos old, to Matthew WETHERBY, to be a house joiner Loose Papers: son of Molly Kebb
T:12	14 May 1799	Nehemiah WADE, 15 yrs old 1 May 1799, to Thomas WILKISON, to be a taylor
T:22	11 Jun 1799	Polly MOORE, 9 yrs old, to John ROBERTSON
T:35	12 Jul 1799	Samuel KEVAN, 15 yrs old, to Archibald MORRISON, to be a hatter
T:38	8 Jul 1799	John PHILIPS, apprentice of, ads. Andrew REDMOND, complaint for apprentice absenting himself without cause
T:38	8 Jul 1799	John SWAIN, 13 yrs old 1 Dec 1798, to Benjamin H. CANBY, to be a tanner
T:60	12 Aug 1799	Joseph HAWKINS, apprentice, vs Thomas FRANCIS, for ill treatment
T:87	9 Sep 1799	Rebekah BROOMHILL to John SCHOOLEY
T:87	9 Sep 1799	Ann MCDANIEL, 12 yrs old 12 Mar 1800, to James ROACH
T:88	10 Sep 1799	William GLADHILL, 10 yrs old 23 Jun 1799, to John DAVIS, to be a farmer Loose Papers: son of Mary Gladhill
T:96	10 Sep 1799	Elizabeth VICKERS, 5 yrs old 5 May 1799, to Joseph ROBERTS
T:97	10 Sep 1799	Buley ASHTON, 12 yrs old 29 Jan 1800, to Jonathan NUTT

Apprentices, Poor Children and Bastards 73

T:98	10 Sep 1799	Abraham LAIR, 14 yrs old 15 Apr 1799, to James NIXON
T:100	10 Sep 1799	Isaaiah CARR, 5 yrs old 13 Oct 1799, to Robert WAID Loose Papers: son of Elizabeth Carr, given name Izack
T:104	11 Sep 1799	Samuel HARRIS, 19 yrs old 6 Jan 1800, to Isaac HARRIS, to be a tanner
T:104	11 Sep 1799	Francis BOWEN, 18 yrs old, to Isaac HARRIS, to be a tanner
T:111	12 Sep 1799	Amos MOORE, 6 yrs old 20 Oct 1798, to James CAMPBELL Loose Papers: indenture found
T:122	14 Oct 1799	Elisha FERGUSSON, 12 yrs old 2 Sep 1799, to Thomas BARKLEY Loose Papers: orphan, surname Ferguson, son of Mary Ferguson, indenture found
T:129	15 Oct 1799	John BRADY, 16 yrs old 27 Mar 1799, to Thomas Cradill WILLS, to be a joyner & house carpenter Loose Papers: indenture found
T:135	15 Oct 1799	Rt. BRABHAM, 12 yrs old 13 Feb 1800, to Robert FULTON, to be a wheelwright
T:141	11 Nov 1799	Zeebar DUNLAP, born Dec. Court 1795, to be bound to fit person
T:141	11 Nov 1799	Benjamin WATSON, 5 yrs old in Mar 1800, to be bound to a fit person
T:196	9 Dec 1799	Mary STICKLER, 2 yrs old 30 Oct 1799, to Joseph SMITH, Sr.,
T:196	9 Dec 1799	Richard RAMSEY to Enoch FRANCIS, to be a miller Loose Papers: son of Mary Ramsey
T:196	9 Dec 1799	Anne CRAGE, 7 yrs old 28 May 1799, to Ezekial POTTS Loose Papers: Jonathan Milbourn gr-father, John Peacock step-father
T:196	9 Dec 1799	John HOWELL, 7 yrs old 10 May 1799, to Abner CRAVEN, formerly bound to John Oxley
T:210	10 Dec 1799	Elijah WILLIAMS, 13 yrs old 10 Jun 1799, to Wm. BEVERIDGE, to be a blacksmith
T:210	10 Dec 1799	William BRADY to Jesse MCVEIGH, to be a taylor Loose Papers: near 14 yrs

T:211	10 Dec 1799	Leah BALL, 13 yrs old 9 Dec 1799, to John WEST
T:238	14 Jan 1800	Jesse DODD, 15 yrs old 11 Dec 1799, to Joseph BENTLEY, to be a hatter
T:240	14 Jan 1800	Thomas MCCOUATT, orphan of Thomas McCouatt, to Adam LYNN, to be a silversmith & jeweller
T:277	14 Apr 1800	William BEST, 17 yrs old 11 Jun 1800, to Jacob CARNES, to be a taylor
T:280	14 Apr 1800	Abraham VICKERS, 11 yrs 6 mo old 13 Oct 1799, to William VICKERS
T:280	14 Apr 1800	Aquilla VICKERS, 4 yrs old 13 Aug 1799, to William VICKERS
T:280	14 Apr 1800	Catherine PHILIPS, 5 yrs old 20 Dec 1799, to Bernard TAYLOR
T:280	14 Apr 1800	Bill , (a negro) 5 yrs old 10 Aug 1800, to David GOODEN, to be a shoemaker
T:284	15 Apr 1800	Catharine LAYER, 13 yrs old 30 Apr 1800, to Elizabeth SCOTT
T:287	15 Apr 1800	John FILPOTT, 10 yrs old, to Jesse TAYLOR
T:296	16 Apr 1800	Mason TILLETT, apprentice, vs Amos DONHAM, for ill treatment (Sybbil Tillett filed complaint)
T:310	13 May 1800	Isaiah NICHOLS, 7 yrs old 13 May Last, to William NICHOLS Loose Papers: 13 May 1800, to be a farmer, indenture found
T:310	13 May 1800	Jane CRAIG, 10 yrs old 24 May 1799, to William PIGGOTT Loose Papers: 24 May 1800
T:361	14 Jul 1800	Sihon SWAIN, 10 yrs old 20 Apr 1800, to Patrick MERRICK, to be a cooper
T:365	14 Jul 1800	Alexander HUNT, 8 yrs old, to Saml. DAVIS, to be a farmer Loose Papers: in May 1800, son of Martha Hunt
T:365	14 Jul 1800	Thomas EVANS, 17 yrs old, to Enoch WHITACRE, to be a hatter
T:370	15 Jul 1800	Francis BOWEN an apprentice of Isaac HARRIS, detained by John Dulin & Elizabeth Bowen
T:396	11 Aug 1800	Francis BOWEN to John DULIN

Apprentices, Poor Children and Bastards 75

U:2	8 Sep 1800	Rachel FITZGERALD, 8 yrs old 13 Aug 1800, to John AXLINE
U:12	8 Sep 1800	Billy HOPKINS, a free negro, son of Minty Hopkins, a free negro, 7 yrs old 15 Aug 1800, to Dublin BITZETT
U:30	9 Sep 1800	Nancy HACKETT, 9 yrs old 23 Feb 1801, to James ELLIOTT
U:61	13 Oct 1800	John BUSSLE to Walter S. WARRANT, to be a taylor Loose Papers: surname Bussell, orphan, Randolph Mott, gdn., of Frederick Co., VA, to Walter S. Warren
U:66	14 Oct 1800	William LESTER, 7 yrs old 22 May 1800, to Jacob SANNS Loose Papers: son of Sarah Lester
U:85	10 Nov 1800	James SHERVIN apprentice of James N. FISHBACK, complaint by apprentice, complaint dismissed 9 Mar 1801, U:244
U:118	14 Nov 1800	John NEALE, 2 yrs 2 mo old 10 Nov 1800, to Thomas DAVIS, to be a farmer Loose Papers: orphan, son of Mary Neale, indenture found
U:152	8 Dec 1800	Catharine LAYER, 13 yrs old 30 Apr 1800, to Stephen SCOTT
U:165	9 Dec 1800	Winifred HUNT, 6 yrs old in Jan 1801, to Reuben SETTLE
U:168	12 Jan 1801	Ann (Nancy) HACKETT to Daniel WHITE, (formerly bound to James Elliott)
U:169	12 Jan 1801	Thomas HACKETT, 7 yrs old 1 Jan 1801, orphan of Thomas Hackett, dec'd, to Daniel WHITE
U:169	12 Jan 1801	James STEVENSON, 17 yrs old 16 Feb 1801, to Jesse MCVEIGH, to be a taylor
U:171	12 Jan 1801	Thomas HALL, orphan of Thomas Hall, dec'd, to David GOODEN, to be a shoemaker
U:194	10 Feb 1801	Betty to Isaac VANDEVENTER, Jr., (formerly bound to John Erskins)
U:194	10 Feb 1801	Walker LANGLEY, 16 yrs old 14 Feb 1801, to Joseph ROBERTS, to be a blacksmith Loose Papers: Walter, son of Sarah Langley
U:195	10 Feb 1801	Amasa POOL to John IREY, to be a blacksmith (formerly bound to Noah Johnson)

U:195	10 Feb 1801	John PHILIPS, 6 yrs old 27 Feb 1801, to Samuel HOLLAM Loose Papers: to Israel Williams, indenture found
U:237	9 Mar 1801	Amos PIERCE, 16 yrs old 1 Apr 1801, to James COCKRANE, to be a blacksmith (formerly bound to Richard Matthews) Loose Papers: orphan
U:300	13 Apr 1801	John STOKER, 17 yrs old 25 Feb 1801, to William SKINNER, to be a fan maker
U:306	13 Apr 1801	Benjamin BAGLEY, 3 yrs old 7 Mar 1801, to Sandford RAMEY Loose Papers: son of Catherine Bagley, to Sandford Wren
U:306	13 Apr 1801	John SNIDER, 8 yrs old 27 Oct 1800, to John STOUTSBERGER Loose Papers: surname Snyder, son of Mary Snyder
U:306	13 Apr 1801	James MCDANIEL, free negro 10 yrs old in Sep 1801, to Edward GLEESON
U:308	13 Apr 1801	Middleton HARRIS, 12 yrs old 19 Jul 1801, to Richard SKINNER Loose Papers: son of Rebeckah Batson
U:310	14 Apr 1801	Henry BURDINE, 17 yrs old 1 Oct 1800, to William SMITH, to be a blacksmith
U:310	14 Apr 1801	Lurana THATCHER, 11 yrs old 12 Apr 1801, to Caleb GREGG
U:310	14 Apr 1801	Harry , a free black boy, to Richard CONNER, to be a shoemaker
U:312	14 Apr 1801	Jonah TOMKINS to John SCHOOLEY
U:324	11 May 1801	James HAGARMAN, 14 yrs old 17 Jan 1801, to James GUNN Loose Papers: surname Hinksman, consent of Samuel Hinksman
U:327	11 May 1801	Elizabeth PARKER, 5 yrs old in May 1801, to Thomas HUMPHREY Loose Papers: 5 yrs old 5 Apr 1801, to Thomas and Mary, indenture found
U:329	11 May 1801	Asaph DAVIS, 16 yrs old in Mar 1801, to John DRISH, to be a house carpenter
U:337	12 May 1801	William HUNTER, 3 yrs old in Mar 1801, to George SMITH, farmer,

Apprentices, Poor Children and Bastards

V:44	12 Oct 1801	Catharine PHILIPS, 6 yrs old 8 Feb 1802, to Israel WILLIAMS Loose Papers: 7 yrs old 23 Feb 1802, indenture found
V:50	12 Oct 1801	Lewis TURNER to John BOYD, to be a house joiner
V:50	12 Oct 1801	Major Fielding TURNER to John B. RATTEE, to be a plaisterer
V:51	12 Oct 1801	Thomas SMITH, 18 yrs old 20 Nov 1800, to Benjamin WALKER, to be a shoemaker
V:52	12 Oct 1801	Alfred WRIGHT, 5 yrs old 16 Aug 1801, to Jacob CALOR Loose Papers: son of Ann Morgan, her name was Ann (W)Right when she had Alfred. The child's father's name was Beshers
V:120	14 Dec 1801	Samuel MINER, 14 yrs old 12 Mar 1801, to Nero LAWSON Loose Papers: orphan, to be a farmer, indenture found
V:120	14 Dec 1801	Nathaniel MINER, 13 yrs old 24 Aug 1801, to Nero LAWSON Loose Papers: orphan, to be a farmer, indenture found
V:156	8 Feb 1802	Joseph HEATON, 6 yrs old 22 May 1802, to James ROSE
V:157	8 Feb 1802	John HOUGH, 16 yrs old 15 Jan 1803, to Charles JOHNSON, to be a carpenter
V:158	8 Feb 1802	Samuel VOLLUM, 17 yrs old 20 Feb 1802, to be bound out, to be a miller Loose Papers: surname Follin, son of Bathsheba Follin, bound to James Fox
V:158	8 Feb 1802	Mary HUGHES, 14 yrs old 29 Mar 1801, to Joseph HOLMES Loose Papers: surname Hews, dau of Mary Hues
V:160	8 Feb 1802	George Dorson HILL, 14 yrs old 16 Oct 1801, to Samuel GUY Loose Papers: son of Roseanna Hill
V:160	8 Feb 1802	Costolon Dorson HILL, 12 yrs old 19 Jan 1802, to Samuel GUY, 12 Apr 1802, V:235, order of 8 Feb rescinded and C.D. Hill bound to John Kile Loose Papers: son of Roseanna Hill, age as of 15 Dec 1801, 19 Jan 1802 date of consent

V:167	9 Feb 1802	Duanna BURGOYNE, 5 yrs old 31 Jul 1802, to Adam HOUSHOLDER, Jr. Loose Papers: dau of Sarah Burguoin, indenture found
V:187	8 Mar 1802	Tamzon PATTERSON, 3 yrs old 1 Oct 1801, to John LOGAN Loose Papers: dau of Marey Bails
V:232	12 Mar 1802	Tacy DUNLOP, 3 yrs old, to Thomas & wife FRANCIS
V:235	12 Apr 1802	Thomas PHILIPS, 14 yrs and 21 days old 12 Apr 1802, to Christian HOPE, to be a mill wright Loose Papers: son of Polley Phillips, indenture found
V:235	12 Apr 1802	Thomas WALKER, 16 yrs old 9 Jun 1802, to Thomas MILLS, to be a house carpenter and joiner
V:235	12 Apr 1802	William DOVE to Samuel GUY, to be a house carpenter and joiner
V:240	12 Apr 1802	Thomas FOLLIN, 17 yrs old 17 Jan 1803, to Enoch FRANCIS, to be a cooper and miller Loose Papers: orphan, indenture found
V:249	13 Apr 1802	Grace MCCULLEY, 10 yrs old in May 1802, to Joseph KNOX, 14 Apr 1802 - V:262, order of 13 Apr rescinded and bound to John Adams Loose Papers: surname McCaulley, indenture found
V:261	14 Apr 1802	Elijah WILLIAMS, apprentice, vs William BEVERIDGE, complaint for ill treatment, V:266, 10 May 1802, complaint dismissed
V:263	10 May 1802	James HUNT, 9 yrs old, to Jacob BROWN
V:265	10 May 1802	Elizabeth HUNT, 15 yrs old 12 Jul 1802, to William ROBERTS
V:266	10 May 1802	Jacob GOODHEART, 15 yrs old, to John WEAST, to be a weaver
V:269	11 May 1802	Sally HUET, 3 yrs old 9 Jan 1802, to George ROWAN
V:271	11 May 1802	Francis COLLIER, 18 yrs old 13 Jul 1802, to John MYERS, to be a cabinetmaker Loose Papers: born July 23, 1784
V:274	12 May 1802	Nathaniel ODEN, 10 yrs old in Dec 1801, to Nathaniel SKINNER
V:274	12 May 1802	James ODEN, 8 yrs old in Dec 1801, to Nathaniel SKINNER

Apprentices, Poor Children and Bastards 79

V:284	12 May 1802	Elizabeth TERRELL, orphan of Margaret Terrell, to John MCCORMICK
V:287	14 Jun 1802	Elam CARTER, son of Hannah Carter, to Joseph BEARD, to be a cabinet maker
V:294	14 Jun 1802	Henry PURDY, alias Henry Swarts, vs William SMITH, for ill treatment
V:302	15 Jun 1802	Wm LEWIS to be summoned for absenting himself from his master's service
V:351	12 Jul 1802	John WATKINS, 4 yrs old 8 Aug 1802, to Cndora LUCUS
V:351	12 Jul 1802	Bernard ONEALE, 8 yrs old 17 Jun 1802, to Peter CARR Loose Papers: consent of Elizabeth O'Neal
V:358	9 Aug 1802	James FERGUSON, 10 yrs old 10 Oct 1802, to Ezar DILLON Loose Papers: son of Marey Ferguson, age as of 10 Oct 1801
V:361	9 Aug 1802	Abner BAILS, 10 yrs old 18 Feb 1802, to John LOGAN, to be a shoe and boot maker Loose Papers: son of Frances Beale, indenture found
V:423	13 Sep 1802	Stephen MCDANIEL, 7 yrs old, to James MITCHELL
V:423	13 Sep 1802	John SWEAN, 15 yrs old 1 Dec 1802, to Richard GREEN, to be a taylor Loose Papers: son of Marthew Frost, age as of 1 Dec 1801, to Richard Green, Sr.
V:435	14 Sep 1802	William MCFARLAND, 17 yrs old in Apr 1802, to Jacob PETIT, to be a stone mason Loose Papers: son of Mary McFarling, to Jacob (or Joab) Petit
V:452	11 Oct 1802	Israel PHILIPS, 11 yrs 7 mo old 1 Oct 1802, to Christian HOPE, to be a mill wright Loose Papers: son of Sally Phillips, age 12 yrs 1 Mar 1803, indenture found
V:456	11 Oct 1802	Betty KINGTON, 10 yrs old, to John SKILMAN Loose Papers: surname Knighton, dau of Betty Knighton, indenture found
V:456	11 Oct 1802	William KINGTON, 8 yrs old, to John SKILMAN Loose Papers: surname Knighton, son of Betty Knighton, to be a farmer, indenture found

W:26	13 Dec 1802	Richard ROACH, 14 yrs old, to Abraham SILKET, to be a blacksmith
W:28	13 Dec 1802	Jonathan NIXON, 17 yrs old 17 Nov 1802, to Joshua GREGG, to be a hatter, W:95, 14 Feb 1803, order of 13 Dec 1802 rescinded
W:29	13 Dec 1802	Emly MCABOY, (alias Kidwell), 4 yrs old about 15 Jun 1802, to James HATCHER
W:30	13 Dec 1802	Elizabeth CROMLY, 4 yrs old 25 Jul 1802, to Jacob COSS
W:32	13 Dec 1802	Margaret VANANDER, 10 yrs old 18 Aug 1802, to Solomon HOGE
W:67	10 Jan 1803	Cornelius PALMER, 14 yrs old 21 Feb 1803, to Charles HUMPHREY, to be a blacksmith Loose Papers: son of Mary Smith
W:72	11 Jan 1803	Thomas H. PEALE, 15 yrs old 15 May 1803, to Joseph BEARD, to be a cabinet maker and joiner
W:73	11 Jan 1803	James TAVENDER, 18 yrs old next Jan., to James ROSE Loose Papers: son of Susanah Tavender
W:95	14 Feb 1803	John MANSFIELD, child of John Mansfield, to be bound
W:95	14 Feb 1803	James MANSFIELD, child of John Mansfield, to be bound Loose Papers: to Joseph Knox to be a wheelwright, indenture found
W:98	14 Feb 1803	Benjamin WILLIAMS, 13 yrs old, to Mesheck LACY, to be a hatter
W:98	14 Feb 1803	Elizabeth VICKERS, 5 yrs old 5 May 1799, to James WALTERS
W:100	15 Feb 1803	Elihue GOING, 18 yrs old in Apr 1803, to William WRIGHT
W:121	16 Apr 1803	David PUSEY, 17 yrs old 11 Nov 1802, to MOORE AND PHILLIPS, to be a tanner and currier, indenture found
W:123	16 Apr 1803	William MITCHELL, 13 yrs old 25 Mar 1804, to Joseph COMBS, to be a house carpenter and joiner Loose Papers: Mary Mitchell, mother, petitioned court to have order rescinded
W:127	9 May 1803	John WAUGH, 8 yrs old, to Richard FREEMAN
W:141	9 May 1803	Isaac JONES, 16 yrs old 21 Dec 1802, to John GEORGE, to be a farmer

Apprentices, Poor Children and Bastards 81

W:141	9 May 1803	Sarah JONES, 5 yrs old 1 May 1803, to John GEORGE
W:141	9 May 1803	Israel WILSON, 5 yrs old 24 May 1803, to Moses MILLER, to be a blacksmith
W:142	9 May 1803	Isaiah NICKOLS to William NICHOLS, (formerly bound to William Nickols, dec'd) Loose Papers: 11 yrs old 13 May Last, to William Nickols, Jr., indenture found
W:142	9 May 1803	Jane CRAIG, 13 yrs old 12 May 1803, to Israel POOL
W:146	9 May 1803	Philip BURKS, 3 yrs old 1 Oct 1802, to Constantine HUGHS, indenture found
W:146	9 May 1803	William HARPER, 16 yrs old 25 Jul 1803, to Samuel SMITH, to be a house carpenter and joiner
W:163	13 Jun 1803	Thomas COATS, 16 yrs old 2 Apr 1803, to Israel HICKS, to be a sadler
W:164	13 Jun 1803	Simon SHORE, 14 yrs old, son of Rebeckah Shore, to Silas REESE, to be a blacksmith
W:196	16 Jun 1803	Stephen MANSFIELD to be bound to some proper person
W:239	11 Jul 1803	John SHELL to William DOOD, until 19 yrs old Loose Papers: 12 yrs old, son of Barsheby Shell, widow, to William Dodd
W:255	11 Jul 1803	John WAR, 11 yrs old 5 May 1803, to Richard FREEMAN
W:256	8 Aug 1803	Melindy ROACH, 3 yrs old 8 Feb 1803, to Thomas EWERS Loose Papers: dau of Hannah Roach(spelled Rotch here), to be a weaver
W:327	12 Aug 1803	John GOODHART, 18 yrs old 25 Apr 1804, to John FRYE, to be a blacksmith
W:341	12 Sep 1803	Elizabeth COLLINS to Thomas BISCOE Loose Papers: 7 yrs old 1 Apr 1803, dau of Elizabeth Collins
W:345	12 Sep 1803	John SAMPLE, 7 yrs old, to be bound to some fit person
W:348	13 Sep 1803	Polly MARKS to be delivered up by James Powell to the Overseers of the Poor who will bind her out
W:348	13 Sep 1803	Polly CAMPBELL to be delivered up by Edward McGinnis to the Overseers of the Poor who will bind her out

W:348	13 Sep 1803	Peggy ROBERTS to be delivered up by Griffith Roberts to the Overseers of the Poor who will bind her out
W:352	13 Sep 1803	Henry CRANE to Joseph HUNT, for 4 yrs Loose Papers: from 13 Sep 1803, to be a stone mason, indenture found
W:353	13 Sep 1803	John MOORE, 14 yrs old 25 Dec 1802, to Michael EVERHEART, to be a farmer Loose Papers: indenture found
W:353	13 Sep 1803	Israel WILSON, 5 yrs old 24 May 1803, to Moses MILLAR, to be a blacksmith
W:354	13 Sep 1803	Amelia KIDWELL, 5 yrs old 10 Jul 1803, to Peter CARR
W:355	13 Sep 1803	Vincent GILL, 5 yrs old, to John ROBERTS
W:355	13 Sep 1803	Mary Cammell BAYLY, 5 yrs old in Jan 1803, to Edward MCGINNIS
W:363	14 Sep 1803	William DECKER to Archibald FLEMING, Sr., W:448, 18 Nov 1803, order with correct name - John L. Decker Loose Papers: John Lawson Decker, 10 yrs old 30 Jun 1803, son of Mary Decker, to be a farmer, indenture found
W:368	10 Oct 1803	George SMALLWOOD, 16 yrs old 25 Apr 1803, to Edward STONE, to be a cooper Loose Papers: orphan
W:373	10 Oct 1803	George MCNELY, 5 yrs old 5 Jan ___, to Michael ASHFORD
W:374	10 Oct 1803	Jemima HENDERSON to John HAVENNER
W:374	10 Oct 1803	Catharine WALKER to Christian SEGAR
W:375	10 Oct 1803	Lydia ANDERSON to Dennis BRIDGES
W:375	10 Oct 1803	Betty ANDERSON to John BRIDGES
W:375	10 Oct 1803	William LACY, 15 yrs old 1 Jul 1803, to Charles JOHNSON, to be a carpenter
W:393	11 Oct 1803	Lindsy THOMAS, 16 yrs old 8 Jan ___, to Jacob FADLY, to be a wheelwright Loose Papers: Lindzy, age as of 1803, son of Joseph Thomas, dec'd
W:425	15 Nov 1803	Sarah PATTERSON, 5 yrs old 1 Oct 1803, to Esther GIBSON Loose Papers: dau of Polley Bails
W:452	12 Dec 1803	Robert BROWN, 15 yrs old 5 Feb 1803, to Robert FULTON, to be a wheelwright Loose Papers: indenture found

Apprentices, Poor Children and Bastards 83

W:460	12 Dec 1803	George SEAGER, 3 yrs old 13 Sep 1803, to Samuel GREGG, Sr.,
W:469	13 Dec 1803	William GRIFFITH, 9 yrs old in Nov 1803, to Joseph DOUGLAS
X:2	9 Jan 1804	Ralph GRAY to Henry LONG
X:16	13 Feb 1804	Georg SPENCE, 14 yrs old 11 Jan 1804, to Joseph KNOX, to be a wheel maker
X:16	13 Feb 1804	Elizabeth HIDE, 8 yrs old 1 Aug 1804, to Samuel TODD Loose Papers: on request of John Wofter, Boston Wofter & Crs. Costlo
X:17	13 Feb 1804	John WINEGROVE, 4 yrs old 1 Jul 1803, to William and Sarah TRAYHORN Loose Papers: Elizabeth Costelo's twin
X:17	13 Feb 1804	Nancy WINEGROVE to William and Sarah TRAYHORN Loose Papers: Elizabeth Costelo's twin
X:18	13 Feb 1804	James PAXON, 17 yrs old 8 May 1804, to Thomas PHILIPS, to be a tanner and currier Loose Papers: surname Paxson, reuquest of his gr-father James Paxson, sent from over Allegany Mt. by his mother. His father several years past went down the Mississippi - not heard from, indenture found
X:24	13 Feb 1804	Ann HACHET to William JAY Loose Papers: surname Hacket
X:24	13 Feb 1804	Thomas HACHET, 9 yrs old 1 Jan 1804, to William JAY Loose Papers: surname Hacket
X:84	9 Apr 1804	John SWAIN, 16 yrs old 1 Dec 1803, to Charles GULLAT, to be a taylor
X:85	9 Apr 1804	Elijah SKINNER, 14 yrs old 28 Mar 1804, to Mesheck LACEY, to be a hatter, Y:139, 12 Aug 1805, order rescinded
X:93	10 Apr 1804	Daniel MCALLISTER to David ENGLISH, to be a plaisterer
X:96	10 Apr 1804	Jacintha CUISAR, 7 yrs old, to Samuel and Eliza CLAPHAM, his wife Loose Papers: dau of Cassandra Cuisar
X:99	10 Apr 1804	Samuel HARPER, 6 yrs old, to Thomas N. BINNS Loose Papers: orphan
X:100	10 Apr 1804	Mahlon COMBS, 16 yrs old in Jan 1804, to William SMALLEY

X:106	11 Apr 1804	Major Feeldon TURNER to Martin KITSMILLER, to be a tanner Loose Papers: orphan
X:126	14 May 1804	John HARRIS, 13 yrs old 10 Nov 1804, son of Rebeckah Batson, to Jesse MCVEIGH, to be a taylor Loose Papers: Richard Batson joined in request
X:132	14 May 1804	Shepherd EATON, 14 yrs old 1 Jan 1804, to James EATON
X:132	14 May 1804	Mary Ann FROS, 10 yrs old 5 Sep 1804, to John HAMMERLEY Loose Papers: surname Frost, dau of Matty Frost
X:136	14 May 1804	John CAMMELL, 6 yrs old 3 Jun 1804, to James BEST, to be a farmer Loose Papers: son of Jane Cambel
X:136	14 May 1804	Hannah LONG, 4 yrs old 30 Oct 1804, to Jacob SMITH Loose Papers: request of Chatherena Long
X:136	14 May 1804	Elijah JAMES, 15 yrs old 15 Mar 1804, to Edmund LOVET, to be a blacksmith
X:136	14 May 1804	Jane CASLO, 12 yrs old 18 May 1804, to Gabriel MCGEATH Loose Papers: surname Costlo, request of Sebastian and Mary Woofter
X:136	14 May 1804	William BUTLER, 12 yrs old 1 Nov 1803, to William GREGG Loose Papers: son of Jacob & Sarah Butler
X:143	15 May 1804	William MITCHELL apprentice to Joseph COMBS, on motion of Mary Mitchell, Combs summoned to shew cause why his apprentice shall not be taken from him and bound to another
X:212	9 Jul 1804	Robert WALKER, 10 yrs old 12 Oct 1804, to Jonas POTTS, to be a miller or merchant (name of Jonas Potts from Rough Minute Book)
X:236	14 Aug 1804	Sarah PATTERSON, 7 yrs 10 mo old 13 Aug 1804, to Abner PATTERSON Loose Papers: surname Bayles, twin child of Mary Bayles, Sarah Patterson, orphan, 6 yrs old in Oct 1804, indenture found

Apprentices, Poor Children and Bastards 85

X:236	14 Aug 1804	Tamason BAYLES, 7 yrs 10 mo old 13 Aug 1804, to James PATTERSON Loose Papers: given name Tamson, twin child of Mary Bayles, Tamason Patterson, orphan, 6 yrs old in Oct 1804, indenture found
X:270	10 Sep 1804	Mahlon WILSON, 11 yrs old 11 Jun 1804, to Lewis MASSEY, to be a saddler
X:282	10 Sep 1804	John COATES, 12 yrs old 31 Jan 1804, to Israel HICKS, to be a saddler Loose Papers: son of Elizabeth Coates
X:286	11 Sep 1804	Betty CROSS, 8 yrs old in Jul 1804, to Robert WADE, (name of Robert Wade from Rough Minute Book)
X:286	11 Sep 1804	Margaret ROBERTS to John SCHOOLEY
X:301	8 Oct 1804	Walter LANGLEY to William SMITH, to be a blacksmith (formerly bound to Joseph Roberts)
X:301	8 Oct 1804	William MCMULLEN to Hugh DOUGLAS, order rescinded 12 Feb 1805, X:438
X:302	8 Oct 1804	George MCMULLEN to Armistead LONG, X:319, 9 Oct 1804, order rescinded
X:306	8 Oct 1804	Sarah MONTGOMERY, 12 yrs old, to Mary STEERS, X:344, 15 Nov 1804, order rescinded and new order giving age as 11 yrs on 5 Dec 1804 Loose Papers: indenture found
X:306	8 Oct 1804	Ralph GRAY apprentice of Henry LONG, discharged from his apprenticeship
X:313	8 Oct 1804	James CRAVEN to William H. CRAVEN, to be a hatter Loose Papers: orphan 14 yrs old 13 Jan 1805, indenture found
X:316	9 Oct 1804	William ROBINSON, apprentice, vs Robert PICKEN, request for release from apprenticeship
X:319(1)	9 Oct 1804	George MCMULLEN to Robert CAMPBELL
X:319(1)	9 Oct 1804	Rosannah MCMULLEN to Robert CAMPBELL, order rescinded 9 Apr 1805, Y:8
X:319(2)	9 Oct 1804	Peyton WALKER to Armistead LONG
X:319(2)	9 Oct 1804	William HALL, 10 yrs old, to Isaac VANDEVENDER

X:322	12 Nov 1804	Jonathan MOORE, 10 yrs old 11 Jul 1804, to Joseph GREGG Loose Papers: son of Margaret Bails
X:329	13 Nov 1804	Peter MASH apprentice of Nicholas GRIMES, Grimes to shew cause why Mash shall not be discharged. Y:145, 13 Aug 1805, order binding Mash to Grimes rescinded, it appearing he is an illegitimate child Loose Papers: to Abiel Jenners to be a farmer, indenture found
X:330	12 Nov 1804	John COLLINGS, 11 yrs old 19 Aug 1804, to Jeremiah HAMPTON
X:402	11 Dec 1804	Ludwell GILES, 12 yrs old 30 Mar 1805, to Martin KITSMILLER, to be a tanner
X:403	11 Dec 1804	William TROST, 9 yrs old 13 Jun 1805, to Conrod VIRTS
X:403	11 Dec 1804	Tamzin QUEEN to Samuel MCPHERSON
X:403	11 Dec 1804	Nancy QUEEN to Elizabeth QUEEN
X:411	14 Jan 1805	John GILES, 14 yrs old 23 Sep 1804, to Martin KITSMILLER, to be a tanner & currier
X:416	14 Jan 1805	Thomas COLLINS, 18 yrs old 13 May 1805, to Thomas BISCOE
X:416	14 Jan 1805	John COLLINS, 16 yrs old 4 Dec 1805, to Thomas BISCOE
X:419	16 Jan 1805	Addison HARRISON to Joseph BEARD, to be a cabinet maker
X:425	11 Feb 1805	David FARNSWORTH, 16 yrs old 12 Nov 1804, to Richard MATTHEWS, to be a sadler Loose Papers: age as of 12 Nov 1805, orphan, son of Hannah Bond
X:426	11 Feb 1805	George MCMULLIN to Peter CARR, formerly bound to Robert Camel
X:438	12 Feb 1805	William MCMULLIN to William WRIGHT, formerly bound to Hugh Douglas
Y:8	9 Apr 1805	Rosannah MCMULLIN, 4 yrs old 20 Jul 1805, to Michael EVERHEART, (formerly bound to Robert Campbell)
Y:8	9 Apr 1805	Henry GOODHEART, 10 yrs old 18 Dec 1804, to Henry LONG, to be a blacksmith
Y:11	9 Apr 1805	William ROBINSON, 20 yrs old 1 Jul 1805, to Armistead LONG, Y:77, 10 Jun 1805, order rescinded, not having jurisdiction
Y:12	9 Apr 1805	William MITCHELL to William BROWN, (son of Hy.),

Apprentices, Poor Children and Bastards

Y:14	10 Apr 1805	Esible VANNANDER, 7 yrs old 15 Nov 1804, to John EWERS Loose Papers: Isabel Vanander, dau of Jane Vanander, to John & Sarah, his wife
Y:15	10 Apr 1805	Amos BOLTON, supposed to be 17 yrs old, to George FORTNEY, to be a blacksmith
Y:29	13 May 1805	Henry HUTCHISON, 10 yrs old, to William WRIGHT, to be a bricklayer Loose Papers: age given by Joshua Hutchison
Y:30	13 May 1805	Neilson HUTCHISON, 12 yrs old, to William WRIGHT, to be a bricklayer Loose Papers: given name Nelson, age given by Joshua Hutchison
Y:37	13 May 1805	Abner BEALE to Robert MCCULLOCK Loose Papers: son of Frances Beale
Y:39	13 May 1805	William MCPHERSON to James SKINNER, to be a waggon and fan maker Loose Papers: 18 yrs old 1 Jun 1805
Y:50	14 May 1805	Joseph MATTHEWS, 12 yrs old 18 Jan 1805, to John SHAVER
Y:55	14 May 1805	Hannah HOPE, 14 yrs old 23 Apr 1805, to Christopher HOPE
Y:55	14 May 1805	Dawson FISHER, 8 yrs old 28 Nov 1805, to Benjamin STEER Loose Papers: to be a farmer, indenture found
Y:56	14 May 1805	John TURNER, 14 yrs old 3 Aug 1805, to Martin KITSMILLER, to be a courier and tanner
Y:128	15 Jun 1805	Thomas DOWLING, 16 yrs old 5 Jun 1805, to Thomas PHILLIPS, to be a tanner Loose Papers: son of Rachel Martin
Y:143	13 Aug 1805	Addison Harding CLEARKE, 15 yrs old 10 Jul 1805, to James RUSSELL, to be a sadler Loose Papers: indenture found
Y:143	13 Aug 1805	David MATTHEWS, 10 yrs old 11 Sep 1805, to George HUFF, to be a sadler
Y:144	13 Aug 1805	Hannah HOPE, 14 yrs old 23 Apr 1805, to William HOUGH, (Waterford),
Y:145	13 Aug 1805	Henry , a black boy, vs Richard CONNER, for ill treatment
Y:167	9 Sep 1805	Samuel KENT, 13 yrs old 1 Feb 1806, to Charles GULLATT

Y:175	18 Sep 1805	John CARNES, 17 yrs old 26 Mar 1806, to Joseph BENTLEY, to be a hatter Loose Papers: age as of 1805, son of Sarah Carnes
Y:185	11 Sep 1805	Nicholas GARRETT, 16 yrs old 15 Dec 1805, to Isaac VANDEVANTER, to be a cooper
Y:185	11 Sep 1805	William MINICH, 8 yrs old in Feb 1806, to Isaac STEERE, Jr. Loose Papers: surname Minick, son of Elizabeth Minick
Y:185	11 Sep 1805	Elijah MINICH, 8 yrs old in Feb 1806, to Thomas STEERE Loose Papers: surname Minick, son of Elizabeth Minick
Y:191	11 Sep 1805	Lydia CROZIER, 11 yrs old 9 Feb 1806, to John CAMPBELL Loose Papers: dau of Sarah Crozier, to John Campbell, Sr.
Y:201	14 Oct 1805	Thomas GOINGS, 13 yrs old 1 Nov 1805, to John GRUBB, to be a miller
Y:210	15 Oct 1805	Henry CRAINE to William WRIGHT, formerly bound to Joseph Hunt
Y:210	15 Oct 1805	Benjamin MURPHEY, 18 yrs old 2 Mar 1806, to John DAYLEY, to be a hatter, indenture found
Y:210	15 Oct 1805	Mary LIVINGSTONE, 8 yrs old 2 Dec 1805, to Jacob SMITH
Y:279	10 Dec 1805	Lydia SHIPMAN, 10 yrs old 3 Nov 1805, to Jonas JANNEY
Y:280	10 Dec 1805	John SHIPMAN, 9 yrs old 9 Mar 1806, to Jonas JANNEY
Y:280	10 Dec 1805	Marten KYSER to John P. SAPPINGTON, to be a taylor
Y:290	14 Jan 1806	James O'HARROW, 16 yrs old 18 Feb 1806, to William JOHNSTON, to be a bricklayer
Y:291	14 Jan 1806	Frances O'HARROW, 13 yrs old 1 Sep 1806, to John BOGUE
D.B. 2G:146	3 Feb 1806	John SURGNOR, (son of Hugh Surgnor), to Aaron DIVINE, for 7 years, to be a boot and shoe maker. Indenture recorded 11 Feb 1806

Apprentices, Poor Children and Bastards

Y:327	11 Feb 1806	Joseph EDWARDS, 15 yrs old 1 Aug 1806, to William WRIGHT, to be a cooper Loose Papers: indenture found
Y:327	11 Feb 1806	Richard CHERRY, 17 yrs old 20 Feb 1806, to Pressley CORDELL, to be a silversmith, watch and clock maker Loose Papers: indenture found
Y:327	11 Feb 1806	George SPENCE, 16 yrs old 21 Apr 1805, to William SMITH, to be a farmer, former order to bind him to Joseph Knox rescinded
Y:405	15 Apr 1806	Addison HARRISON to William SMITH, to be a joiner (formerly bound to Joseph Beard)
Y:410	16 Apr 1806	George VANANDER, 16 yrs old, to ___ GARDNER, to be a shoemaker
Y:410	16 Apr 1806	Josiah TALLEY, 16 yrs old 15 Dec 1805, to Isaac MILLER, to be a joiner and fann maker Loose Papers: son of Susannah Grubb alias Talley
Y:410	16 Apr 1806	William Barnes HOLMES, 10 yrs old 2 Jun 1806, to Blackstone JANNEY Loose Papers: son of Martha Holmes
Y:410	16 Apr 1806	John CARNES, 17 yrs old 26 Mar 1806, to William HOUSER Loose Papers: a very bad boy, son of Sarah Carns, to William Howser, indenture found
Y:410	16 Apr 1806	Nancy QUEEN, 4 yrs old 30 Jan 1806, to James RUSSELL, (former order to be bound to Elizabeth Queen rescinded) Loose Papers: orphan, indenture found
Y:410	16 Apr 1806	Jacob SHRY to John RAZOR
Y:428	12 May 1806	Walter BOZZELL, 16 yrs old 9 Apr 1806, to William JONES, to be a tanner Loose Papers: son of Maryan Pool
Y:428	12 May 1806	Thomas TAYLOR, 12 yrs old in May 1806, to Thomas TALBOTT, Jr.,
Y:428	12 May 1806	John MCCANN, 13 yrs old 20 Apr 1806, to William WOODFORD
Y:433	13 May 1806	Joseph BEALLE to Isaac NICKOLS Loose Papers: 12 yrs old 15 Sep 1806, to be a farmer, to Isaac, Jr., indenture found
Y:433	13 May 1806	Lewis HUNT to Joseph HUNT, (former order to be bound to William Smith set aside)

Y:435	13 May 1806	Martin KYSER, 11 yrs old 20 May 1806, to Joshua JACOBS, to be a taylor (former order to be bound to John Sappington set aside) Loose Papers: orphan, indenture found
Z:10	14 Jul 1806	Jacob SCHRY apprentice to John RAZOR, discharged from covenants of his indenture
Z:74	9 Sep 1806	Ambrose POPKINS, 6 yrs old 11 Aug 1806, to Robert WARE, to be a cooper Loose Papers: indenture found
Z:75	9 Sep 1806	Hugh O'HARROW, 14 yrs old 10 Jul 1806, to Henry LAFEVER, to be a farmer
Z:75	9 Sep 1806	Manasses O'HARROW, 11 yrs old 20 Jul 1806, to Henry LAFEVER, to be a farmer
Z:81	10 Sep 1806	Lydia CROZIER, 11 yrs old 9 Feb 1807, to John BALL Loose Papers: orphan, to be a housekeeper, indenture found
Z:198	9 Dec 1806	Westley HENDERSON, 5 yrs old 2 Jan 1806, to Jacob AXLINE Loose Papers: age as of 1805, son of Elizabeth Henderson
Z:198	9 Dec 1806	Thomas SHEPHERD to Leven SMALLWOOD, to be a carpenter and house joiner
Z:198	9 Dec 1806	William JONES, 17 yrs old 3 Dec 1806, to Jacob CARNES, to be a farmer
Z:201	9 Dec 1806	Ann HACKETT to Nathan BROWN, (former order to be bound to William Guy set aside)
Z:208	9 Dec 1806	Andrew , a free black 15 yrs old 15 Aug 1806, to Jesse HIRST, to be a farmer (formerly bound to James Moore)
Z:209	9 Dec 1806	Willis FOSTER, 7 yrs old in Sep 1806, to Joab PETTITT, to be a stonemason Loose Papers: Jane Kent says "son of my daughter and Edmond Foster", indenture found
Z:209	9 Dec 1806	William GALT, 7 yrs old 1 May 1806, to William BROWN, (son of Henry), to be a farmer
Z:215	12 Jan 1807	Robert BEATTY, orphan of William Beatty, to be bound to some suitable person
Z:217	13 Jan 1807	Michael CAVAN to Joseph BEARD, to be a cabinet maker, James Cavan his guardian

Apprentices, Poor Children and Bastards 91

Z:217	13 Jan 1807	Owen Rodgers ROACH, 12 yrs old 13 Oct 1806, to William GOODWIN, to be a shoemaker Loose Papers: son of Margaret Roach, indenture found
Z:217	13 Jan 1807	William MINICK to Isaac STEERE, Jr.,
Z:218	13 Jan 1807	Elijah MINICK to Thomas STEERE
Z:228	9 Feb 1807	Henry HOPE, 15 yrs old 15 May 1807, to Christian HOPE, to be a millright Loose Papers: age as of 11 May, indenture found
Z:234	10 Feb 1807	William MOORE, 16 yrs old 25 Dec 1806, to Edward DORSEY, to be a carpenter and joiner Loose Papers: indenture found
Z:234	10 Feb 1807	Francis O'HARROW, 13 yrs old 1 Sep 1806, to John MYERS, formerly bound to John Bogue (appears to read "to whom she was formerly bound")
Z:236	10 Feb 1807	Jacob FOUCH, 13 yrs old 28 Jan 1807, to Stephen COOKE, to be a farmer Loose Papers: son of Elizabeth Smith, his father is dead, indenture found
Z:237	10 Feb 1807	Eliza COOTES, 3 yrs old 5 Feb 1807, to George FORTNEY Loose Papers: indenture found
Z:239	10 Feb 1807	Reuben CONNER to Robert MOFFETT Loose Papers: orphan, 13 yrs old 14 Sep 1807, to be a farmer, indenture found
Z:240	11 Feb 1807	Samuel FITZSIMMONS, 10 yrs old in Nov 1806, to George RHODES, to be a blacksmith
Z:255	10 Mar 1807	Cressey WEBB, 15 yrs old 25 Sep 1807, to John SCHOOLEY, Jr.,
Z:270	12 Mar 1807	George MCNEALLY to be bound , formerly bound to Charles Gullatt Loose Papers: 19 Mar 1807, orphan 10 yrs old 26 Jan 1808 to James Greenlease to be a farmer, indenture found
Z:293	13 Apr 1807	Peter RUST, 17 yrs old 14 Feb 1807, to Joshua GREGG, to be a hatter
Z:299	15 Apr 1807	Josiah TALLEY, 17 yrs old 13 Dec 1806, to John SAPPINGTON, to be a taylor Loose Papers: son of Susannah Talley
Z:299	15 Apr 1807	William BRIGHT to John MARSHALL

Z:300	15 Apr 1807	Robert Harrison DOUGLAS, 15 yrs old 6 Feb 1807, to Asa MOORE, and Thomas Phillips, to be a tanner and currier Loose Papers: orphan, son of Mary Offutt, indenture found
Z:306	11 May 1807	Thomas GLADDELL, 14 yrs old 11 Mar 1807, to Simon YAGEY, to be a cooper Loose Papers: surname Gladhill, to Yakey
Z:311	11 May 1807	Jacob WALTMAN, 17 yrs old in Jun 1807, to Leven SMALLWOOD, to be a carpenter and joiner
Z:316	11 May 1807	Ludwell GILES to Henry GLASSGOW, to be a cordwainer, formerly bound to Martin Kitzmiller
Z:329	12 May 1807	Samuel HARPER to James GARNER, to be a coppersmith, formerly bound to Thomas Binns
Z:430	14 Jul 1807	John RINE, Jr., 9 yrs old 26 Aug 1807, to Robert WILSON, to be a farmer
1:80	15 Sep 1807	George MCGWIN, 8 yrs old 5 May 1808, to Elias COCKRELL, to be a farmer Loose Papers: son of Rachel McGwin
1:81	15 Sep 1807	Reed POULTON, 16 yrs old 16 Feb 1807, to Dennis Gillum JONES, to be a cabinet maker Loose Papers: indenture found
1:111	12 Oct 1807	Daniel BRYAN to John BOYD, for 4 yrs, to be a carpenter and joiner, Charles Lewis his guardian
1:127	18 Oct 1807	Stephen MANSFIELD, 8 yrs old 1 Jul 1807, to Joseph STEERE, to be a farmer
1:234	16 Dec 1807	John RINE to Robert WILSON
1:241	11 Jan 1808	Daniel COCKRILL, 16 yrs old 29 May 1808, to William CLENDENNING, to be a joiner and cabinet maker Loose Papers: son of Jean Cockrill
1:344	12 Apr 1808	Sarah MONTGOMERY, 15 yrs old 5 Dec 1808, to Timothy HIXON
1:351	13 Apr 1808	Jacob EDWARDS, 14 yrs old, to John NEARE
1:352	13 Apr 1808	William NIGHTING to Josiah CRAVEN, to be a blacksmith, 1:376 & 2:36 Elizabeth Nighting, his next friend
1:355	13 Apr 1808	Thomas HASSETT, 17 yrs old 12 Oct 1808, to George WALTERS

1:366	9 May 1808	John BARBER, 8 yrs old 12 Jul 1808, to Bernard MANN Loose Papers: b. 12 Jul 1801, son of James Barber, dec'd and Mary Barber now wife of Eliakim Anderson
1:375	10 May 1808	Daniel JANNEY, 16 yrs old 6 Sep 1807, to MOORE, and Phillips, to be a tanner Loose Papers: son of Ruth Janney
1:375	10 May 1808	Henry HOPE, 16 yrs old 11 May 1808, to Lindsey THOMAS, to be a turner & wheelmaker (formerly bound to Christian Hope)
1:377	10 May 1808	Jane MCGEATH to Casper ECKART, and Nancy, his wife
1:382	10 May 1808	Michael CAVAN to Joseph PURCELL, former order binding him to Joseph Beard rescinded
1:385	11 May 1808	Martin KYSER, 12 yrs old 20 May 1807, to Thomas BERKBY, to be a wheelwright (formerly bound to Joshua Jacobs) Loose Papers: son of Cassandra Kyser widow of Montgomery Co., MD, to Birkby, indenture found
2:4	13 Jun 1808	Polly WAUGH, 14 yrs old 1 Aug 1808, to Enoch FRANCIS
2:19	14 Jun 1808	William MINICK vs Isaac STEER, Jr., complaint of ill treatment
2:21	14 Jun 1808	Henry HOPE, 16 yrs old 11 May 1808, to Stephen DONALDSON, Jr., to be a blacksmith. Former order is rescinded
2:81	11 Jul 1808	Thomas GOINGS, 16 yrs old 1 Nov 1808, to Cornelius SHAWN, to be a miller, formerly bound to John Grubb
2:124	12 Sep 1808	Peter MANLY to be bound, formerly bound to Joseph Lay
2:127	12 Sep 1808	Mary SMITH to William WERTZ
2:130	12 Sep 1808	Middleton HARRIS, 19 yrs old 19 Jul 1808, to Peter SKINNER, formerly bound to Richard Skinner
2:132	12 Sep 1808	Elijah MASON, 8 yrs old (emancipated by will of Mary Porter), to John FLETCHER, to be a wheelwright Loose Papers: 4 yrs 3 mo old, indenture found

2:133	13 Sep 1808	William SMITH, 12 yrs old 5 Sep 1808, to Jacob CRUMBAKER, to be a blacksmith
2:133	13 Sep 1808	George SMITH, 13 yrs old 1 Apr 1808, to John GEORGE, Jr., to be a miller
2:134	13 Sep 1808	Esther SEARS, 10 yrs old 12 Sep 1808, to Joseph DOUGLAS
2:139	13 Sep 1808	John MYERS, orphan of Benjamin Myers, dec'd, bound by his mother and guardian, to Joseph BEARD, to be a cabinet maker Loose Papers: son of Elizabeth Myers
2:139	13 Sep 1808	Stacy LACEY, 16 yrs old 10 Nov 1808, to Joseph TALBOTT, to be a sadler Loose Papers: age is 15 not 16, and corrected 9 Jan 1809
2:144	15 Sep 1808	Elizabeth STONE, 9 yrs old in Oct 1808, to Barton LUCAS
2:144	15 Sep 1808	Ambrose POPKINS, 8 yrs old 11 Aug 1808. Formerly bound to Robert Ware, to be bound
2:149	10 Oct 1808	Polly SMITH, orphan, 3 yrs old, to William VERTS
2:151	10 Oct 1808	George DUNN, alias McKimmey, to Stephen DONALDSON, Jr., to be a blacksmith
2:235	12 Dec 1808	Mason SHIPMAN, 20 yrs old, to Joseph EIDSON, to be a carpenter and joiner Loose Papers: son of Deborah Shipman
2:240	13 Dec 1808	Thomas HOUGH vs John MYERS, complaint for ill treatment discharged
2:248	9 Jan 1809	Daniel SMITH, 19 yrs old 1 Mar 1809, to William JOHNSTON, to be a blacksmith. Formerly bound to Thomas Ewers.
2:249	9 Jan 1809	Maria ROACH, 7 yrs old 4 Mar 1809, to George TAVENER, Sr.,
2:250	9 Jan 1809	Hendley RUSSELL, mulatto, 9 yrs old in Apr 1809, to Joshua OSBORN, to be a farmer
2:250	9 Jan 1809	Middleton WARWICK, mulatto, 7 yrs old in Dec 1808, to Joshua OSBORN, to be a farmer
2:254	9 Jan 1809	Frederick BURNES, alias Worthington, 4 yrs old 27 Dec 1808, to Nathan NICHOLS, to be a farmer Loose Papers: indenture found
2:256	9 Jan 1809	Polley WAUGH, 14 yrs old 14 Aug 1808, to David ORRISON, formerly bound to Enoch Francis

Apprentices, Poor Children and Bastards 95

2:256	9 Jan 1809	Stacy LACEY, 15 yrs old 4 Nov 1808, to Joseph TALBOTT, order correcting age
2:263	13 Feb 1809	Moses HICKS, 15 yrs old 25 Mar 1809, to Joshua GREGG, to be a hatter
2:263	13 Feb 1809	Eliakim HICKS, 13 yrs old 7 Nov 1809, to Eliakim ANDERSON, Jr., to be a farmer
2:269	13 Feb 1809	Micanda SILCOTT, 7 yrs old in Nov 1808, to Jonah SANDS
2:271	14 Feb 1809	Sampson REED, 12 yrs old 3 Feb 1809, to William DODD
2:271	14 Feb 1809	Mary GROOMS, 10 yrs old 5 May 1808, to Jesse HURST
2:271	14 Feb 1809	Peter JACOBS, 13 yrs old 4 Mar 1809, to Henry MONINGER, to be a blacksmith
2:271	14 Feb 1809	David HERVEY, 11 yrs old 27 Feb 1809, to Joshua PUSEY
2:271	14 Feb 1809	Viney HERVEY, 13 yrs old 4 Aug 1809, to David JANNEY
2:271	14 Feb 1809	Jacob HERVEY, 8 yrs old 15 Jan 1809, to Robert BRADEN
2:271	14 Feb 1809	William HERVEY, 14 yrs old 9 May 1809, to be bound
2:271	14 Feb 1809	Henry HERVEY, 17 yrs old 20 Aug 1809, to be bound
2:382	11 Apr 1809	Thomas HATCHETT, 13 yrs old 1 Feb 1809, to Philip COOPER, farmer,
2:389	18 May 1809	Landon YOUNG, 9 yrs old 25 Mar 1809, to John PANCOAST, Sr., to be a farmer Loose Papers: son of Leticia Young, indenture found
2:426	12 Jun 1809	John TAYLOR to Levi JAMES, to be a saddler
2:429	12 Jun 1809	Lynna , a free black girl 4 yrs old, to William BEAVERS
2:491	10 Jul 1809	Hiram ORAM, 8 yrs old 1 Jan 1810, to George FAIRHURST, to be a farmer Loose Papers: orphan, indenture found
2:491	10 Jul 1809	Richard CASTOR to Isaac HARRIS, to be a tanner Loose Papers: son of Mary Castor
2:491	10 Jul 1809	Elizabeth CREAMOUR, 10 yrs old 11 Dec 1809, to John WILLIAMS, & Lydia, his wife Loose Papers: dau of Catherine Divine, surname may be Souder, indenture found

2:491	10 Jul 1809	Jacob SNIDER, 12 yrs old 25 Sep 1809, to William HOUGH, (son of William), to be a farmer
3:27	15 Aug 1809	John SPENCER, orphan of John Spencer, Jr., to John SPENCER
3:27	15 Aug 1809	Cecilia SPENCER, orphan of John Spencer, Jr., to John SPENCER
3:108	11 Sep 1809	Jarrett LOCKER, 14 yrs old 16 Jul 1809, to Isaac STEERE, miller,
3:108	11 Sep 1809	Susanna MANLEY, 12 yrs old 25 Dec 1809, to Samuel ROBERTS Loose Papers: dau of Sarah Manley
3:110	11 Sep 1809	James MCDONALL, 18 yrs old in Sep 1809, to Benjamin JAMES
3:116	11 Sep 1809	Douglas CARMICHAEL, son of Mary Carmichael, apprentice of Colmore BRASHEARS, discharged from apprenticeship Loose Papers: given name Daniel
3:117	11 Sep 1809	William SEARS, 12 yrs old 1 Apr 1809, to Martin KITZMILLER, to be a tanner Loose Papers: stepson of John Scrivener
3:126	9 Oct 1809	Peyton SILCOTT, alias Chambling, 9 yrs old 28 Oct 1809, to Abraham SILCOTT, to be a blacksmith Loose Papers: son of Lydia Silcott
3:131	9 Oct 1809	Caleb WILSON, 8 yrs old, to Timothy TAYLOR
3:131	9 Oct 1809	Rebekah WILSON, 11 yrs old, to Timothy TAYLOR
3:131	9 Oct 1809	Orpha WILSON, 14 yrs old, to Levi GIBSON
3:137	10 Oct 1809	Henry CARNS, 13 yrs old 12 Jan 1810, to Joseph GARDENER, to be a shoemaker Loose Papers: son of Sarah Carnes
3:137	10 Oct 1809	George W. HENRY to William GOODWIN, to be a shoe and boot maker
3:151	16 Nov 1809	Henry CARN, orphan, to Jotham WRIGHT, to be a taylor. The former order binding him is rescinded Loose Papers: indenture found
3:178	16 Nov 1809	Elijah TARLTON, 16 yrs old 26 Dec 1809, to Samuel HOUGH, to be a hatter

3:241	11 Dec 1809	Pleasant, daughter of Phebe, 5 yrs old 25 Dec 1809, to Eli JANNEY Loose Papers: Phebe a person of color, indenture found
3:241	11 Dec 1809	William HUNTER, 12 yrs old 1 Jan 1809 to John JEFFERSON Loose papers: son of Elizabeth Jones
3:323	13 Mar 1810	Mary STONE, 13 yrs old 8 Aug 1810, to Jotham WRIGHT, 3:333, 14 Mar 1810, order rescinded. Also in Book 4:33 and 4:38. Book 4:pages 1-98 appear to be rough minutes from which orders in Book 3 pages 260-450 were prepared.
3:323	13 Mar 1810	Harriot MORRIS, about 12 yrs old, to William ROBERTS, (also in 4:34)
3:333	14 Mar 1810	Mary FEAGINS, 13 yrs old 8 Aug 1810, to Jotham WRIGHT, (also in 4:38) Loose Papers: orphan, indenture found
3:410	14 May 1810	Margaret DOWNS, 14 yrs old 19 Jun 1810, to Jacob WALTMAN, (also in 4:74) Loose Papers: orphan, to Jacob Jr., indenture found
3:419	14 May 1810	William SEIRS, 13 yrs old 25 Apr 1810, to Thomas C. WILLS, to be a carpenter and joiner (also in 4:80), formerly bound to Martin Kitzmiller [as William Sears]
3:419	14 May 1810	Sarah HOOD, 12 yrs old 7 May 1810, to Samuel DANNIEL, (also in 4:80) Loose Papers: dau of Linny Hood, to Samuel Daniel and Sarah, his wife
3:426	15 May 1810	John DOBBINS to Joseph BEARD, to be a cabinetmaker (also in 4:85)
4:149	13 Aug 1810	Thomas McDowell SINCLAIR, orphan of Samuel Sinclair, to William CLENDINON, to be a joiner Loose Papers: son of Edith Sinclair
4:172	18 Sep 1810	Stacy LACY, 17 yrs old 4 Dec 1810, to MOORE, & Phillips, to be a tanner and currier (formerly bound to Joseph Talbott)
4:190	8 Oct 1810	Elizabeth MOCK, 8 yrs old 20 Jan 1810, to Henry LONG
4:201	9 Oct 1810	John RYON released from service to Thomas WILSON

4:203	12 Nov 1810	Squire LITTLE, 12 yrs old 9 Apr 1810, to John RALPH, to be a taylor Loose Papers: son of Sary Little, age as of 1811
4:210	12 Nov 1810	Joseph SIMONS, 16 yrs old 11 Jun 1811, to John L. WYNN, to be a shoe and boot maker Loose Papers: son of Effie Simons
4:253	10 Dec 1810	James BLOCKSTONE, 9 yrs old in Mar 1810, to James WILKINSON, farmer,
4:257	10 Dec 1810	Vincent KELLEY, an orphan, bound to John ROBERTS, Sr., Roberts to show cause why Kelley should not be released. 4:261, 14 Jan 1811, same order. 4:281, 12 Feb 1811, mistake in former order, correct name is Vincent Gill. 4:297, 12 Mar 1811, order binding him to Roberts rescinded
4:261	14 Jan 1811	John EDDING apprentice to Benjamin WILLS, Wills to show cause why Edding should not be released. 4:280, 12 Feb 1811, rule discharged
4:267	14 Jan 1811	James DOBBINS, 15 yrs old, to Henry GLASSGOW to be a shoemaker. 4:282, 12 Feb 1811, at request of Eleanor Dobbins, Henry Glasgow to shew cause why James Dobbins should not be released from service. 4:299, 12 Mar 1811, rule to shew cause discharged Loose Papers: indenture found
4:267	14 Jan 1811	William REED, an orphan, apprentice of John BROWN, millwright, Brown to show cause why Reed should not be released
4:269	14 Jan 1811	Eliakim HICKS, 13 yrs old 7 Nov 1810, to Eliakim ANDERSON, Jr., to be a cooper
4:275	11 Feb 1811	Owen R. ROACH, 15 yrs old 13 Oct 1810, to Stephen CLAYTON, to be a blacksmith. (formerly bound to Wm. Goodwin) [4:289, 11 Mar 1811, same order]
4:279	12 Feb 1811	Clement WYNN to John L. WYNN, to be a shoe and boot maker
4:287	11 Mar 1811	Elias POOL, 11 yrs old, to Joseph PARKER, farmer,
4:289	11 Mar 1811	Thomson BLOCKSON, 11 yrs 6 mo today, to William BLAKELEY, to be a tanner Loose Papers: indenture found

Apprentices, Poor Children and Bastards 99

4:289	11 Mar 1811	James BLOCKSTON, 10 yrs old 12 Mar 1811, to Joseph WILKINSON, farmer, (see 4:253, 10 Dec 1810)
4:290	11 Mar 1811	John BARBER, 10 yrs old 12 Jul 1811, to Bernard MANN, farmer Loose Papers: indenture found
4:295	12 Mar 1811	William VEATCH, 17 yrs old 26 Feb 1811, to William GOODWIN, to be a shoe and boot maker
4:298	12 Mar 1811	Levi JONES to William KIRK, to be a taylor
4:327	15 Mar 1811	Samuel FARRIS, 18 yrs old 11 Jun 1811, to John F. SAPPINGTON, to be a taylor
4:330	9 Apr 1811	Elizabeth MOCK, 8 yrs old 20 Jan 1811, to Samuel ORRISON, (formerly bound to Henry Long)
4:331	9 Apr 1811	Polly MOCK, 11 yrs old 2 Feb 1811, to Adam WERTS
4:341	13 May 1811	Jemima MENIX, 8 yrs old 13 Jun 1811, to Joseph BROWN
4:342	13 May 1811	Ishmael WATERS, 8 yrs old 27 Aug 1810, to Samuel MOORE Loose Papers: son of Mary Waters
4:349	14 May 1811	David STALL, 17 yrs old 17 Apr 1811, to John F. SAPPINGTON, to be a taylor
5:6	10 Jun 1811	Louisa CORNWELL, 10 yrs old, to David GIBSON
5:14	10 Jun 1811	Duanna BURGUOYNE to Dr. Isaac HOUGH
5:14	10 Jun 1811	Nancy MOCK to Mahlon JANNEY, 3rd,
5:15	10 Jun 1811	Charles SIMPSON to John PURCELL, to be a tanner and currier
5:30	13 Jun 1811	Elias POOL to John L. WYNN, to be a shoe and boot maker
5:60	12 Aug 1811	Isaac HOOK, 5 yrs old 19 Jul 1810, to Hugh HUGHS, on motion of Martha Hook
5:60	12 Aug 1811	Elizabeth HOOK, 11 yrs old 28 Nov 1810, to Hugh HUGHS, on motion of Martha Hook
5:94	9 Sep 1811	John PEARCE, 8 yrs old 10 Jun 1811, to John BRADY, to be a cabinet maker and house joiner
5:94	9 Sep 1811	Herod B. PEARCE, 6 yrs old 8 Mar 1811, to John BRADY, to be a cabinet maker and house joiner

5:95	9 Sep 1811	Stephen CURRAN, 13 yrs old 4 Jul 1811, to John HOUGH, to be a carpenter and house joiner Loose Papers: surname Curans, son of Sarah Curans
5:112	14 Oct 1811	John RYAN, 13 yrs old 16 Aug 1812, to Joseph CUMMINS, to be a cooper Loose Papers: son of Sarah Ryan
5:112	14 Oct 1811	Simeon HAINS, 4 yrs old in Mar 1811, to Miriam HOLE, to be a farmer
5:175	16 Nov 1811	John MCCABE, 11 yrs old 4 Jun 1811, to Matthew MITCHELL, and Reuben Schooley, to be a blacksmith
W.B. K:155	22 Nov 1811	Nancy DOWNS "legally bound to" James BATTSON
W.B. K:155	22 Nov 1811	Walter DOWNS "legally bound to" James BATTSON
W.B. K:155	22 Nov 1811	William DOWNS "legally bound to" James BATTSON
5:183	9 Dec 1811	George SINCLAIR to John HOUGH, for 4 yrs, to be a cabinet maker and joiner Loose Papers: consent of Edith Sinclair
5:188	10 Dec 1811	Jesse MELLAN apprentice to Eli MELLAN, Eli to shew cause why Jesse should not be released from his apprenticeship
5:199	13 Jan 1812	Jesse MELLAN, 18 yrs old in Oct 1811, to Eli MELLAN, to be a wheelright
5:203	14 Jan 1812	Elizabeth SHEDACRE, about 9 yrs old, to Ellis JENKINS
5:211	14 Jan 1812	Wm. LIVINGSTON, 12 yrs old 16 Jan 1812, to David JANNEY Loose Papers: son of Pleasant Livingston, to be a farmer, indenture found
5:243	10 Feb 1812	Harriott RINE, 9 yrs old 12 Jan 1812, to William CUMMIN Loose Papers: dau of Sarah Rine
5:250	10 Feb 1812	James SMARR, 17 yrs old 18 Oct 1811, to Martin KITZMILLER, to be a tanner
5:257	9 Mar 1812	Isaac GRIMES, 14 yrs old 21 Sep 1811 (or 1812, written over), to John L. WYNN, to be a boot and shoemaker
5:258	9 Mar 1812	Alfred JONES to Joshua PANCOAST
5:260	9 Mar 1812	Thos. HARDY to Robert SANDFORD

Apprentices, Poor Children and Bastards　　101

5:309	16 Mar 1812	Henry STEWART, 20 yrs old 16 Jun 1811, to Samuel PASSMORE, to be a cabinet maker
5:313	14 Apr 1812	Anderson GEEASLING to Martin KITZMILLER
5:341	12 May 1812	Emily MCABOY, 14 yrs old 10 Jul 1812, to Mary CARR Loose Papers: orphan, indenture found
5:341	12 May 1812	George MCMULLEN, 13 yrs old 15 Jan 1812, to John CARR Loose Papers: to be a farmer, indenture found
6:8	8 Jun 1812	John EVANS to Caleb GALLAGHER, to be a cabinet maker
6:12	8 Jun 1812	Sarah FAGAN, 8 yrs old 5 Feb 1812, to John PANCOAST Loose Papers: dau of Nancy Fagan
6:18	8 Jun 1812	James HENRY, 17 yrs old 13 Apr 1812, to Stephen DANIEL, at request of William Wright, his guardian
6:43	12 Jun 1812	Wm. PARKER, 8 yrs old 13 Aug 1812, to Jas. RUSSELL, to be a farmer Loose Papers: son of Ann Parker
6:78	10 Aug 1812	Adam KENDALL, 6 yrs old 4 Apr 1812, to Wm. KENDALL; to be a cooper
6:80	10 Aug 1812	Rebecca HAVERLIN's children, (of Middleburg), to be bound
6:100	13 Aug 1812	George MCGWIN, 13 yrs old 5 May 1813, to Henry B. DOWNS, farmer,
6:121	14 Sep 1812	David Batson PAINE, 5 yrs old 23 Dec 1812, to John BATSON, to be a farmer
6:121	14 Sep 1812	Joseph POOL to James MOORE
6:129	14 Sep 1812	Amey HUGHES to Daniel FOX
6:132	14 Sep 1812	Adam ZIMMERMAN, Bernard Taylor his guardian, to Aquilla MEAD, to be a tanner
6:149	12 Oct 1812	Jacob VALENTINE, 9 yrs old (or 10), to Joshua HARDY, to be a taylor Loose Papers: b. 5 Apr 1802, formerly bound in Fairfax Co.
6:149	12 Oct 1812	James THOMAS to Richard BROWN, farmer, indenture to Thomas Lacey declared void. 6:163, 9 Nov 1812, former order incorrect, bound to Jos. Brown, not Richard Loose Papers: Thomas Lacey indenture found

6:197	14 Dec 1812	Asa HALSEY, alias Wheeler, to Lewis KLINE, to be a boot and shoe maker Loose Papers: son of Nancy Wheeler
6:202	15 Dec 1812	Robert WALKER, 18 yrs old 12 Oct 1812, to Martin KITZMILLER, to be a tanner
DPP 1:702	9 Jan 1813	John SPOONER, free black age 21, to Wm. M. LITTLEJOHN, for 3 yrs
6:211	11 Jan 1813	John POOL, 15 yrs old 10 Mar 1813, to Aquila BRISCO, to be a bricklayer
6:211	11 Jan 1813	John VENANDERS, 14 yrs old in Mar 1813, to John HUMPHREY Loose Papers: son of Jane Venanders
6:229	8 Feb 1813	Keziah HOOK, 11 yrs old 23 Sep 1812, to Lewis ELLZEY
6:235	9 Feb 1813	Jonathan FERRIS to James MOORE, & Co., to be a carder and spinner in a woolen manufactory Loose Papers: illegitimate, mother dead and father gone for several years
6:237	9 Feb 1813	Charles SHEPHERD, 16 yrs old 26 Nov 1812, to Benjamin PERRY, to be a joiner
6:241	8 Mar 1813	John GREEN, 15 yrs old 8 Mar 1813, to Reuben ROWSEY, wheelwright,
6:250	9 Mar 1813	Henry TINSMAN, 13 yrs old 15 Feb 1813, to Jonathan KIDWELL Loose Papers: son of Phebe Tinsman
6:277	13 Apr 1813	John WALTMAN, 15 or 16 yrs old, to John PALMER, to be a shoemaker. 7:207, 11 Apr 1814, above order rescinded
6:285	10 May 1813	Jesse VIETCH, an orphan, 16 yrs old 5 Dec 1812, to James MOORE, & Co., to be a carder and spinner of wool by machinery Loose Papers: surname Veatch, b. 25 Dec, son of Nancy Veatch of Montgomery Co., MD
6:290	10 May 1813	Mary Ann BARBOUR, 10 yrs old 31 Jan 1813, to Thomas COLLINS
6:290	10 May 1813	James BARBOUR, 8 yrs old 14 Dec 1812, to Thomas COLLINS, to be a stone mason
6:290	10 May 1813	John PEARSON, 16 yrs old 27 Feb 1813, to Thomas COLLINS, to be a stone mason
6:307	14 Jun 1813	John TALBOTT, 17 yrs old 20 Dec 1812, to MOORE & PHILLIPS, to be a tanner and currier Loose Papers: son of Rebekah Talbot

6:310	14 Jun 1813	Baldwin JOHNSTON to MOORE & PHILLIPS, to be a tanner and currier Loose Papers: b. 20 Aug 1799, certified by Ellender Hart
6:310	14 Jun 1813	Levi JONES, b. 18 May 1802, to Joseph THOMAS, to be a bricklayer, order binding him to Wm. Kirk rescinded
6:344	12 Jul 1813	Elijah PALMER, orphan, to James MOORE, & Co., to be a wollen[sic] weaver
7:39	14 Aug 1813	Leven SHEPPARD, orphan of Chs. Sheppard, to John THOMAS, until 20 yrs old, to be a carpenter and joiner, John Littlejohn his guardian
7:45	13 Sep 1813	Robert GARNER, an orphan, 13 yrs old 15 Sep 1813, to George HEAD, Jr., to be a sadler Loose Papers: surname Gardner
7:45	13 Sep 1813	Joseph ELLIS, an orphan, 16 yrs old in Dec 1813, to John G. HUMPHREY, to be a blacksmith Loose Papers: indenture found
7:58	12 Oct 1813	Joseph BROWN, 16 yrs old 3 Oct 1813, Samuel Dunkin, guardian, to Caleb GALLAHAR, to be a cabinet maker
7:59	12 Oct 1813	Lewis ELLIS, b. __Feb 1801, to Garret WALKER, to be a shoemaker Loose Papers: indenture found
7:59	12 Oct 1813	Samuel ELLIS, b. __May 1803, to Ben. WALKER, to be a tanner Loose Papers: indenture found
7:103	13 Dec 1813	Levi HICKS, 11 yrs old in Mar 1813, to Amos GIBSON, to be a miller
7:103	13 Dec 1813	Wm. RILEY, about 17 yrs old, to Lewis KLEIN, to be a boot and shoe maker
7:104	13 Dec 1813	Elias POOL, 13 yrs old 25 Jan 1814, to Henry GLASGOW, to be a boot and shoemaker, order binding him to John Winn rescinded
7:105	13 Dec 1813	Alfred JONES to James MOORE, & Co., to be a carder and spinner of wool by machinery
7:105	13 Dec 1813	Henry WALKER to Joseph TAYLOR, to be a shoe and boot maker Loose Papers: for 3 yrs from 28 Nov 1814, until 21, indenture found

7:109	14 Dec 1813	Thomas JEFFERSON to William KING, to be a boot and shoe maker
7:109	14 Dec 1813	Charles GORDEN to William KING, to be a boot and shoe maker
7:117	10 Jan 1814	William ADAMS, 17 yrs old 4 Apr 1814, to James MOORE, & Co., to be a woolen weaver
7:117	10 Jan 1814	Samuel ADAMS, 14 yrs old 8 Mar 1814, to James MOORE, & Co., to be a carder and spinner by machinery
7:144	14 Feb 1814	Isak YOUNG, 9 yrs old 19 Apr 1814, to Wm. TAYLOR, to be a carpenter Loose Papers: Isaiah Young, indenture found
7:147	14 Feb 1814	Thornton JORDEN, 15 yrs old 15 Aug 1814, to Jas. MOORE, & Co., to be a carder and spinner by machinery
7:147	14 Feb 1814	Wm. JORDEN, 14 yrs old 9 Mar 1814, to Jas. MOORE, & Co., to be a woollen[sic] weaver
7:149	14 Feb 1814	Leven SHEPPARD to Benj. PERRY, to be a carpenter, order binding him to John Thomas rescinded
7:151	15 Feb 1814	Joshua GRAVES, 15 yrs old 14 Oct 1814, to Thornton WALKER, to be a house carpenter and joiner
7:195	19 Mar 1814	James THORNTON to Andrew BIRDSALL, to be a farmer
7:195	19 Mar 1814	Allen RIGGS, 15 yrs old 15 May 1814, to William KING, to be a boot and shoe maker
7:195	19 Mar 1814	Levi JONES, 13 yrs old 10 Apr 1814, to James MACKLAW, to be a miller
7:213	9 May 1814	Anthony LAMBAG to John N. KLINE, for 4 yrs 1 mo., to be a house carpenter Loose Papers: son of Neomi Lambag
7:216	9 May 1814	Peter JACOBS, 18 yrs old 5 Mar 1814, to Joseph GRUBB, to be a stone mason Loose Papers: son of Elizabeth Jacobs
DPP 1:237	28 May 1814	John DOBBINS, 20 yrs old 1 Jun 1814, to Joseph BEARD, to be a cabinet maker (until 21)
7:247	14 Jun 1814	Beninah RICE to John THOMAS, until 22 yrs old, to be a carpenter and joiner (formerly bound to Wm. Roberts)

Apprentices, Poor Children and Bastards

7:249	14 Jun 1814	Jane TAYLOR, 12 yrs old 22 Jun 1814, to George WATERS Loose Papers: to George Walters or Watters
7:249	14 Jun 1814	John WILLIAMS, 12 yrs old, to Andrew BIRDSALL, to be a farmer
7:253	14 Jun 1814	Wm. WILLIAMS, orphan of Joshua Williams, 15 yrs old, to James BRANDON, to be a miller Loose Papers: indenture found
7:253	14 Jun 1814	Cornelius PALMER, b. 12 Jan 1805, to David GALLEHER, to be a farmer
7:256	14 Jun 1814	George HAMMAT to Joseph HILLIARD, to be a bricklayer
7:274	17 Jun 1814	John A. SUTHERLAND to Patrick MCINTYRE, to be a printer
7:282	11 Jul 1814	Caleb SUTHERLAND, Richard H. Henderson guardian, to George HEAD, to be a sadler, indenture to be recorded
7:284	11 Jul 1814	George RIDENBAUGH, 10 yrs old 31 Mar 1814, to John SHOVER, to be a miller
7:292	8 Aug 1814	Levenia MOORE, 12 yrs old 7 Oct 1814, to Stephen MCPHERSON Loose Papers: Levina, dau of Hannah Moore, indenture found
7:300	9 Aug 1814	Sophia JERARD, 10 yrs old 8 May 1814, to Js. MCGEATH Loose Papers: consent of Susannah Jared, to James McGeath
7:300	9 Aug 1814	Sampson REID to William ELLIOTT, to be a house joiner and carpenter, order binding him to Wm. Dodd rescinded
7:335	10 Oct 1814	Thos. BOWLING, 18 yrs old 1 Feb 1814, to David COPELAND, to be a blacksmith Loose Papers: indenture found
7:365	9 Jan 1815	Aaron SCATTERDAY to John UNDERWOOD, to be a stone mason, formerly bound to Wm. Cook
7:365	9 Jan 1815	Polly GOINGS to Samuel BUCK, formerly bound to Wm. Hammerly
7:369	9 Jan 1815	Wm. GREEN to William ELLIOTT, to be a carpenter and joiner Loose Papers: 18 yrs old 15 Mar 1815, consent of William & Elizabeth Wooddy

7:384	13 Feb 1815	Thomas Obadiah CLIFFORD, orphan of Obadiah Clifford dec'd, to Patrick MCINTYRE, to be a printer Loose Papers: for 6 yrs from 13 Feb 1815, until 21, indenture found
7:418	16 Mar 1815	Peter MCNAMARA to Jacob MARTIN, to be a hatter
7:428	17 Mar 1815	Hugh OGDEN, b. 17 Sep 1801, orphan of Charles Ogden, to Peter BEMARDORFER, to be a miller
DPP 1:830	1 Apr 1815	Leroi, free mulatto 13 yrs old, to John MCCORMICK, until 21
7:438	12 Apr 1815	George MCNEALLY, 17 yrs old 26 Jan 1815, to John THOMAS, to be a house joiner Loose Papers: indenture found
7:438	12 Apr 1815	Samuel DAVIS, 11 yrs old 18 Oct 1815, to Henry GLASGOW, to be a shoemaker
7:451	8 May 1815	Hannah HAVERLIN to Elisha JANNEY, Jr.,
7:453	8 May 1815	Eli WILSON, 10 yrs old 9 Feb 1816, to Mahlon WATTERS, farmer,
7:454	8 May 1815	Peyton HOUGH, 17 yrs old in Oct 1815, to MOORE & PHILLIPS, to be a tanner an currier
7:455	8 May 1815	Josiah SEERS, an orphan about 13 yrs old, to John E. PALMER, to be a boot and shoemaker
7:470	12 Jun 1815	Thos. WILDAY to Joshua PUSEY, to be a farmer, formerly bound to Fred Filler Loose Papers: for 12 yrs, 11 mo. 20 da. From 10 Jun 1815
7:484	13 Jun 1815	Samuel TINTZMAN, 10 yrs old in Dec 1815, to David FULTON Loose Papers: surname Tinsman, son of Phoebe Tintzman, to be a farmer, indenture found
7:484	13 Jun 1815	Isaac HOOK to William BROWN, Jr. Loose Papers: consent of Martha Hook, 14 Jun 1815 to Amos Harvey for 12 yrs from 29 Jul 1815 until 21, to be a farmer, indenture found
7:486	13 Jun 1815	Mahala HAMBLETON to Thomas FRANCIS Loose Papers: Mehely, dau of P__cy Hambelton

7:486	13 Jun 1815	Henry TINTZMAN to Thomas FRANCIS Loose Papers: surname Tinsman, son of Pheby Tinsman
7:510	10 Jul 1815	James SPENCE, alias James Brooks, an orphan about 13 yrs old, to Fielding BROWN, to be a blacksmith Loose Papers: for 8 yrs from 3 Aug 1815 until 21, indenture found
7:510	10 Jul 1815	James L. SEAR, orphan b. 25 Jan 1799, to Jesse GOVER, to be a saddler and harness maker
7:510	10 Jul 1815	Samuel CONNOR, orphan about 10 yrs old, to Isaac HARRIS, to be a tanner Loose Papers: indenture found
7:517	10 Jul 1815	John Melcher WALTMAN to Adam GRUBB, to be a stone mason
1:8	14 Aug 1815	Jacob EVERHEART, 19 yrs old 3 Feb 1815, to Edward DORSEY, to be a carpenter and joiner
1:8	14 Aug 1815	Isaac WALKER, 17 yrs old 28 Jul 1815, to Edward DORSEY, to be a carpenter and joiner
1:8	14 Aug 1815	Benjamin WAUGH, 14 yrs old 15 Sep 1815, to Edward DORSEY, to be a carpenter and joiner
1:8	14 Aug 1815	Thomas REILY, about 16 yrs old, to Robert MOORE, to be a boot and shoemaker
1:24	17 Aug 1815	Isaac HOOKE to Amos HARVEY, to be a farmer
1:24	17 Aug 1815	Elizabeth MCGAHA, 11 yrs old 9 Apr 1815, to Jonathan CARTER
1:36	11 Sep 1815	Selina ESKRIDGE, 8 yrs old 7 Mar 1816, to Jonas JANNEY Loose Papers: dau of Catherine Vanpelt, to Jonas & wife
1:50	9 Oct 1815	Bennett BOND, 16 yrs old 2 Jun 1815, to Abel MORRISON, to be a house carpenter
1:69	13 Nov 1815	Nelson MCGEE to William GREGG, & wife Loose Papers: surname McGhee, black boy 6 yrs old 1 Aug 1815, son of Sophia McGhee, to William & Rebeckah Gregg
1:72	13 Nov 1815	John ROBERTSON, 8 yrs old 24 Jul 1815, to Wm. HART Loose Papers: son of Sarah Robertson

Records Found in Court Order Books

1:96	8 Jan 1816	John MENICK to David OGDEN, to be a cabinet maker Loose Papers: surname Minick, orphan, 15 yrs old 15 Sep 1815, indenture found
1:96	8 Jan 1816	Henry GARNER, 15 yrs old 17 Apr 1816, to Benj. MOFFETT, to be a cooper
1:99	8 Jan 1816	Samuel PULLER, until 22 yrs old, to Benj. HAGERMAN, to be a stone mason Loose Papers: indenture found
1:107	12 Feb 1816	Levi CHAPILIER, 14 yrs old in Dec 1815, to Archibald MORRISON, for 4 yrs, to be a farmer
1:107	12 Feb 1816	Richard MULLIN, 12 yrs old 16 Feb 1816, to Wm. WRIGHT, to be a bricklayer Loose Papers: age as of 10 Feb 1816, indenture found
1:107	12 Feb 1816	Laban HOWARD, 16 yrs old 21 Nov 1815, to Jonas ABY, to be a boot and shoemaker
1:108	12 Feb 1816	Jacob TAWNER to Thomas BIRKBY, to be a wagon maker
1:114	12 Mar 1816	Harrison CUMMINGS, 8 yrs old 24 Apr 1816, orphan of Geo. Cummings, to Wm. BROWN, to be a farmer Loose Papers: indenture found
1:114	12 Mar 1816	Elijah MINNIX to William GREGG Loose Papers: son of Elizabeth Minnix
1:122	13 Mar 1816	Charles NEALE, 15 yrs old 5 Apr 1816, to John THOMAS, to be a house carpenter and joiner Loose Papers: indenture found
1:122	13 Mar 1816	Philip THOMAS, 12 yrs old in Apr 1816, to John MOORE, to be a farmer
1:142	13 May 1816	Margaret SPENCE, 9 yrs old 31 Mar 1816, to Constantine HUGHES
1:142	13 May 1816	Wm. PHITZIMONS, 17 yrs old 19 Oct 1815, to Sandford EDMONDS, to be a cabinet maker
1:153	13 May 1816	Elizabeth MOORE, 6 yrs old 4 Aug 1816, to William LODGE Loose Papers: dau of Hannah Moore, indenture found
1:154	13 May 1816	William BOLIN, 17 yrs old 4 May 1816, to Daniel COCKERILL, to be a carpenter and joiner, indenture found

Apprentices, Poor Children and Bastards

1:154	13 May 1816	Benjamin GILDER, 15 yrs old 15 Jun 1816, to James COCHRAN, to be a blacksmith
1:154	13 May 1816	Jacob VALENTINE, b. 5 Apr 1802, to Joshua HARDY, to be a taylor Loose Papers: b. in Fairfax Co., has a brother Michael, indenture found
1:158	13 May 1816	Levin HOWELL to Nelson H. HUTCHISON, to be a bricklayer
1:158	13 May 1816	George HAMMETT, 18 yrs old 9 May 1816, to Wm. WRIGHT, to be a bricklayer
1:167	10 Jun 1816	Frederick WEEDON, 11 yrs old 1 Dec 1816, orphan of Jno. Weadon, to John THOMAS, to be a farmer Loose Papers: son of Margaret Weadon, indenture found
1:169	10 Jun 1816	Washington JARVIS, about 16 yrs old, to Jotham WRIGHT, to be a taylor
1:175	11 Jun 1816	Jas. TRAYHERN, 16 yrs old in Jan 1812(?), to Jotham WRIGHT, to be a taylor
1:180	12 Jun 1816	Polly GOINGS to Robt. R. HOUGH, order binding her to Samuel Buck rescinded
1:183	12 Jun 1816	William DAVIS, 10 yrs old 28 Nov 1816, to Jacob MARTIN, to be a hatter Loose Papers: son of Catharine Davis
1:235	9 Sep 1816	Wm. THOMAS, 10 yrs old 15 Jun 1816, to Joseph BROWN, until 17 yrs old Loose Papers: son of Mary Thomas
1:243	15 Oct 1816	Henly MCCOY, son of Ben. McCoy, dec'd, 16 yrs old 13 Sep 1816, to Martin KITZMILLER, to be a tanner and currier
1:248	15 Oct 1816	Isaias SEARS to Robert GOVER, to be a shoemaker, order binding him to John E. Palmer rescinded
1:270	9 Dec 1816	Mary Ann COCKERILLE, 10 yrs old 10 Dec 1816, to Asa MOORE Loose Papers: dau of Sarah Cockerill, to Asa & Ann
1:274	9 Dec 1816	Benjamin GILDER, 15 yrs old 15 Jun 1816, to Wm. CHAPPALEAR, to be a boot and shoe maker
1:277	13 Jan 1817	Richard MULLEN to John REESE, to be a plaisterer, formerly bound to William Wright Loose Papers: indenture found
1:282	13 Jan 1817	Daniel SHIPES, 11 yrs old 15 May 1817, to John D. BROWN, to be a tanner

1:285	14 Jan 1817	Henley MCCOY to Martin KITZMILLER, until 21 which will be 13 Sep 1822, to be a tanner (see 1:243, 15 Oct 1816)
1:289	11 Feb 1817	William Henry FYE, 14 yrs old 25 Dec 1816, to Joseph P. THOMAS, to be a bricklayer
1:289	11 Feb 1817	John FYE, 14 yrs old 25 Dec 1816, to Joseph P. THOMAS, to be a bricklayer
1:295	11 Feb 1817	Benjamin BAGLEY, 20 yrs old 9 Mar 1817, illegitimate, to Nelson HUTCHISON, to be a bricklayer (until 21)
1:299	10 Mar 1817	George WARTERS, 13 yrs old 24 Nov 1817, orphan of Enos Warters, to John BRADFIELD, to be a farmer Loose Papers: indenture found
1:303	11 Mar 1817	Washington EARP, 17 yrs old 4 Jun 1817, to Jacob MARTIN, to be a hatter Loose Papers: son of Verlinda Earp of Montgomery Co., MD
1:304	11 Mar 1817	George GERMAN to Richard VANPELT, to be a blacksmith Loose Papers: b. 4 Oct 1803, twin son of Eleanor German relict of John German of Fairfax Co., indenture found
1:304	11 Mar 1817	Peter GERMAN to Richard VANPELT, to be a blacksmith Loose Papers: b. 4 Oct 1803, twin son of Eleanor German relict of John German of Fairfax Co., indenture found
order not found:	11 Mar 1817	Sarah GERMAN to Jane CAMEL Loose Papers: b. 12 Oct 1806, Eleanor German agreed to bind her dau to Jane Camel, wife of Robert Camel
1:309	13 Mar 1817	Leven SHEPHERD apprentice of Benjamin PERRY, released from apprenticeship and indenture cancelled
1:326	15 Apr 1817	Jno. W. ROSE to Jacob MARTIN, to be a hatter Loose Papers: 20 yrs old 19 Oct 1817, son of Sibby Sanford
1:342	12 May 1817	Jno. C. NEWTON, b. 21 Feb 1801, to Jno. HAMMERLY, to be a house carpenter
1:407	13 Aug 1817	Richard MULLEN to David COPELAND, to be a blacksmith, orderbinding him to John Reese rescinded

Apprentices, Poor Children and Bastards 111

1:412	14 Aug 1817	Alex COMBS to Benj. MAULSBY, to be a saddler, for a term of six years Loose Papers: name Alexander, on request of Martin & Martha Cordell, to Benjamin Maulsby
2:12	13 Nov 1817	Samuel DAVIS, 13 yrs old 18 Oct 1817, to Jacob MARTIN, to be a hatter Loose Papers: son of Catherine Davis
2:12	13 Nov 1817	Henry DAVIS to Jno. MONROE, to be a house carpenter and joiner
2:21	8 Dec 1817	Diana WAUGH, 3 yrs 9 mo old, dau of Polly Waugh, to Joseph PATTERSON
2:21	8 Dec 1817	Ferdinando BOWLINS, about 14 yrs old, orphan of John Bowlins, to Acquilla MEADE, to be a tanner
2:27	8 Dec 1817	Hiram DUTY, 10 yrs old in Jan 1817, to Elisha CHICK, to be a farmer
2:41	12 Jan 1818	Charles FOX, 9 yrs old 10 Dec 1817, to Jonas JANNEY, to be a farmer Loose Papers: son of Gracy Fox, indenture found
2:44	12 Jan 1818	Levi HIX to Elisha JANNEY, to be a farmer, order binding him to Amos Gibson rescinded
2:51	13 Jan 1818	Levi JONES, 15 yrs old 18 May 1818, to Wm. KING, to be a shoemaker Loose Papers: son of Elizabeth Jones
2:77	10 Mar 1818	William SPENCER to John CARNEY, to be a boot and shoe maker
2:122	11 May 1818	Eliza Ann WRIGHT to Joseph WOOD, until 18 which will be 13 Feb 1830 Loose Papers: dau of Jane Ann Wright
2:127	12 May 1818	Morris PARKER to William KING, to be a shoe and boot maker
2:133	8 Jun 1818	Israel TRAYHORN to Jesse GOVER, to be a sadler
2:133	8 Jun 1818	Colvin POWELL, 9 yrs old 14 Aug 1818, to William LODGE Loose Papers: son of Mary Powell, to be a farmer, indenture found
2:200	10 Aug 1818	Michael Wm. FACKLER, 15 yrs old 30 Apr 1818, to Joseph STEER, to be a blacksmith Loose Papers: son of Elizabeth Fackler

2:200	10 Aug 1818	Franklin John FACKLER, 11 yrs old 3 Dec 1817, to Joseph STEER, to be a blacksmith Loose Papers: son of Elizabeth Fackler
2:229	14 Aug 1818	Edward LANDY to David NIXON, until 21 yrs old, to be a farmer
2:245	14 Sep 1818	John RUSSELL to Thomas PHILLIPS, to be a tanner and currier Loose Papers: son of Sarah Russell
2:256	12 Oct 1818	Catherine MULLEN, about 12 yrs old, orphan of Joseph Mullen, to Isaac HARRIS Loose Papers: John Mullen her gr-father
2:274	10 Nov 1818	Stephen MOSS, 11 yrs old 22 Nov 1818, to Wm. KING, to be a boot and shoe maker Loose Papers: birth month Oct, son of Mary Moss
2:274	10 Nov 1818	Catherine MASS, 8 yrs old 11 Jun 1818, to Jotham WRIGHT Loose Papers: age as of 16 Jun 1818, dau of Mary Mass, widow
2:362	8 Mar 1819	James JOHNSON, about 14 yrs old, orphan of John Johnson, to Benjamin HAGERMAN, to be a stone mason, Casper Johnson, his guardian consented
2:402	13 Mar 1819	Wm. FRYE to Jno. COPELAND, for 5 yrs or until 21, to be a miller
2:447	12 May 1819	Reasin GREGG to David OGDEN, for 7 yrs from 26 Mar 1819, to be a cabinetmaker
2:462	14 Jun 1819	Hiram ORAM, 18 yrs old 1 Jan 1820, to Charles GULLATT, until 21, to be a taylor
2:465	14 Jun 1819	Jos. BARNETT to Truman GORE, until 21, to be a house joiner, Mary Barnett his guardian
3:28	10 Aug 1819	Ann HEVELIN, alias Heblin, dau of Rebecca Hevelin alias Heblin, about 16 yrs old, to be bound out
3:28	10 Aug 1819	Eliza HEVELIN, alias Heblin, dau of Rebecca Hevelin alias Heblin, about 14 yrs old, to be bound out
3:39	12 Aug 1819	Leven HAGERMAN, 12 yrs old 5 Feb 1818, son of S. Cassey, to John HARRIS, to be a taylor
3:73	13 Sep 1819	Henry DAWS, a bastard, apprentice to J.S. HENCHER, Hencher to shew cause why order binding Daws to him should not be rescinded

Apprentices, Poor Children and Bastards 113

3:73	13 Sep 1819	John TURNER, orphan, 14 yrs old 13 Sep 1819, to John MONROE, to be a house joiner
3:82	11 Oct 1819	Henry DAWS, alias Stater, to Wm. KING, to be a boot & shoemaker
3:82	11 Oct 1819	Aris WALKER, b. 19 Jun 1803, to Craven WALKER, to be a house carpenter
3:82	11 Oct 1819	Wormly WALKER, b. 9 Aug 1809, to Craven WALKER, to be a house carpenter
3:82	11 Oct 1819	Lott GRAVES, about 16 yrs old, to James MILLER, to be a taylor Loose Papers: orphan, indenture found
3:82	11 Oct 1819	Isaac MOORE, son of Edon B. Moore, to Patrick KING, to be a sadler
3:97	8 Nov 1819	Anthony WELCOME, 9 yrs old, child of James Welcome, to Anthony LUCAS, to be a farmer
3:106	10 Nov 1819	Robert DOUGAN, orphan, 16 yrs old, to John SURGENOR, to be a boot & shoemaker
3:107	10 Nov 1819	William HENRY, orphan, 11 yrs old, to James BROWN, to be a blacksmith
3:119	11 Nov 1819	John ENZER, son of Margaret Jenkins, to Wm. KING, to be a boot & shoemaker
3:128	12 Nov 1819	Kerzia HARNED, dau of Nathaniel Harned, dec'd, about 8 yrs old, to Aaron JANNEY Loose Papers: given name Kezia, indenture found
3:147	14 Dec 1819	___ NEWLON, child of Geo. Newlon, dec'd, to John JOHNSTON, to be a carpenter
3:147	14 Dec 1819	Isaac MOORE, orphan of Eden Moore, dec'd, to Wm. MOORE, to be a farmer, Patrick King having refused to comply with requisitions of law Loose Papers: 14 yrs old 25 Sep 1820, indenture found
3:161	11 Jan 1820	Samuel MULLEN to be bound
3:168	14 Feb 1820	Lewis FIGH, 17 yrs old 25 Jul 1820, to Isaac P. THOMAS, to be a turner & chair maker, indenture found
3:169	14 Feb 1820	William MILLER, son of John Miller who has absconded, to John HARDY, to be a boot & shoemaker Loose Papers: 13 yrs old 25 Mar 1819, indenture found

3:173	15 Feb 1820	Samuel DAVIS to Wm. KING, to be a boot & shoemaker, formerly bound to Jacob Martin Loose Papers: son of Catharine Davis
3:239	8 May 1820	Wm. CRIDER, 16 yrs old 14 Jun 1820, son of Frederick Crider, dec'd, to be bound
3:239	8 May 1820	Frederick CRIDER, 13 yrs old 27 Feb 1820, son of Frederick Crider, dec'd, to be bound
3:256	12 Jun 1820	Daniel HINES, 16 yrs old 9 Jan 1820, son of John Hines who is absent from this commonwealth, to Richard ROACH, to be a blacksmith Loose Papers: surname Hynes, indenture found
3:268	14 Jun 1820	John ADAMS, 12 yrs old 15 Nov 1819, son of Elizabeth Adams, to Joseph FREDD
3:268	14 Jun 1820	Thomas MERCER to Isaac BROWN, to be a farmer
3:280	16 Jun 1820	Nimrod BARR, order binding him to __ Evans rescinded Loose Papers: bound to Henry Evans, indenture found
3:280	16 Jun 1820	Henson SIMPSON, about 15 yrs old, orphan of Henson Simpson, dec'd, to Thomas RUSSELL, to be a taylor Loose Papers: Jas. Simpson guardian
3:311	14 Aug 1820	Powell SHRY, 20 yrs old 15 Nov 1820, to Abraham BROWN, to be a blacksmith
3:328	16 Aug 1820	James WRIGHT, 9 yrs old 16 Aug 1820, to Asa BROWN, to be a saddler & harness maker Loose Papers: b. Jul, son of Christiana Wright, indenture found
3:337	18 Aug 1820	Kitty MORELAND, 16 yrs old, dau of David Moreland, who is absent from this commonwealth, and Bridgett, alias Mary, Moreland, to R.R. HOUGH, 3:382, 10 Oct 1820, order rescinded
3:355	11 Sep 1820	Ignatius DEAN, 18 yrs old in Mar 1820, to John REESE, to be a plaisterer Loose Papers: to John Ruse(?), indenture found
3:370	13 Sep 1820	Henry DAWES to Samuel TUSTIN, to be a carriage maker, formerly bound to Wm. King

Apprentices, Poor Children and Bastards

3:382	10 Oct 1820	James SPENCE to Adam HOUSEHOULDER, to be a farmer, former order binding him to Fielding Brown rescinded
3:382	10 Oct 1820	James RHINE, 15 yrs old, son of Sarah Rhine, to John SURGHNOR, to be a boot and shoe maker
4:7	13 Nov 1820	Joseph LYONS, about 16 yrs old, son of Jos. Lyons, dec'd, to Daniel VERNON, to be a miller
4:8	13 Nov 1820	Hugh Franklin LYONS, about 7 yrs old, son of Jos Lyons, de'd, to Samuel SMITH, Jr., to be a farmer
4:8	13 Nov 1820	Robert LYONS, about 11 yrs old, son of Jos. Lyons, dec'd, to Seth SMITH, to be a fan and plough maker
4:8	13 Nov 1820	William HARNED, 14 yrs old 22 Nov 1820, son of N. Harned, dec'd, to William BALL, to be a waggonmaker Loose Papers: son of Nathaniel Harned, indenture found
4:8	13 Nov 1820	Elijah MASON, a yellow boy, to John HARDY, to be a boot and shoemaker Loose Papers: mulatto, about 16 yrs 5 mo old, indenture found
4:8	13 Nov 1820	Nancy LEWIS, dau of Z. Lewis who has absconded, to John JOHNSON, of Union Loose Papers: dau of Zachariah Lewis, age 13, indenture found
4:53	11 Dec 1820	Solomon LITTLETON, orphan of Sampson Littleton, to Hugh THOMPSON, to be a tanner
4:53	11 Dec 1820	Alfred JONES, 15 yrs old 23 Sep 1820, son of Elizabeth Jones, to Amasa HOUGH, to be a farmer Loose Papers: indenture found
4:56	12 Dec 1820	Anthony WELCOME, orphan boy of color, Anthony LUCAS, Lucas to show cause why order binding Welcome should not be rescinded
4:56	12 Dec 1820	Nancy MOCK, orphan, vs Mahlon JANNY, (of Amos), to show cause why order binding her should not be rescinded
4:69	8 Jan 1821	Emily TRIBBY, 13 yrs old, to S.A. JACKSON

4:73	9 Jan 1821	Anthony WELCOME, order binding him to Anthony Lucas rescinded
4:84	12 Feb 1821	Emily POLTON bound to Samuel A. JACKSON, to shew cause why order binding her should not be rescinded. 4:120, 14 Mar 1821, rule dismissed, the girl considered to be an apprentice of Jackson Loose Papers: for 4 yrs from May 1821 until 18, indenture found
4:84	12 Feb 1821	William MERCER, son of Henry Mercer who has departed this commonwealth, to John BROWN, farmer,
4:90	13 Feb 1821	William, a boy of color, apprentice of Thomas J. NOLAND, to show cause why indenture should not be rescinded
4:95	14 Feb 1821	William SPENCE to Isaac WRIGHT, to be a bricklayer
4:95	14 Feb 1821	Henson SPENCE, child of Nancy Spence, to be bound
4:95	14 Feb 1821	Vincent SPENCE, child of Nancy Spence, to be bound
4:121	14 Mar 1821	Nepolian BALL, orphan of Stephen Ball, to Daniel MOCK, until 17 yrs old, to be a farmer
4:150	10 Apr 1821	George GLASGOW, 13 yrs old 8 Sep 1821, son of Henry Glasgow, to James GARRISON, to be a hatter Loose Papers: son of Henry & Catharine Glasgow, indenture found
4:153	14 May 1821	John ROBINSON, 12 yrs old 21 Mar 1822, to Thomas WILKINSON, to be a taylor
4:164	14 May 1821	Joseph BARNETT to Joseph HILLIARD, to be a bricklayer
4:164	14 May 1821	Joseph MULLEN to Joseph HILLIARD, to be a bricklayer
4:164	14 May 1821	Polly MULLEN, about 13 yrs old, to William HUNT Loose Papers: given name Mary, indenture found
4:168	14 May 1821	Joseph COCKERILL to Thomas H. KERBY, to be a blacksmith
4:172	15 May 1821	Wm. LEWIS, about 7 yrs old, son of Zachairah Lewis who has absconded from the commonwealth, to Henry PLAISTER, Jr., to be a farmer

Apprentices, Poor Children and Bastards 117

4:172	15 May 1821	Moses HARNED, about 7 yrs old, son of Nathaniel Harned, dec'd, to Jacob GOUGHNER, to be a farmer Loose Papers: to Jacob Gochnauer, Jr.
4:187	11 Jun 1821	Elizabeth WRIGHT, 8 yrs old 16 May 1821, to John SULLIVAN, consent of Catherine Wright Loose Papers: date 16 Apr, consent of Christiana Wright, her mother, indenture found
W.B. N:357	11 Aug 1821	Matilda BUTLER to be bound out until 28 yrs
W.B. N:357	11 Aug 1821	Margaret VOLLUM to be bound out until 19 yrs
4:337	12 Nov 1821	Frederick WEEDON to John THOMAS, Jr., formerly bound to John Thomas, Sr. Loose Papers: both indentures found
4:384	10 Dec 1821	Wm. COPELAND to be bound Loose Papers: child of Jane Copeland
4:384	10 Dec 1821	Susan COPELAND to be bound Loose Papers: child of Jane Copeland
4:432	11 Mar 1822	Daniel MOFFETT, 11 yrs old 12 Feb 1823, orphan of Wm. Moffett, to Wm. WILSON, to be a farmer
4:496	14 May 1822	Sarah R. LOWE to Thoms R. MOTT
5:9	10 Jun 1822	Pierce NOLAND, 14 yrs old 8 Mar 1822, to David OGDEN Loose Papers: son of Elizabeth Noland
5:63	12 Aug 1822	William MORAN, son of John M. Moran, dec'd, to be bound
5:124	14 Oct 1822	William MORAN, 16 yrs old, to Martin KITZMILLER, to be a tanner
5:63	12 Aug 1822	John MORAN, son of John M. Moran, dec'd, to be bound
5:74	13 Aug 1822	Hanson SPENCE, 10 yrs old 25 Dec 1822, to James GARRISON, to be a hatter
5:216	13 Jan 1823	Alfred POOL, 8 yrs old 1 Jan 1823, son of Susanah Pool, to John BRADY, to be a cabinet maker
5:234	10 Feb 1823	Owen , commonly called Jefferson, negro boy 16 yrs old 4 Feb 1823, to Charles BINNS, Jr., to be a farmer

Records Found in Court Order Books

5:250	10 Mar 1823	Catharine ARNOT, 8 yrs old 8 Mar 1823, orphan of Wm. Arnot, to Wm. SUMMERS Loose Papers: orphan of Wm Arnot, dec'd and Ann Arnot, widow
5:255	11 Mar 1823	Burrell LEACH, 16 yrs old 20 Jun 1823, to Jacob MANN, of Middleburg, to be a tanner & currier
5:255	11 Mar 1823	James GEEN, b. 10 Nov 1810, to John BRADY, to be a cabinet maker
5:255	11 Mar 1823	John Bennett EVANS, b. 1 Apr 1814, to be bound
5:256	11 Mar 1823	Catherine MASS vs Jotham WRIGHT, petition to cancel indenture for failure to provide raiment & education. 5:290, 15 Mar 1823, indenture cancelled
5:289	15 Mar 1823	James NEWLON to Jas. MCDANIEL, to be a boot & shoe maker
5:290	15 Mar 1823	Catherine MASS to be bound
5:305	12 May 1823	Berkley POULTON, 14 yrs old 14 Oct 1823, son of John Poulton who has left his family, to Enos TRAYHORN Loose Papers: left wife and 5 children
5:305	12 May 1823	John POULTON, 12 yrs old 9 Nov 1823, son of John Poulton who has left his family, to William DANIEL, Jr.,
5:305	12 May 1823	Adrain POULTON, 10 yrs old 15 Feb 1823, son of John Poulton who has left his family, to William BRADFIELD, of Pumpkin Town,
5:305	12 May 1823	Eviline Ann POULTON, 7 yrs old 1 Sep 1823, dau of John Poulton who has left his family, to Minor REED
5:305	12 May 1823	Patrick BURNS, about 10 yrs old, parents unknown, to Asahel EVANS
5:305	12 May 1823	Moses ARNET, 10 yrs old 28 Jun 1823, to John SMITH, (son of William),
5:312	12 May 1823	Wm. GHEEN, orphan of Jas. Gheen, dec'd, to John BRADY, to be a cabinet maker
5:312	12 May 1823	Andrew CAMPBELL, 11 yrs old 18 Nov 1823, orphan of Wm. Campbell, to John VANSICKLE, to be a farmer, Jane Campbell, mother, gave consent

Apprentices, Poor Children and Bastards

5:326	9 Jun 1823	James ADAMS, about 12 yrs old in Jan 1823, orphan of Jos. Adams, to David FULTON, to be a farmer, Elizabeth Adams, mother, gave consent Loose Papers: age as of 13 Jan 1823
5:337	10 Jun 1823	David WALTMAN, 15 yrs old, to Henry T. BAYNE, to be a taylor
5:400	13 Aug 1823	Alfred JACKSON, an orphan about 14 yrs old, to Jos. EIDSON, (or some other suitable person), to be a carpenter
5:438	8 Sep 1823	John DULANEY, 18 yrs old 14 Feb 1824, to John H. MONROE, to be a house joiner
5:503	8 Dec 1823	Uriah GILL, orphan of Daniel Gill, dec'd, to Samuel TRAYHORN, to be a boot & shoe maker
6:14	12 Jan 1824	Mary Ann ARNET, 14 yrs old 2 Mar 1824, dau of Wm. Arnet, dec'd, to Jonah NICHOLS
6:14	12 Jan 1824	John ARNET, 7 yrs old 22 Dec 1823, son of Wm. Arnet, dec'd, to Absolom BEANS
6:14	12 Jan 1824	Andrew FOLEY, 14 yrs old 15 Mar 1824, to Joseph HOUGH
6:19	13 Jan 1824	Nathaniel ALLISON to Thomas RUSSELL, to be a taylor
6:31	9 Feb 1824	James MCGAHA, orphan, 15 yrs old in Apr 1824, to Samuel KALB, to be a farmer Loose Papers: son of Nancy Anna Caler
6:63	9 Mar 1824	Francis BOGUE, orphan of John Bogue, dec'd, to Thomas RUSSELL, to be a taylor, Frances Bogue, his mother, consented
6:64	9 Mar 1824	William VANHORNE, 16 yrs old 2 Mar 1824, orphan, to Joseph EIDSON, to be a house joiner, Nancy Vanhorn, his mother, consented
6:109	10 May 1824	Mandy WATTS apprentice of Thomas H. KIRBY, Kirby has failed to comply with his covenant with O.P. 6:312, ordered to appear
6:138	14 Jun 1824	William CRIDER apprentice of Thomas H. KIRBY, why apprentice should not be released
6:197	9 Aug 1824	Elijah SMITLEY, 16 yrs old 25 Mar 1824, to Wm. SUMMERS, Jane Smitley, his mother, consented

Records Found in Court Order Books

6:197	9 Aug 1824	Edmund SMITLEY, 14 yrs old Apr 1824, to Wm. SUMMERS, Jane Smitley, his mother, consented Loose Papers: as of 28 Apr
6:241	13 Sep 1824	Collin CORDELL, 15 yrs old 11 Sep 1824, to Thomas RUSSELL, to be a taylor
6:261	11 Oct 1824	Wallace , free boy of colour, to Thomas BISCOE, to be a farmer. 6:260, former order binding him to Thomas Brown rescinded Loose Papers: to be a stone mason, indenture to Brown found
6:362	14 Feb 1825	John HELPON, 14 yrs old 4 Jun 1825, orphan of Michael Helpon, to Wm. KING, to be a boot & shoemaker
6:366	14 Feb 1825	Thomas DAWLIN, 16 yrs old 29 May 1825, to Samuel HAMMONTREE, to be a cabinet maker
6:385	14 Mar 1825	George SMALLWOOD, 9 yrs old in Jun 1824, to Israel MYRES, until 17 yrs old Loose Papers: for 8 yrs from 10 Jun 1824, to Israel Myers, indenture found
6:385	14 Mar 1825	Mary SMALLWOOD, 11 yrs old in Jun 1824, to Wm. SCHOOLEY
6:403	11 Apr 1825	Wm. GLASGOW, 15 yrs old 13 Oct 1825, to James GILMORE, Catharine Glasgow his mother consented
6:438	10 May 1825	Henry LANGLEY, 17 yrs old in Feb 1825, son of Elick Langley, to James BROWN, to be a blacksmith
7:35	16 Jun 1825	Hannah Binns GOFF, orphan of Adam Goff, dec'd, to John SURGHNOR
7:35	16 Jun 1825	George L. GOFF, orphan of Adam Goff, dec'd, to Samuel GILPIN, to be a hatter
7:35	16 Jun 1825	Elleanor S. GOFF, orphan of Adam Goff, dec'd, to be bound
7:35	16 Jun 1825	Landon LYDER to Wm. BRADFIELD, to be a boot & shoemaker, on motion of Letitia Lyder Loose Papers: Letitia his sister and guardian
7:35	16 Jun 1825	Jacob LYDER to Abraham CORRELL, to be a plaisterer, on motion of Letitia Lyder Loose Papers: Letitia his guardian
7:36	16 Jun 1825	Nathaniel ALLISON an apprentice of Thomas RUSSELL, petition to remove him from Russell and bind him to some other person, Hilleary Allison, next friend

7:60	11 Jul 1825	Thomas JACOBS, orphan of Thomas Jacobs, dec'd, to John W. CROUSE, to be a taylor
7:120	13 Sep 1825	Wm. CHAMBLING, 12 yrs old 28 Dec 1824, orphan of Jas. Chamblin, to John PENN(?), to be a cooper
7:126	10 Oct 1825	William BECK, 15 yrs old 18 Jun 1826, orphan, to Joshua PUSEY, to be a farmer, Eleanor Beck his mother consented
7:127	10 Oct 1825	George B. SHOEMAKER, 7 yrs old 20 Dec 1825, to David FULTON, to be a farmer Loose Papers: (age corrected 7:370)
7:145	14 Nov 1825	Wallace, a free boy of colour, to Thomas BISCOE, to be a stone mason
7:145	14 Nov 1825	Manly WATTS, 13 yrs old 16 Dec 1825, to James M. DANIEL, to be a boot & shoemaker, formerly bound to Thomas H. Kirby who has left the commonwealth
7:202	9 Jan 1826	Bently MOORE, 18 yrs old 28 Mar 1825, orphan of Abner Moore, dec'd, to Wm. J. HANBY, to be a boot and shoemaker
7:213	10 Jan 1826	Edward LOWE, 15 yrs old 4 Mar 1826, orphan of Thos. Lowe, dec'd, to , to be a boot & shoe maker (on motion of John Surghnor)
7:221	11 Jan 1826	Hannah GOFF, orphan of Adam Goff, to be bound
7:228	13 Feb 1826	Wm STEWART, Jr., about 9 yrs old, son of Wm. Stewart, to David JURY, to be a farmer, parents unable to support him
7:229	13 Feb 1826	Henry NEWTON, 14 yrs old 20 Sep 1825, son of Ann Conner, late Newton, to Samuel G. HAMILTON, to be a boot & shoemaker, Ann Conner gave consent
7:229	13 Feb 1826	Sandford McNealy ANDREWS, 20 yrs old 28 Jul 1826, to Wm. LAFABER, to be a farmer, former order to be a blacksmith rescinded
7:230	13 Feb 1826	Jonah MCCUTCHEON, orphan, 16 yrs old 15 Feb 1826, to Samuel HOUGH, to be a carder & spinner Loose Papers: age as of 5 Feb 1826
7:230	13 Feb 1826	Sydney, alias Sydnor, BENNETT, orphan 10 yrs old in Mar 1825, to Samuel\ HOUGH, to be a weaver Loose Papers: son of Chas. Bennett, dec'd

7:251	14 Mar 1826	Francis WORRAN, 16 yrs old 18 Mar 1826, to Benjamin DAWES, to be a boot & shoemaker
7:251	14 Mar 1826	Robert BRIGGS, 18 yrs old 4 Feb 1826, to Benjamin DAWES, to be a boot & shoemaker
7:251	14 Mar 1826	Spencer WORRAN, 18 yrs old 5 Jul 1826, to Benjamin DAWES, to be a boot & shoemaker
7:255	15 Mar 1826	Martin NEWLIN, between 14 & 15 yrs old, to William W. HAMMONTREE, to be a chair maker
7:256	15 Mar 1826	James Henry STEWART, about 12 yrs old, son of Wm. Stewart, to Robert WHITACRE, to be a farmer, parents unable to support him
7:275	11 Apr 1826	Silas GORDON, 14 yrs old 5 Feb 1826, orphan, to John HARRIS, to be a taylor
7:288	8 May 1826	George MCKIM, 13 yrs old, son of James McKim, to Samuel HOUGH, to be a weaver, father unable to support him
7:295	9 May 1826	James Henry STEWART, about 12 yrs old, son of Wm. Stewart, to James THOMAS, to be a butcher, order binding him to Robert Whitacre rescinded
7:297	12 Jun 1826	Nancy GOFF, 8 yrs old 11 Mar 1826, orphan of Adam Goff, dec'd, to John BRADY Loose Papers: indenture found
7:297	12 Jun 1826	Margaret GOFF, 8 yrs old 11 Mar 1826, orphan of Adam Goff, dec'd, to Samuel HAMMETT
7:297	12 Jun 1826	Ellen GOFF, 11 yrs old in Dec 1825, orphan of Adam Goff, dec'd, to Benjamin BRADFIELD Loose Papers: indenture found
7:311	13 Jun 1826	Jno. WRIGHT, 11 yrs old 25 Feb 1826, to Silas GARRETT, to be a farmer, Christiana Wright his mother, consented Loose Papers: given name John
7:359	15 Aug 1826	John HENRY, 19 yrs old 16 Aug 1826, son of Stephen Henry, dec'd, to Benj. DAWES, to be a boot & shoemaker

Apprentices, Poor Children and Bastards 123

7:364	15 Aug 1826	William CONNER to William KITZMILLER, Martin Kitzmiller, to whom Conner was bound in 1821, having died, indenture is transferred Loose Papers: indenture found
7:370	16 Aug 1826	George B. SHOEMAKER, __ yrs old 4 Nov 1825, to David FULTON, to be a farmer Loose Papers: 11 yrs old 4 Nov 1825, mother is dead and father has run away
8:71	12 Feb 1827	William BALLINGER, son of Henson Ballinger, dec'd, to John ROGERS, to be a farmer
8:71	12 Feb 1827	Charles BALLINGER, son of Henson Ballinger, dec'd, to John ROGERS, to be a farmer
8:76	12 Feb 1827	John H.G. RODGERS, orphan, about 11 yrs old, to William HANNAH, to be a blacksmith
8:101	12 Mar 1827	Samuel BALL, a free boy of colour, 17 yrs old in Mar 1827, son of Hester Ball, to Wm. BLACKNELL, to be a barber & hairdresser Loose Papers: indenture found
8:146	10 Apr 1827	John URTON, about 14 yrs old, to Thomas FRAZIER, to be a farmer
8:166	14 May 1827	Mandly M. HAINES, orphan of Stacey Haines, dec'd, to Joseph HAINES, to be a stonemason. 8:171, Edward W. Hains not Joseph Haines, order corrected 16 May 1827
8:179	11 Jun 1827	Henry JONES, a free boy of colour, 17 yrs old 28 Aug 1826, to Wm. HANNAH, to be a blacksmith
8:188	12 Jun 1827	Thos. JACOBS, 18 yrs old 16 Mar 1828, orphan of Thos. Jacobs, dec'd, to John W. CROWSE, to be a taylor. 8:253, 14 Aug 1827, order rescinded Loose Papers: indenture found
8:188	12 Jun 1827	George Washington BOWMAN, 17 yrs old 10 Jan 1827, orphan of John Bowman, dec'd, to B.W. SOWER, to be a printer
8:226	9 Jul 1827	Silas JORDAN, 15 yrs old 10 Jan 1827, to Jno. HARRIS, to be a taylor
8:246	13 Aug 1827	Wm. B. MOFFETT, 16 yrs old 6 Aug 1827, orphan of Nancy Moffett, to Evan J. OWENS, to be a shoe & boot maker. 8:381, 12 Dec 1827, order rescinded

Records Found in Court Order Books

8:253	14 Aug 1827	Thomas JACOBS, 17 yrs old in Mar 1827, orphan of Thos. Jacobs, dec'd, to David M. WALLACE, to be a taylor Loose Papers: indenture found
8:286	10 Sep 1827	Jacob SMITH, orphan, 18 yrs old 18 Dec 1826, to John BRADY, to be a cabinet maker
8:286	10 Sep 1827	Lemuel SMITH, orphan, 16 yrs old 11 Nov 1826, to John BRADY, to be a cabinet maker
8:291	10 Sep 1827	Linton ANDERS, orphan, 12 yrs old, to Henson LOWE, to be a farmer and post & fence maker
8:291	10 Sep 1827	Abalino HOLE, orphan, 17 yrs old 15 Apr 1827, to Wm. HAMMONTREE, to be a chairmaker & painter
8:292	10 Sep 1827	Thos. EVANS, 17 yrs old 13 Dec 1827, to Thomas RUSSELL, to be a taylor
8:305	8 Oct 1827	William HOOK, orphan, 19 yrs old 1 Jan 1828, to Joseph TAYLOR, to be a boot & shoe maker, formerly bound to Elijah James
8:305	8 Oct 1827	James Henry STEWART apprentice to James THOMAS, petition of Catharine Stewart, mother, for release from indenture. 8:338, 14 Nov 1827, to remain with Thomas
8:319	12 Nov 1827	William DAVIDSON, infant child of John Davidson who has absconded from the commonwealth, to be bound
8:319	12 Nov 1827	Mary Catharine DAVIDSON, infant child of John Davidson who has absconded from the commonwealth, to be bound
8:338	14 Nov 1827	George GOFF, orphan of Adam Goff, dec'd, to Samuel GILPIN, to be a hatter
8:354	16 Nov 1827	Emily, a free girl of colour, 15 yrs old, to Jacob SUMMERS, formerly bound to John Bell
1:61	13 Jul 1829	John TURNBULL, 18 yrs old in May 1829, orphan of Jno. Turnbull, dec'd, to Wm. MCCLOSKY, to be a shoe and boot maker Loose Papers: indenture found
1:61	13 Jul 1829	James HIGBY, orphan, 18 yrs old in May 1829, to Wm. MCCLOSKY, to be a shoe and boot maker Loose Papers: indenture found

1:61	13 Jul 1829	Benjamin DUVALL, 16 yrs old in Oct 1828, orphan of Aaron Duvall, to Wm. MCCLOSKY, to be a shoe and boot maker Loose Papers: indenture found
1:61	13 Jul 1829	Josiah ADAMS, orphan, 19 yrs old in Dec 1828, to Wm. MCCLOSKY, to be a shoe and boot maker Loose Papers: indenture found
1:67	13 Jul 1829	Presley PARKER to Jno. MORRIS, to be a shoe and boot maker Loose Papers: 14 yrs old 14 Feb 1829, indenture found
1:177	10 Nov 1829	Wesley CROSS, free negro, son of Violett Cross alias Nickens, to Benjamin SHREVE, Jr., Shreve to shew cause why supposed indenture should not be revoked Loose Papers: age 15, step-son of Richard Nickens, indenture found
1:217	11 Jan 1830	John WHEELER, free boy of colour, 14 yrs old, to William W. KITZMILLER, to be a tanner
1:217	11 Jan 1830	Madison M. CARTY, free boy of colour, 11 yrs old, to William W. KITZMILLER, to be a tanner
1:217	11 Jan 1830	Manly SLACK, 13 yrs old 25 Aug 1830, son of Polly Slack, to David FULTON, to be a farmer
1:228	8 Feb 1830	Nathan TIMBERS, a free boy of colour, about 13 yrs old, to Wm. PEACOCK, to be a farmer
1:244	9 Feb 1830	Wm. SPENCE an apprentice of Isaac WRIGHT, indenture rescinded
1:272	10 Mar 1830	Wesley MANLY, a free boy of colour, b. 21 Sep 1821, son of Fanny Manly, to Thomas RUSSELL
1:313	13 Apr 1830	Washington HOLE, b. 5 Mar 1813, to Thomas LITTLETON, to be a cabinet maker
1:322	10 May 1830	Zachariah KNOTT, 12 yrs old 6 Jun 1830, orphan of Lewis Knott, dec'd, to Hugh MCNULTY, to be a taylor
1:322	10 May 1830	Mary TERRY, about 10 yrs old, to Smith JAMES Loose Papers: Mary Ann, 9 yrs old in Feb 1830, indenture found

1:328	10 May 1830	Wm. BUTLER, about 13 yrs old, to Jno. SCHOOLEY, to be a farmer
1:332	11 May 1830	Milly NORRIS, a free girl of color, child of Lucy Norris, bound to John FULTON, Fulton to show cause why indenture should not be cancelled
1:332	11 May 1830	Joannah, a free girl of color, bound to Thomas TAYLOR, to show cause why indenture should not be cancelled
1:334	11 May 1830	Richard MORAN, 16 yrs old 3 Apr 1830, to D.T. MATHIAS, to be a house joiner & carpenter
1:336	11 May 1830	Thomas EVANS to Benjamin MITCHELL, indenture to Thomas Russell, now deceased, transferred to Mitchell
1:399	12 Jul 1830	Alexander NEWTON, 16 yrs old 18 Jul 1830, orphan of Robert Newton, dec'd, to Alexander BRACKENRIDGE, to be a blacksmith
1:400	12 Jul 1830	David CONNOR, 18 yrs old 29 Aug 1830, orphan of David Connor, dec'd, to Alexander BRACKENRIDGE, to be a blacksmith
1:89	14 Mar 1831	Henry HAMILTON, infant child of John Hamilton, dec'd, to be bound
1:89	14 Mar 1831	Alexander HAMILTON, infant child of John Hamilton, dec'd, to be bound
1:89	14 Mar 1831	Presley HAMILTON, infant child of John Hamilton, dec'd, to be bound
1:89	14 Mar 1831	Washington HAMILTON, infant child of John Hamilton, dec'd, to be bound
1:89	14 Mar 1831	Elizabeth HAMILTON, infant child of John Hamilton, dec'd, to be bound
1:131	11 Apr 1831	Lorenz M. RUNNELLS, about 12 yrs old in Jun 1830, to Gideon HOUSHOLDER, to be a farmer
1:131	11 Apr 1831	John CRUPPER, 16 yrs old 8 Oct 1830, to David OGDEN, to be a cabinet maker
1:147	9 May 1831	Charles William JACOBS, 16 yrs old 9 Jul 1831, orphan of Thomas Jacobs, dec'd, to Thomas W. BROOKS, to be a taylor Loose Papers: indenture found

Apprentices, Poor Children and Bastards 127

1:148	9 May 1831	George HARROVER, b. 10 Oct 1816, orphan of Thomas and Sinah Harrover, to Henry STEPHENS, to be a miller and carder of wool Loose Papers: indenture found
1:149	9 May 1831	Wilson LUCAS, son of Thomas Lucas, to George HEAD, to be a sadler
1:149	9 May 1831	Jeffrey LUCAS to Richard D. EMERSON, to be a shoemaker Loose Papers: son of Thomas Lucas
1:150	9 May 1831	Cassandra HARROVER, b. 18 Oct 1819, dau of Thomas and Sinah Harrover, dec'd, to Henry STEPHENS Loose Papers: both parents of Fairfax Co., indenture found
1:224	11 Jul 1831	Henry CAMPBELL, orphan of Joseph Campbell, dec'd, to Wm. KING, to be a boot & shoemaker
1:228	11 Jul 1831	George CREAGOR, will be 21 yrs old 21 Nov 1835, to Daniel G. SMITH, to be a white smith
1:240	9 Aug 1831	James H. STEWART an apprentice of James THOMAS, Thomas to shew cause why indenture should not be cancelled. 1:264, 12 Sep 1831, indenture revoked
1:249	1 Aug 1831	William GALLIHER, orphan of John Galliher, dec'd, to Caleb C. SUTHERLAND, to be a sadler
1:276	13 Sep 1831	Charles , free boy of colour, son of Betsey Shumach, to Samuel BALL, to be a barber (for 4 yrs)
1:286	10 Oct 1831	James H. STEWART, 17 yrs old 17 Jun 1831, orphan of Wm. Stewart, to R.D. EMERSON, to be a boot & shoe maker
1:383	13 Feb 1832	Armstead QUICK, 15 yrs old 11 Feb 1832, son of Maria Quick, to George DAY, to be a tin plate worker. 2:31, 15 Mar 1832, tinner & copper worker
2:16	13 Mar 1832	Presley HAMILTON, 14 yrs old 25 Jan 1832, orphan, to Newton KEENE, to be a farmer Loose Papers: indenture found
2:62	10 Apr 1832	Alexander POLAND, 14 yrs old 18 Jul 1832, orphan, to John WADE, to be a farmer

2:84	15 May 1832	James DOWDELL, 13 yrs old 30 Sep 1831, orphan of John Dowdell, dec'd, to David M. WALLACE, to be a tailor Loose Papers: indenture found
2:135	15 Jun 1832	Mandly HAMERLY, about 16 yrs old, orphan of Jno. Hamerly, dec'd, to David M. WALLIS, to be a taylor Loose Papers: indenture found
2:148	9 Jul 1832	George FORTNEY, 15 yrs old 3 Dec 1832, orphan of John Fortney, dec'd, to Francis L. BOGUE, to be a taylor Loose Papers: indenture found
2:148	9 Jul 1832	Robert HINTON, 16 yrs old 1 Mar 1832, orphan of Robert Hinton, dec'd, to Francis L. BOGUE, to be a taylor Loose Papers: indenture found
2:173	14 Aug 1832	Charles Fenton HAINS, 14 yrs old 23 Dec 1832, son of Joseph & Mary Hains, to Thomas BIRKBY, to be a carriage maker
2:214	10 Sep 1832	John FOUCH to Benjamin MAULSBY, to be a sadler & harness maker
2:233	8 Oct 1832	Armistead T. POMROY, 13 yrs old 20 Jan 1832, orphan, to John BRADY, to be a cabinet maker Loose Papers: Armistead T.M. Pomroy, son of Nancy Pomroy, widow, orphan of F. Pomroy, indenture found
2:250	12 Nov 1832	Solon RECTOR, b. 4 Feb 1819, orphan of Hy. & Eliz. Rector, dec'd, Herod Osborn, his guardian, to Joseph B. FOX, to be a farmer
2:250	12 Nov 1832	Julia KNOTT, 14 yrs old, to Wm. ELGIN
2:259	13 Nov 1832	James TRAHORN, orphan, 17 yrs old 16 Dec 1832, to be a blacksmith Loose Papers: to Abel Jones, indenture found
2:259	13 Nov 1832	Christopher RIVERS, orphan, 14 yrs old 8 Jul 1832, to Wm. F. CLARKE, to be a tailor
2:271	15 Nov 1832	Armstead Thompson Mason HAINS, 4 yrs old 1 Jan 1833, to Geo. HEAD, to be a sadler
2:290	10 Dec 1832	James MANSFIELD, about 13 yrs old, to Thomas MATTHEWS, to be a wool manufacturer

Apprentices, Poor Children and Bastards 129

2:302	12 Dec 1832	Harrison GREEN, 17 yrs old 11 Jun 1832, son of Mary Green, to Robert GOVER, to be a boot & shoemaker
2:321	14 Jan 1833	James M. CAMPBELL, 15 yrs old 1 Nov 1833, to James KITTLE, to be a cabinet maker
2:343	12 Feb 1833	Robert JACKSON, son of Alexander Jackson (a free man of colour), vs Beverly HUTCHISON, Hutchison to shew cause why indenture should not be cancelled. 3:17, 12 Mar 1833, indenture cancelled Loose Papers: age 14, indenture found
2:345	12 Feb 1833	Carline JACKSON, Nelly Jackson, mother, an apprentice of Jotham WRIGHT, petition to be released from indenture denied Loose Papers: indenture found
3:32	14 Mar 1833	James NEILSON, orphan, about 17 yrs old, to Charles A. JOHNSON, to be a hatter
3:40	15 Mar 1833	Elias Mason GREEN, orphan of John Green, to Eli SCHOOLEY, to be a farmer
3:94	11 Jun 1833	Joanna GANT, Lucy Gant, her mother, a free woman of colour, a servant of Thomas TAYLOR, Taylor to shew cause why indenture should not be cancelled. 3:118, 8 Jul 1833, same order, 3:142, 14 Aug 1833, same order, 3:196, 15 Oct 1833, court refused to set aside indenture
3:99	12 Jun 1833	Alexander DUVAL, 14 yrs old 11 Jun 1833, son of Harriet Duval, to John SURGHNOR, to be a boot & shoemaker
3:107	13 Jun 1833	James TIMMS, orphan, 15 yrs old 19 Aug 1833, to Alexander P. BRACKENRIDGE, to be a blacksmith, to serve until 19 Aug 1838
3:111	14 Jun 1833	John GUIDER, 12 yrs old, a free boy of colour, son of Charles & Kate Guider, to John A. BINNS, 5:349, 14 Aug 1837, order rescinded, J.A. Binns dead, indenture found
3:111	14 Jun 1833	Sarah GUIDER, about 9 yrs old, a free girl of colour, dau of Charles and Kate Guider, to Jas. L. MARTIN Loose Papers: indenture found
3:113	14 Jun 1833	John HAMERLY, 14 yrs old 4 Feb 1833, to Thomas LITTLETON, to be a cabinet maker Loose Papers: indenture found

3:121	8 Jul 1833	Albert G.C. CLARKE, 12 yrs old in Feb 1833, son of John F. Clarke, to Lemuel WATSON, to be a waggonmaker
3:241	9 Dec 1833	John SHIPLEY, 15 yrs old 26 Jul 1833, son of Ann L. Shipley, who consented, to Thos. W. BROOKS, to be a tailor
3:264	14 Jan 1834	Georgianna JACKSON, orphan, about 10 yrs old, to Edwin A. STOVER, to be a house servant
3:288	11 Feb 1834	George FORTNEY, orphan, 16 yrs old 3 Dec 1833, to Jno. SURGHNOR, to be a boot & shoemaker Loose Papers: indenture found
3:288	11 Feb 1834	Thomas SPATES, orphan, 16 yrs old 12 Mar 1834, to John SURGHNOR, to be a boot & shoemaker Loose Papers: indenture found
3:307	11 Mar 1834	Thomas COX, son of Samuel Cox, to John A. MCCORMCK, to be a blacksmith (for 4 yrs from 1 Jan 1834) Loose Papers: colored boy age 17, indenture found
3:307	11 Mar 1834	Peter LEE, about 14 yrs old, free boy of colour, to Stephen J. DONOHOE, to be a farmer
3:336	14 Apr 1834	Chs. JACKSON, orphan of Jno. W. & Polly Jackson, dec'd, to Isaac HOUGH, to be a millwright
3:345	12 May 1834	George REED, son of Charlotte Reed, to Rodney C. BRADEN, to be a fuller, carder & weaver
3:347	12 May 1834	Harriett SCOTT to Jacob ECKMAN
4:28	13 Aug 1834	William ROBEY, 17 yrs old 21 Aug 1834, to Edward HAMMAT, to be a farmer
4:42	8 Sep 1834	Martha Ann TRAYHORN, 12 yrs old in Jan 1835, dau of James Trayhorn, dec'd, to James MCILHANEY Loose Papers: indenture found
4:44	8 Sep 1834	William W. DIVINE, son of Aaron Divine, apprentice of Thos. W. BROOKS, Brooks to shew cause why his indenture should not be cancelled
4:97	9 Dec 1834	James BUTLER, about 10 yrs old, orphan of Geo. Butler, to Luke GOINGS, to be a farmer

4:147	12 Mar 1835	William WARD, will be 21 yrs old 30[sic] Feb 1839, son of James Ward, to Edward R. EDWARDS, to be a baker
4:161	13 Apr 1835	Addison CAMPBELL, orphan of Joseph Campbell, dec'd, to B.W. SOWER, to be a printer. 4:344, 14 Dec 1835, order rescinded
4:166	14 Apr 1835	Samuel WOODDY, apprentice of, vs Simon SMALE, for ill treatment
4:196	12 May 1835	James Hanson JOHNSON, 14 yrs old 24 Aug 1834, to Jno. BRADY, to be a cabinet maker
4:247	13 Jul 1835	John BROOKS to Isaac MOORE, to be a weaver
4:262	11 Aug 1835	James H. MUSE, 15 yrs old 23 Feb 1835, orphan of Walker Muse dec'd, to John F. BARRETT, to be a tailor
4:330	11 Nov 1835	John REDMON, 9 yrs old this fall, son of George Redmon, to Reuben JENKINS, to be a farmer Loose Papers: free boy of colour, indenture found
4:332	11 Nov 1835	William ROSE, orphan of John Rose, dec'd, to Daniel G. SMITH, to be a white smith
4:344	14 Dec 1835	Addison CAMPBELL, 16 yrs old 30 Oct 1835, orphan of Joseph Campbell, to George RICHARD, to be a printer, Margaret McKim his mother consented. 5:51, 11 Apr 1836, order rescinded
4:359	11 Jan 1836	Thomas RIVERS, 9 yrs old 4 Jul 1835, son of Charles Rivers, to Albert G. CHAMBLIN, to be a tanner Loose Papers: indenture found
5:14	9 Feb 1836	Mary Ann POOL, about 11 yrs old, dau of Susanna Denty, to Dr. Geo. LEE Loose Papers: 11 yrs old in Aug 1835, dau of Susanna Denty, formerly Pool, indenture found
5:30	15 Mar 1836	John SIMPSON, about 18 yrs old, orphan of William Simpson, dec'd, to John SURGHNOR, to be a boot & shoemaker
5:74	13 Jun 1836	Joseph L. DAVIS, in 15th yr, orphan of Samuel Davis, to William TATE, to be a farmer

5:96	15 Jun 1836	John Henry SCHOOLEY, 14 yrs old 19 Sep 1836, orphan of Aaron Schooley, dec'd, to Geo. RICHARD, to be a printer Loose Papers: indenture to Geo. Richards found
5:170	10 Oct 1836	Henry GALE, alias Harris, 12 yrs old 1 Jan 1836, to Jacob FADELY, to be a farmer. 5:219, 9 Jan 1837, Eliza Harris, mother requested order be revoked. 5:231, 13 Feb 1837, order revoked
5:218	9 Jan 1837	William BOSWELL, orphan, 12 yrs old 17 Jul 1836, to Wm. TORRISON, to be a blacksmith
5:221	9 Jan 1837	George BOSWELL, orphan of Walter Boswell, dec'd, to Thomas BIRKBY, to be a wheelwright and carriage maker
5:221	9 Jan 1837	Robert BOSWELL, orphan of Walter Boswell, dec'd, to Thomas BIRKBY, to be a wheelwright and carriage maker
5:231	13 Feb 1837	Henry HOLMES, 20 yrs old 22 Feb 1837, orphan of Jacob Holmes, dec'd, to George KABRICK, to be a carpenter
5:231	13 Feb 1837	Joseph D. HOLMES, 16 yrs old 25 Dec 1836, orphan of Jacob Holmes, dec'd, to George KABRICK, to be a carpenter
5:238	13 Feb 1837	Solon RECTOR, orphan of Henry Rector, to George KABRIDGE, to be a house carpenter (until 20 yrs old)
5:248	13 Mar 1837	Alcinda SILCOTT, 8 yrs old 14 Apr 1836, orphan of John Silcott, dec'd, to Abraham SILCOTT
5:295	8 May 1837	James William SAUNDERS, orphan of William Saunders, dec'd, to James SAUNDERS, to be a farmer
5:295	8 May 1837	John WILSON, orphan of Wm. Wilson, dec'd, to David LOVETT, to be a farmer
5:296	8 May 1837	William BOZZELL, about 18 yrs old, son of Walter Bozzell, dec'd, to John WILLIAMS, to be a blacksmith
5:297	8 May 1837	Benjamin MANLY, 8 yrs old, to Peyton H. DAVIS, to be a farmer Loose Papers: coloured bastard child, indenture found
5:326	14 Jun 1837	William WAR, orphan of Benjamin War, dec'd, to James GARRISON, to be a hatter

Apprentices, Poor Children and Bastards 133

5:339	10 Jul 1837	James H. TRAHERN, orphan of James Trahern, dec'd, to James W. BRAWNER, to be a sadler Loose Papers: b. 18 Dec 1827, son of Pricila Trahern, James Henry Trahern, indenture found
5:343	11 Jul 1837	Daniel Thomas WRIGHT, son of Isaac Wright, to Geo. RICHARD, to be a printer Loose Papers: 16 yrs old 5 Jul 1837, alias Thomas Daniel Wright, to Geo. Richards, indenture found
5:349	14 Aug 1837	John GUIDER, about 15 yrs old, orphan of Charles and Kate Guider, dec'd, to John ROSE, to be a farmer Loose Papers: free boy of colour, indenture found
6:41	8 Jan 1838	Thomas LYNCH to Wm. MAVIN, & Robert, to be a house carpenter, until 1 Jan 1841
6:87	14 Mar 1838	William P. SOWER, 14 yrs old 18 Aug 1838, son of Brook W. Sower, to B. MAULSBY, to be a sadler Loose Papers: to Benjamin Maulsby
6:207	14 Jan 1839	Samuel BARNES, mulatto bastard, to Leven RICHARD, indenture binding him to Thomas Francis transferred to Leven Richard
6:363	15 Oct 1839	Charles FENTON, about 9 yrs old, a free boy of colour, to William STEER, to be a farmer Loose Papers: indenture found
6:388	9 Dec 1839	John ELLIOTT, 3 yrs old 30 Sep 1839, a free boy of colour, to Hanson ELLIOTT, to be a farmer
7:30	10 Mar 1840	Elias M. GREEN, orphan of John Green, dec'd, to David CONNER, to be a blacksmith
7:151	9 Nov 1840	Wm. M. CORDELL, 17 yrs old 14 Dec 1840, orphan of Martin Cordell, dec'd, to James MCDONOUGH, to be a wheelwright Loose Papers: Wm. Martin Cordell, son of Martha Cordell
7:178	14 Dec 1840	Lewis GOINGS, son of Mary Goings, to Wm. H. FRENCH, to be a farmer
7:186	11 Jan 1841	Mary SMITH, 13 yrs old in Apr 1841, to John W. LICKEY
7:187	11 Jan 1841	Howard P. SMITH, 10 yrs old 10 May 1841, to Addison OSBURN

7:191	12 Jan 1841	Amanda POLON, 4 yrs old 23 Apr 1840, to Isaac HOGUE Loose Papers: indenture found
7:191	12 Jan 1841	James Henry NISEWANGER, son of Susan Niswanger, to Alfred LOGAN, to be a shoe and boot maker Loose Papers: 18 yrs old 15 Apr 1841, indenture found
7:194	8 Feb 1841	Jack NOGGLE, 8 yrs old 22 May 1841, free boy of colour, to Thomas FRED Loose Papers: to be a farmer, indenture found
7:220	11 Mar 1841	Albert LEWIS, 12 yrs old 27 Aug 1841, son of Elizabeth Lewis, to Matson JAMES, to be a farmer Loose Papers: indenture found
7:248	11 May 1841	Wm. ORR, son of __ Orr, dec'd, and Tamar Orr, to Geo. W. NOLAND, to be a tailor Loose Papers: 15 yrs old 12 Oct 1841, indenture found
7:267	16 Jun 1841	Charles William LUCAS, 14 yrs old 16 Dec 1840, a free boy of colour, son of Charles & Delia Lucas, to Alfred LOGAN, to be a shoe & boot maker. 7:352, 11 Nov 1841, terms of indenture different Loose Papers: indenture found
7:267	16 Jun 1841	Virginia HOLLIDAY, 4 yrs old 3 Jan 1840, to John PANCOAST, to learn housework
7:283	12 Jul 1841	Catharine, about 3 yrs old, a free negro, to Charles TAYLOR, to be a housekeeper Loose Papers: age as of 12 Jun 1841, indenture found
7:318	14 Sep 1841	Priscilla, 6 yrs old in Jan 1842, a negro, to Humphrey SHEPHERD, to be a housekeeper
7:325	11 Oct 1841	Fanny JACKSON, 7 yrs old in May 1841, dau of Mary Jackson, to Wm. TAYLOR Loose Papers: indenture found
7:337	8 Nov 1841	Geo. BROOKS, 11 yrs old, to Henry T. BAYNE, to be a tailor
7:374	15 Dec 1841	Joseph WADE, 17 yrs old 23 Jan 1842, to Geo. W. NOLAND, to be a tailor
8:43	15 Mar 1842	Amanda HOWARD, mulatto, 12 yrs old, to Mary A. HOUGH, to be a housekeeper

Apprentices, Poor Children and Bastards 135

8:55	9 Mar 1842	John BROOKS, 19 yrs old 13 Apr 1842, to Abraham EVERHEART, to be a carder & fuller
8:82	12 Apr 1842	Amanda NOGGINS, 6 yrs old 25 May 1842, free girl of colour, to Joab OSBURN, to be a housekeeper, indenture found
8:132	11 Jul 1842	Joseph TIMBERS, 5 yrs old, coloured boy, to Samuel PAXSON Loose Papers: free coloured boy, 6 yrs old 15 Aug 1842, to be a farmer, indenture found
8:165	14 Sep 1842	William TIMBERS, free boy of colour, 11 yrs old 16 Aug 1842, to Edwin PURCEL, to be a farmer, indenture found
8:165	14 Sep 1842	John Cornelius MOCK, 9 yrs old 1 Aug 1842, son of Kitty Mock, to Uriah BEANS, to be a farmer Loose Papers: indenture found
8:348	15 Mar 1843	Thadeus THOMAS, free boy of colour, 15 yrs old, to William THOMAS, to be a farmer
8:380	8 May 1843	Thadeus THOMAS, free boy of colour, 15 yrs old, to Samuel L. GOVERNEUR, to be a farmer
8:454	16 Aug 1843	Thomas William GRIFFITH, b. 29 Mar 1832, son of Margaret Griffith, to Bernard TAYLOR, to be a farmer, indenture found
8:468	12 Sep 1843	James BALL, 7 yrs old 24 Feb 1843, son of Eliza Ball, to Ben SMITH, (coloured man), to be a blacksmith
8:468	12 Sep 1843	(nameless) BALL, b. 23 Aug 1843, son of Eliza Ball, to Ben SMITH, (coloured man), to be a blacksmith
9:8	14 Nov 1843	Ann Amelia, negro, 6 yrs old in Jan 1842, to Humphrey SHEPHERD, to be a housekeeper
9:18	18 Nov 1843	Amandy TRIBBEE, 13 yrs old, dau of Emily Tribbee, to be a housekeeper
9:137	11 Jun 1844	Andrew MORGAN, 4 yrs old 19 Feb 1844, to Jesse GRAYSON Loose Papers: to be a farmer, Grayson a colored man, indenture found
9:137	11 Jun 1844	Charles MORGAN, 7 yrs old 1 Mar 1844, to Jesse GRAYSON Loose Papers: to be a farmer, Grayson a colored man, indenture found

Records Found in Court Order Books

9:180	12 Aug 1844	Charles SKINNER, negro, 10 yrs old in Oct 1844, to Franklin OSBURN, former indenture to Joab Osburn assigned to Franklin Osburn
9:180	12 Aug 1844	Amanda NOGGINS, negro, 8 yrs old 25 May 1844, to Martha OSBURN, former indenture to Joab Osburn assigned to Martha Osburn
9:181	12 Aug 1844	Joseph WISE, orphan, 15 yrs old, to be bound
9:358	13 May 1845	America POLAND, coloured, 5 yrs old 25 Mar 1846, to Thomas BEAVERS, to be a housekeeper Loose Papers: child of white mother, indenture found
9:358	13 May 1845	Adolphus Descletian FITCH, white bastard, 9 yrs old in Feb 1845, to Garrett WALKER, to be a farmer Loose Papers: indenture found
9:358	13 May 1845	Isabella HOLADAY, coloured, 4 yrs old 25 Mar 1845, to Craven PEARSON, to be a farmer Loose Papers: child of white mother
9:358	13 May 1845	Letitia HALL, 4 yrs old, child of Eliza Hall, to Henry H. NICHOLLS, to be a housekeeper
9:457	14 Oct 1845	John WIGGINTON, orphan, to Edward HANES, to be a stone mason Loose Papers: 12 yrs old, son of Wm. Wigginton, dec'd, indenture found
10:10	13 Jan 1846	Richard GUIDER, free boy of colour, about 14 yrs old, to Chs. F. FADELY Loose Papers: to be a hack & stage driver, indenture found
10:14	13 Jan 1846	Ryland W. TRACY, 5 yrs old, to Thomas FORREST, to be a farmer Loose Papers: indenture found
10:19	9 Feb 1846	Lavina SUTHERLAND, about 13 yrs old, to Alexander POLAND, to be a housekeeper & seamstress
10:32	9 Mar 1846	Joseph TRIBBY, child of Emily Tribby, to John STONE, to be a farmer
10:32	9 Mar 1846	Jesse TRIBBY, child of Emily Tribby, to Even EVENS, to be a farmer
10:32	9 Mar 1846	Mary TRIBBY, child of Emily Tribby, to Jacob CRIM, to be a housekeeper

Apprentices, Poor Children and Bastards 137

10:103	10 Jun 1846	Wilson GANT, 7 yrs old 1 Apr 1846, son of Amelia Gant, to Wm. H. HOUGH, to be a farmer
D.B. 4X:39	2 Nov 1846	Sarah Frances ROBERTSON, a free negro, to William GIBSON, & Sarah N., his wife, to be an apprentice and servant for 10 yrs
10:247	9 Feb 1847	John SOWER, 14 yrs old, son of Brook W. Sower, to Thomas C. CONNOLLY, to be a printer
10:247	9 Feb 1847	Thomas T. SEEDERS, 15 yrs old, son of William Seeders, dec'd, to Thomas C. CONNOLLY, to be a printer
10:352	12 Jul 1847	Tilghman MOCK to George JOHNSON, to be a farmer Loose Papers: 9 yrs old 15 Apr 1847, indenture found
11:88	8 May 1848	Joseph Henry ALLENSWORTH, free boy of colour, 7 yrs old 7 Feb 1848, son of Kitty Allensworth, to Manuel TRENARY, to be a millwright. 11:121, 10 Jul 1848, terms of indenture modified
11:88	8 May 1848	Peter S. CLEMENTS, 16 yrs 6 mo. old, to John W. DAILEY, to be a shoemaker Loose Papers: age on 1 May 1848, son of Sarah Bollen
11:98	12 Jun 1848	Wilson GANT, 9 yrs old 1 Apr 1848, son of Amelia Gant, to Wm. H. HOUGH, to be a farmer, indenture found
11:120	10 Jul 1848	Wm. GILBERT, free boy of colour, 12 yrs old in Apr 1848, to Thomas COCKLIN, to be a farmer Loose Papers: indenture found
11:120	10 Jul 1848	Basil MYERS, free negro, 6 yrs old 8 Oct 1848, to Thomas COCKLIN, to be a farmer Loose Papers: indenture found
11:183	8 Jan 1849	Jos. N. THORNTON, son of Mary Thornton, to George W. DORRELL, to be a farmer Loose Papers: alias Adison, coloured boy about 10 yrs old, indenture found
11:219	17 May 1849	Charles W. SPATES, son of Any A. Frits, to Mandly HAMMERLY, to be a tailor, for 8 yrs
11:225	11 Jun 1849	John W. SHORES, son of Priscilla Shores, to Joseph EVERHEART, to be a farmer
11:232	12 Jun 1849	Thomas HOLLADAY to John VANSICKLER, to be a farmer

11:253	9 Jul 1849	John Henry STINCHECOMBE to Daniel I. (or J.) FOUCHE, to be a carpenter Loose Papers: about 17 yrs old, indenture found
11:270	15 Aug 1849	David C. ADAMS, orphan, 15 yrs old 17 Jun 1849, to John W.B. BEACH, to be a shoemaker
11:284	12 Sep 1849	John JOHNSON, negro, son of Sally Johnson, dec'd, to Thomas PURSEL, to be a house servant
11:289	8 Oct 1849	Jefferson GILBERT, son of Margaret Gilbert, to Alfred WRIGHT, to be a farmer
11:289	8 Oct 1849	Robert GANT to Wilson NORRIS, to be a farmer
11:326	14 Jan 1850	George CLARKE, negro, son of Susan Clarke, to John THOMAS, Sr., to be a farmer
11:356	12 Feb 1850	George STEWART, 8 yrs old, to Benjamin BIRDSALL, to be a farmer
12:10	11 Jun 1850	James Edward KIDWELL, about 10 yrs old, illegitimate son of Fanny Kidwell, to Robert THOMAS, to be a blacksmith Loose Papers: indenture found
12:31	8 Jul 1850	Dardana HOLLIDAY, mulatto child of Mahala Holladay, to Mary MCPHERSON, to be a housekeeper
12:35	12 Aug 1850	Henry, 13 yrs old, a boy of colour, to Josiah J. SETTLE, 12:40, 13 Aug 1850, Charles Gant, father of Henry. 12:50, 9 Sep 1850, order revoked
12:63	15 Oct 1850	Letitia HALL, about 8 yrs old, a free girl of colour, to Maria NICHOLS, to be a housekeeper, indenture found
12:81	16 Nov 1850	Madison GOWEN, 6 yrs old in Dec 1850, son of Martha Ann Gowen, to Samuel PAXTON, to be a farmer

Apprentices, Poor Children and Bastards   139

INDENTURES on File (No Orders Found)
Most indicate by Authority of Act of Assembly

5 Oct 1815	Sanford McNealy ANDRES, bastard, to Wm. LAFAVER, for 12 yrs from 28 Jul 1816, to be a blacksmith & farmer
14 Nov 1817	Agnes, girl of colour, to Martha THOMAS, for 7 yrs from Mar 1818, to be a housewife
20 Feb 1836	Henry ALEXANDER, mulatto, 6 yrs old 25 Dec 1836, to Thomas M. HUMPHREY, to be a house carpenter
23 Mar 1819	Amos, boy of colour, to Turner OSBURN, for 13 yrs from 15 Jun 1819, to be a farmer
8 Feb 1806	Tince ASHBEY, orphan, 16 yrs old, to Thomas DRAKE, Jr.,
20 Apr 1810	Amar BALES, bastard, 2 yrs 8 mo 15 da. old, to James PATTERSON, Sr., to be a farmer
24 May 1833	Samuel BARNS, bastard mulatto, 12 yrs old 25 Dec 1832, to Thomas FRANCIS, to be a farmer
29 Mar 1811	Felix BASSEL, free mulatto, to William NICHOLS, until 2 Sep 1822 when he will be 21, to be a farmer
9 Mar 1803	Thomas H. BEALL, 15 yrs old 15 May 1803, to Joseph BEARD, to be a cabinet maker & joiner
11 Dec 1809	Eliza BEATY, illegitimate orphan, 8 yrs old 6 Jan 1809, to James HATCHER, to be a housekeeper
3 Feb 1825	Lawson BEATTY, boy of colour, 11 yrs old, to William WILSON, to be a farmer
22 Nov 1820	Bill, (or William), coloured boy, to David REESE, for 7 yrs from 16 Apr 1821, to be a farmer
13 Feb 1833	Bill, orphan of colour between 9 & 10 yrs old, to Robert BAYLY, to be a farmer
11 Jan 1806	Mahlon BISHOP, 3 yrs old 10 Sep 1805, to Thomas HATCHER, & Thomas Hatcher, Jr.,
19 Nov 1810	Mariah BOARDLY, black girl, to Stephen BEARD
20 Jun 1835	Lydia Jane BOGESS, bastard, 2 yrs old 8 Dec 1834, to George PETTIT, to be a housekeeper
11 Jan 1825	Catharin BOLIN to George WARNER, for 8 yrs from 29 Jul 1824, to be a housekeeper
4 Feb 1822	Eliza BOLTON to Joseph GORE, Jr., for 6 yrs from 20 Oct 1822, to be a housekeeper
12 Feb 1829	Aquilla BOUGHMAN, 12 yrs 12 da. old, to Edward HAINES, to be a bricklayer & stonemason

140 INDENTURES on File (No Orders Found)

19 Jan 1818	James Voloney BOYD, 14 yrs old 9 Jan 1818, to Walter LANGLEY, to be a blacksmith
2 Feb 1805	Henson BRADY, 6 yrs old 30 Nov 1805, negro orphan, to Mahlon HOUGH, to be a farmer
2 Apr 1806	William BRADY, 14 yrs old 2 Jun 1800, to Jesse MCVEIGH, to be a taylor
25 Jun 1805	Willis BRADY, orphan, 8 yrs old 23 Oct 1805, to Ezra FOX, to be a farmer
25 Nov 1820	Eliza BROOKBANK to Issachar BROWN, for 5 yrs from 16 Mar 1821, to be a housekeeper
8 Mar 1817	George BROOKBANK, bastard, to Elizabeth RODGERS, for 10 yrs from 1 Jun 1817, to be a farmer
5 Mar 1817	Josiah BROOKBANK, bastard, to William MARSHALL, for 14 yrs from 29 Dec 1817, to be a farmer
31 Dec 1804	Tapley BRUMBACK, 12 yrs old 19 Mar 1804, to Joseph CLOWES
11 Sep 1809	Arnold BURGOIN, 6 yrs old 10 Aug 1809, to Samuel LINDSEY, to be a farmer
22 Jun 1808	Ann Matilda BUTLER, black orphan, 8 yrs old 13 Feb 1809, to Sarah WOODDY, to be a housekeeper
26 Aug 1808	Ann Matilda BUTLER, black orphan, 8 yrs old 13 Feb 1809, to Richard H. HENDERSON, to be a housekeeper
14 Dec 1820	Ruth BUTLER, illegitimate, to John CRIM, for 11 yrs from 1 Apr 1821, to be a housewife
29 Mar 1808	John CAMPBELL, orphan, to Enos BEST, for 11 yrs 2 mo from 3 Apr 1808, to be a farmer
13 Feb 1833	Caroline , free girl of colour about 10 yrs old, to Robert BAYLY, to be a house servant
20 Jun 1825	Fenton Lewis CARTWRIGHT, mulatto, to John B. YOUNG, to be a house servant
20 Apr 1805	James CASTOR, orphan, 15 yrs old 26 Dec 1804, to Benjamin SHREVE, to be a farmer
18 Jun 1838	Catharine , alias Catharine Cross or Catharine Goens, free mulatto, 8 yrs old 7 Aug 1838, to George RICHARD, to be a family servant
16 Dec 1805	Catherine CHILTON, orphan, 12 yrs old 8 Feb 1806, to William BROWN, to be a housekeeper
22 Apr 1818	Armistead CLASBY to Mahlon RUSSELL, for 16 yrs from 11 Sep 1818, to be a farmer
16 Nov 1767	George CLINTON to Henry VANOVER, to serve 11 yrs 2 wks, to be a shoemaker
11 Apr 1804	Mahlon COCKERILL, 16 yrs old in Jan 1804, to William SMALLEY, to be a farmer

Apprentices, Poor Children and Bastards 141

1 Jan 1820	John COLEMAN, colored boy, 11 yrs old 11 Jul 1819, to William BROWN, to be a farmer
13 Jul 1809	Richard CONNER, orphan, 13 yrs old 3 Mar 1809, to Isaac HARRIS, to be a tanner
31 Mar 1821	William CONNER, son of David Conner, to Martin KITZMILLER, for 10 yrs from 5 Nov 1820, to be a tanner & currier
29 Jun 1805	John COOPER, orphan, 6 yrs old 9 Apr 1805, to George RAZOR, Jr., to be a farmer
9 Mar 1812	Jonathan COST, 18 yrs old 22 Oct 1811, to Edward DORSEY, to be a carpenter & joiner
13 Sep 1817	Mariah COWGILL, baseborn, 6 yrs old 4 May 1817, to Isaac COWGILL, to be a housekeeper
12 Jun 1759	George CRAWFORD to Joseph YEATS(YATES), for 2 yrs 4 mo.
13 Jan 1823	Eli CROSS, coloured, to William BROWN, for 13 yrs from 1 Sep 1822, to be a farmer
7 May 1816	Mary CROSS, coloured bastard, to Garret WALKER, for 11 yrs from 15 Jan 1816, to be a spinster [I think they meant spinner]
11 Dec 1804	Sarah CROSS, 15 yrs old 7 Aug 1804, to Benjamin DANIEL, to be a housekeeper
28 Mar 1821	William CROSS, alias Clifford, coloured, to James D. FRENCH, for 12 yrs from 20 Mar 1821, to be a farmer
22 Sep 1813	Charles CUMMINS, baseborn, 15 yrs old 5 Jun 1813, to Stephen MCPHERSON, to be a blacksmith
2 Jan 1808	Sanford DAVIS, orphan, to Benjamin PHILLIPS, to serve until 15 Aug 1813 when he will be 21, to be a blacksmith
3 Nov 1820	Harriet DAVIS, illegitimate dau of Nancy Davis, 6 yrs old 6 Mar 1820, to Catherine HATCHER, to be a housekeeper
12 Jul 1814	Henry DAWS, bastard, to James W. HANCHER, for 16 yrs from 24 Oct 1814, to be a carpenter
25 Jun 1836	Samuel DIXSON, alias Samuel Risby, mulatto son of Sally Risby, 15 yrs old 25 Jun 1836, to David REECE, to be a farmer
28 Jan 1805	Andrew DORNON, orphan, 15 yrs 8 mo & 26 da. old, to William CARTER, to be a farmer
22 Jun 1812	Hamton DUNHAM, poor boy, 9 yrs 1 mo. 11 da. old, to Joseph BURSON, to be a farmer
13 Apr 1830	Amon DUVALL, 15 yrs old 10 Feb 1829, to Robert H. GOVER, to be a boot & shoe maker

INDENTURES on File (No Orders Found)

13 Jun 1808	Elisha , mulatto orphan, 6 yrs old 12 Jun 1808, son of Judy and with her consent, to Henry TAYLOR, to be a farmer
2 Sep 1808	Eliza , black orphan, 2 yrs old 15 Jul 1808, to Thomas MINA, to be a housekeeper
9 Apr 1810	John ELLIOT, coloured orphan, 11 yrs old 15 Sep 1810, to George YOUNG, to be a farmer
16 Dec 1824	Emily , coloured, to Amasa HOUGH, for 10 yrs from 1 Jun 1825, to be a housekeeper
20 Mar 1838	Elijah ERTON, bastard, about 12 yrs old in Jan 1838, to James SANDIFORD, to be a carpenter & house joiner
23 Jul 1805	Malinda FARGUSON, orphan, 2 yrs 11 mo. old, to Thomas TORBERT, to be a spinner, knitter, etc.
9 Mar 1812	George FARMER, negro, 11 yrs old 1 Jan 1812, to Israel JANNEY, to be a farmer
12 Nov 1811	Sanford FERRIL, poor boy, 13 yrs 7 mo. 12 da. old, to John PEARCE, to be a blacksmith
22 Jun 1812	Malinda FORGISON, poor girl, 9 yrs 10 mo 15 da. old, to Elizabeth TORBERT, to be a spinner on the big & little wheels
5 Jun 1819	Bennet FRANCE, bastard, son of Elizabeth France, to John WINN, for 12 yrs, to be a farmer
2 Sep 1812	Sinthy FRANCE, poor girl, 5 yrs 5 mo. 25 da. old, to Joshua GREGG, & Lydia, to be a spinner on the big & little wheel
19 Feb 1813	Fanny FRANCE to Amos HARVEY, & Elizabeth, to serve until 30 Mar 1820 when she will be 18, to be a housekeeper
16 Oct 1812	Mary FRANCIS to Issacher BROWN, to serve until __ Mar 1818 when she will be 18, to be a housekeeper
7 Aug 1819	Pressly FRANCIS to Benjamin BRADFIELD, to serve for 11 yrs from 10 Sep 1819, to be a farmer
7 Aug 1821	Richard FRANCIS to Samuel CROOK, for 13 yrs from 7 Oct 1821, to be a farmer
6 Apr 1811	William FRAIZOR, poor boy, 15 yrs 8 mo 22 da. old, to Amos PIERCE, to be a blacksmith
12 May 1810	Martha FROST, coloured orphan, 8 yrs old 10 Nov 1810, to Moses DOWDELL, to be a housekeeper
25 Aug 1808	Rachel FULTON, orphan, 3 yrs old 4 Apr 1808, to Susanna FULTON, to be a housekeeper
12 Dec 1836	Charles GANT, bastard mulatto of free parents, 7 yrs old 7 Mar 1836, to John BEAVERS, to be a farmer

Apprentices, Poor Children and Bastards 143

20 Jun 1825	Betsey GASKINS, coloured, 10 yrs old, dau of Nelly Gaskins, to John LEWIS, to be a spinster [spinner?]
13 Feb 1835	James GASKINS, black boy, 18 yrs old 18 Feb 1834, to John BEAVERS, to be a farmer
17 Mar 1829	Margaret Douglas GOFF, orphan of Adam Goff, 10 yrs old 11 Mar 1828, to Samuel KENNERLY, to be a housekeeper
11 Dec 1837	Elihu GOING, free mulatto bastard, 5 yrs old 14 Aug 1833, to John MARTIN
8 Jun 1813	Patrick GOINGS, mulatto bastard, 7 yrs old 17 Mar 1813, to Robert CAMPBELL, to be a farmer
26 Nov 1817	Dennis GRAYSON, 13 yrs old 24 Dec 1814, son of Amy Grayson, free woman of colour, to John KILE
26 Nov 1817	Willis GRAYSON, 17 yrs old 8 Jun 1817, son of Amy Grayson, free woman of colour, to John KILE
27 Jun 1817	John GREGORY, illegitimate, 10 yrs old 3 Nov 1817, son of Hannah Kidwell, to John ROSS, to be a farmer
3 Oct 1825	Eli GUIDER, free negro bastard, 18 yrs old, to John SURGHNOR, to be a shoemaker
14 Feb 1814	Harriot , bastard mulatto, to Amos BEALES, for 14 yrs from 7 Feb 1814, to be a seamstress
13 Jun 1803	Harry , free black, to Richard CONNER, until 17 Aug 1810, to be a shoemaker
20 Feb 1836	Harvey HOLIDAY, mulatto, 5 yrs old 20 Nov 1835, to Thomas G. HUMPHREY, to be a farmer
27 Dec 1819	Armstead HOWELL to William S. SAUNDERS, for 12 yrs from 1 Jul 1819, to be a taylor
12 Jan 1811	John HURDLE, poor boy, 3 yrs 8 mo. old, to Thomas FRANCIS, to be a farmer
1 Jun 1838	George C. JACKSON, son of S.A. Jackson, to C.C. MCINTYRE, until 1 Jun 1842, to be a printer
13 Jun 1835	Joseph JACKSON, coloured bastard, 7 yrs old, to Thomas CAMRON, to be a farmer
23 Feb 1833	James , coloured bastard, 10 yrs old, to Arthur ORRISON, to be a farmer
16 Jun 1829	George JOHNSON, coloured bastard, 5 yrs old in Oct 1829, to John SWART, to be a farmer
16 Oct 1807	George KEAN, mulatto, to Stacy TAYLOR, to be a farmer
2 Jan 1808	Thomas KIDWELL, alias Philips, bastard, to Benjamin PHILIPS, until Dec 1818 when he will be 21, to be a blacksmith

INDENTURES on File (No Orders Found)

21 Jun 1820	Albert KILE, 3 yrs old 15 Jun 1820, son of Elizabeth Kile, single woman, to Benjamin MITCHELL, Jr.,
18 Oct 1778	Kitty, negro about 6 yrs old, to Edward STABLER, & Mary,
7 Mar 1822	Jesse LANE, coloured, to John CLINEDIENST, for 5 yrs from 15 Jun 1822, to be a tanner & currier
8 Nov 1831	Simon LEE, coloured bastard, 2 yrs old, to John W. DAVIS, to be a farmer
1 Jun 1811	William LEE, poor boy, 11 yrs 5 mo. old, son of Elizabeth Lee, to Thomas LITTLETON, to be a farmer
15 Oct 1838	John W. LEWIS, bastard, 6 yrs old 4 Apr 1838, to Birket JETT, to be a farmer
23 Aug 1821	Solomon LITTLETON to Hugh THOMPSON, for 4 yrs from 7 Jul 1821, to be a tanner & currier
5 Apr 1819	Volney LUCUS, coloured, to Jonas POTTS, for 14 yrs from 15 Feb 1820, to be a farmer
15 Jan 1828	Lydia, coloured, to Daniel JANNEY, to be a housekeeper
12 Feb 1804	John MAHONEY, poor boy, to John HOLDING, to be a farmer
12 Feb 1804	Thomas MAHONEY, poor boy, to John HOLDING, to be a farmer
10 Mar 1829	George MANLY, free boy of colour, 10 yrs old, to Christopher STONEBURNER, to be a farmer
3 Oct 1820	Maria, coloured, to Jane HOUGH, for 13 yrs, to be a housekeeper
10 Apr 1810	John MARKER, orphan, 7 yrs old 15 May 1810, to Peter COMPHER, to be a farmer
3 Jun 1839	Henry A. MASON, coloured bastard, 7 yrs old 1 Feb 1839, to John WEADON, to be a house servant
7 Mar 1839	Jesse MASON, coloured bastard, 14 yrs old 17 Apr 1839, to William CARR, to be a farmer
16 Nov 1838	Nancy MASON, free coloured bastard, 4 yrs old 16 Apr 1838, to Washington BEAVERS, to be a housekeeper
9 Feb 1829	Wesly MASON, free mulatto, b. 21 Sep 1821, to Thomas RUSSELL, to be a house servant
29 Apr 1817	Catharine MCAFFREY to Jonas JANNEY, for 7 yrs from 2 Apr 1818, to be a housekeeper
9 Apr 1810	Mason MCCASTOR, coloured orphan, 5 yrs old 9 Jan 1810, to James SMALWOOD, to be a farmer
3 Feb 1814	Jesse MCCONNAHAY, poor boy, b. 29 Apr 1805, to Cyrus BURSON, to be a farmer

Apprentices, Poor Children and Bastards 145

27 Dec 1820	Landon MCFARLING, (a twin), to Thomas TRIBBY, for 14 yrs from 20 Nov 1821, to be a farmer
27 Dec 1820	Milton MCFARLING, (a twin), to Thomas TRIBBY, for 14 yrs from 20 Nov 1821, to be a farmer
21 Mar 1815	Washington MCFARLING to Thomas TRIBBY, for 14 yrs from 1 Jan 1816, to be a farmer
22 Jul 1848	Harriet Ann MCGINNIS, about 4 yrs old, dau of Charlotte McGinnis, to Mary BOUTS, for 5 yrs
9 Aug 1806	Eli MCKEMEY, 9 yrs old 2 Feb 1806, to John LOVE, to be a farmer
23 Oct 1812	Burniar MCKNIGHT, poor boy, 14 yrs 7 mo 13 da. old, to David JINKINS, to be a blacksmith
7 Mar 1821	Nimrod MCKNIGHT to Isaac YOUNG, for 5 yrs from 15 Mar 1821, to be a farmer
12 Dec 1836	Henry M. MCPHERSON, free negro bastard, 6 yrs old 24 Jun 1836, to John BEAVERS, to be a farmer
12 Dec 1836	Peter William MCPHERSON, free negro 7 yrs old 13 May 1836, to John BEAVERS, to be a farmer
19 Jun 1806	William MCPHERSON, mulatto orphan, 4 yrs old in Feb 1806, to William CARR, to be a farmer
15 Oct 1787	Fanny MEEGETH, orphan, 12 yrs old 25 Dec 1787, to John MARKS, to be a housekeeper
19 Jul 1819	John MELON, son of a single woman, to John JOHNSON, to serve until 9 Mar 1822, to be a carpenter & joiner
10 Feb 1829	Henry MILHOLLAND, 14 yrs 6 mo old, to John SURGHNOR, to be a boot & shoe maker
25 Apr 1829	Lucindy MONSTER, free coloured, 12 yrs old, to Christopher STONEBURNER, to be a housekeeper
13 Aug 1833	Philip MOYER, now 27 yrs old, , (same as Phillip bound to Samuel Russell in 1819)
12 Aug 1808	Nancy , black orphan, 3 yrs old 10 Jul 1808, to Precilla BEASIX, to be a housekeeper
7 Apr 1814	Nancy , bastard, to Lot T. JANNEY, for 8 yrs from 1 Jan 1815, to be a seamstress
25 Jun 1819	John NICHOLES to Peyton POWELL, for 8 yrs from 22 Oct 1819, to be a blacksmith
11 Mar 1812	Permelia NICHOLS to John YOUNG, & Lois, until 3 Jan 1821, to be a housekeeper
15 Jul 1820	Gabriel NITRE to David COPELAND, for 4 yrs 7 mo., to be a blacksmith
17 Feb 1818	Norvel , coloured, to Andrew GRAHAM, for 16 yrs from 20 Jul 1818, to be a farmer

146 INDENTURES on File (No Orders Found)

23 May 1832	Norvel, coloured bastard, 13 yrs old 18 Feb 1832, to Amasa RITICOR, to be a farmer
19 Mar 1816	John ORRISON to Timothy TAYLOR, for 13 yrs from 26 Feb 1817, to be a farmer
26 Oct 1812	Sarah ORRISON, poor girl, 5 yrs 5 mo 7 da. old, to Joseph FRED, Jr. & Hannah, to be a spinner & seamstress
8 Aug 1805	Ann PAGE, orphan, 11 yrs old 5 Jul 1805, to Samuel MURREY, to be a housekeeper
14 Feb 1805	Robert PAGE, orphan, 13 yrs old 29 Aug 1805, to William WRIGHT, to be a bricklayer
19 Jan 1818	David PAIN, b. 23 Dec 1807, to Hugh WILEY, Jr., for 11 yrs from 23 Dec 1817, to be a shoe & boot maker
26 Dec 1807	Peyton, bastard, 8 yrs old in Apr 1808, to Abraham SILCOTT, to be a blacksmith
17 Nov 1819	Phillip, coloured, to Samuel RUSSELL, for 8 yrs, to be a tanner or farmer
21 Jun 1815	Kitty PHILIPS, coloured, to James SMALLWOOD, for 4 mo. until 18, to be a housekeeper
19 Mar 1816	Alfred POULTON to Daniel COCKRILL, for 6 yrs from 28 Feb 1817, to be a carpenter & joiner
6 Jan 1821	Emila POULTON, dau of Tamer Tribby, to John GRUBB, for 4 yrs from 5 Jul 1821, to be a housekeeper
29 Oct 1812	Thomas POULTON to Joseph TAYLOR, until 1 Oct 1819 when 21, to be a boot & shoe maker
7 Nov 1817	Leven POWELL to William BRADFIELD, for 10 yrs from 19 Apr 1818, to be a boot & shoe maker
22 Jan 1842	Levi PRINCE, son of Matthias Prince, to John BONTZ, until 5 Apr 1848 when 21, to be a boot & shoe maker
30 Dec 1813	Lucindy REDMAN, 4 yrs old 18 Nov 1813, to Thomas RILEY, to be a housekeeper
15 Oct 1832	John REED, bastard, 13 yrs old 4 Feb 1832, to William MILLER, to be a shoemaker
12 Apr 1828	George W. RISBEY, 17 yrs old, to David REECE, to be a farmer
1 Jan 1839	Carter ROBERTSON, free negro, 6 yrs old, to Thomas LITTLETON, to be a farmer
1 Jan 1839	Susan ROBERTSON, free negro, 11 yrs old 25 Dec 1838, to Thomas LITTLETON, to be a housekeeper
13 Jul 1820	Joseph ROBINSON, coloured, to Thomas J. MARLOW, for 16 yrs from 1 Aug 1820, to be a farmer
26 Jun 1838	Mary Ann ROBISON, free coloured, 9 yrs old 15 Mar 1838, to John LOGAN, Sr., to be a house servant

Apprentices, Poor Children and Bastards 147

27 Jan 1824	Payton ROBISON, coloured, to Joseph WOOD, for 8 yrs from 14 Mar 1824, to be a farmer
30 Mar 1822	William H. RUSSELL to Aaron RUSSELL, for 18 yrs from 15 Jun 1822, to be a farmer
27 Feb 1819	Sally, illegitimate yellow girl, 10 yrs old 25 Dec 1818, to Jeremiah HAMPTON, to be a housekeeper
17 Feb 1818	Westley SHRIEVE to Daniel COCKRELL, for 3 yrs from 1 Aug 1818, to be a carpenter & joiner
14 Nov 1837	John Thomas SKINNER, bastard, 9 yrs old 10 Nov 1837, to John A. BEAVERS, to be a farmer
20 Feb 1836	William Randolph SMALLWOOD, bastard, 8 yrs old 8 Aug 1835, to Robert MCCARTY, to be a tanner
29 Jan 1821	Caroline SPARROW, 9 yrs old in Aug 1820, dau of Dinah Sparrow, single woman, to James PLASTER, & wife, to be a housekeeper
10 Feb 1829	Minor SPATES, 16 yrs old, to John SURGHNOR, to be a boot & shoe maker
12 Jun 1819	Elizabeth TAVENOR, illegitimate dau of Mary Tavenor, to John HATCHER, until 18, to be a housekeeper
13 Mar 1838	Morris THOMPSON, bastard, 15 yrs old 24 Sep 1837, to Thomas M. HUMPHREY, to be a carpenter
28 Aug 1819	James Madison THORNTON, illegitimate son of Nancy Thornton, to William GALLEHER, until 21, to be a farmer
26 Sep 1823	Ebeline TILMAN to John FRY, for 9 yrs from 1 Mar 1823, to be a housekeeper
28 Dec 1819	Alfred TIMBERS, coloured, to Andrew OGDEN, for 15 yrs from 1 Nov 1820, to be a farmer
15 Oct 1819	Mary TRACY, 9 yrs old 1 Feb 1820, dau of Sally Tracy, single woman, to William & Margery GALLEHER, to be a housekeeper
3 Aug 1829	Susan TURNBULL, orphan of John Turnbull, 10 yrs old in Apr 1829, to William MCCLOSKY, to be a housekeeper
26 Jan 1818	Agnes TURNER to Israel PHILIPS, for 1 yr from 10 Jan 1819, to be a housekeeper
23 Dec 1820	Alexander TURNER to Joseph TAYLOR, for 4 yrs from 4 Jul 1821, to be a shoe & boot maker
20 Feb 1819	Joseph URTEN, illegitimate, 11 yrs old 24 Jul 1819, to Jacob MANN, to be a farmer
8 Apr 1816	Nimrod VICKERS to George RHODES, for 5 yrs from 14 Feb 1816, to be a blacksmith

INDENTURES on File (No Orders Found)

15 Jan 1842	Joseph WADE, 17 yrs old 23 Jan 1842, to George W. NOLAND, to be a tailor
9 Nov 1816	Wallace, coloured, to Thomas BROWN, for 10 yrs from 20 Sep 1817, to be a millwright
11 May 1818	Enos WARTERS to Nathan NICHOLS, for 9 yrs from 13 Jan 1819, to be a farmer
13 Feb 1810	Peyton WATKINS, 7 yrs old 13 Feb 1810, orphan of colour, to Armistead LONG, to be a farmer
16 Mar 1819	Samuel WAUGH, illegitimate, 19 yrs 1 mo 4 da. old, to Nelson GREEN, to be a boot & shoe maker
21 Nov 1832	Maddison WHEELER, free coloured bastard, 14 yrs old 10 Apr 1832, to James L. MARTIN, to be a tanner
13 Feb 1835	William WILLIAMS, mulatto, 4 yrs old 8 Aug 1834, to John BEAVERS, to be a farmer
12 May 1826	Mary WINTERS, coloured, to John RAMSEY, for 10 yrs, to be a housekeeper
13 Aug 1844	Joseph WISE, orphan, 15 yrs old, to Edward HAINES, to be a stone mason
26 Mar 1819	Harrison Douglas YOUNG to Isaac H. NICHOLS, for 14 yrs from 11 Aug 1819, to be a farmer
25 Nov 1833	Thompson ZABRA, free coloured, about 13 yrs old, to George GOINES, to be a barber & hairdresser

Apprentices, Poor Children and Bastards   149

Bastard Children

(Listed by Name of Mother)

1757	Abigail THATCHER – child, b. __ _ 1757 at the house of Amos Thatcher
11 Oct 1757	Ann NELSON – child, b. within past 12 mo. She lives at Daniel Sanders'
9 May 1758	On 9 May 1758 the grand jury returned a presentment against Ann HAYS for having a base born child within the past 6 months, John WINN, reputed father
9 May 1758	On 9 May 1758 the grand jury returned a presentment against Ann VINES for having a base born child within the past 6 months
9 May 1758	On 9 May 1758 the grand jury returned a presentment against Barbary RAMEY for having a base born child within the past 6 months
14 Nov 1758	On 14 Nov 1758 the grand jury returned a presentment against Mary ENGLISH for having a base born child within the past 6 months
1759	Elizabeth GRANTHAM __ _ 1759 delivered of a bastard child
	Barbara RAMEY (REMEY) – child, b. __ _ 1759, James WHALEY, Jr., acknowledged father
8 May 1759	On 8 May 1759 the grand jury returned a presentment against Mary PROCTOR, for having a base born mulatto child. Same date, Thomas KELLY for conniving and detaining Mary PROCTOR to cohabit with a negro named Peter
8 May 1759	On 8 May 1759 the grand jury returned a presentment against Lydia DODD for having a base born child within the past 8 months
8 May 1759	On 8 May 1759 the grand jury returned a presentment against Rachel DUNCAN for having a base born child within the past 6 months
13 Nov 1759	On 13 Nov 1759 the grand jury returned a presentment against Sarah ROBERTS for having a base born child within the past 12 months
13 Nov 1759	On 13 Nov 1759 the grand jury returned a presentment against Mary FRANKS for having a base born child within the past 12 months
13 Nov 1759	On 13 Nov 1759 the grand jury returned a presentment against Chloe POOR for having a base born child within the past 12 months

Bastard Children

13 Nov 1759	On 13 Nov 1759 the grand jury returned a presentment against Elizabeth TAPMEN for having a base born child within the past 12 months
11 Nov 1760	On 11 Nov 1760 the grand jury returned a presentment against Sarah OWSLEY for having base born children within the past 6 months
12 Feb 1761	Ann CORNWELL sued by CHWDNS for 500 pounds of tobacco or 50 shillings. Case discontinued 11 June 1761
10 Sep 1761	Catherine STEWART sued by CHWDNS for 500 pounds of tobacco or 50 shillings. Case dismissed 10 Sep 1761, fine being paid
14 Mar 1762	Ann GRIFFIN delivered of a baseborn child within past 12 mo. Case discontinued 12 May 1763
15 Jul 1762	Mary WINSOR sued by CHWDNS for 500 pounds of tobacco or 50 shillings
15 Jul 1762	On 15 Jul 1762 the grand jury returned a presentment against Jemima HARLE for having a base born child. Discontinued 13 Apr 1763
15 Jul 1762	On 15 Jul 1762 the grand jury returned a presentment against Ruth HERLE for having a base born child. Discontinued 13 Apr 1763
15 Jul 1762	On 15 Jul 1762 the grand jury returned a presentment against Sarah OWSLEY for having a base born child.
12 Aug 1762	Elizabeth BLACK sued by CHWDNS for 500 pounds of tobacco or 50 shillings
12 Aug 1762	Lydia DODD – bond given by Josiah MILES for support of her child
16 Sep 1762	On 16 Sep 1762 the grand jury returned a presentment against Rachel HALL for having a base born child
14 Dec 1762	Christian WOODHOUSE –child, Withers SMITH, adjudged father, to pay for support of the child
11 May 1763	On 11 May 1763 the grand jury returned a presentment against Hannah OXLEY for having a base born child within the past 6 months
15 Mar 1764	Ann HAYS sued by CHWDNS for 500 pounds of tobacco or 50 shillings
13 Nov 1764	On 13 Nov 1764 the grand jury returned a presentment against Elizabeth FINICAN for having a base born child within the past 2 months
15 Oct 1766	Jane JEW sued by CHWDNS for 500 pounds of tobacco or 50 shillings. Sheriff's return on summons: "married to Francis Bradock and not found"

Apprentices, Poor Children and Bastards 151

15 Oct 1766	Elizabeth STOKER sued by CHWDNS for 500 pounds of tobacco or 50 shillings. Case dismissed Apr 1767 "No inhabitant". Sheriff's return indicates a resident of Prince William Co.
15 Oct 1766	Sarah MATHENEY sued by CHWDNS for 500 pounds of tobacco or 50 shillings. Case dismissed 10 Mar 1767 agreed
11 May 1767	On 11 May 1767 the grand jury returned a presentment against Jane McDaniel for having a base born child
11 May 1767	On 11 May 1767 the grand jury returned a presentment against Elizabeth MARLBROUGH for having a base born child
11 May 1767	On 11 May 1767 the grand jury returned a presentment against Mary WILSON for having a base born child
9 May 1768	On 9 May 1768 the grand jury returned a presentment against Hannah OXLEY for having a base born child
14 Nov 1769	On 14 Nov 1769 the grand jury returned a presentment against Ann JENKINS for having a base born child
12 Feb 1770	Mary WILKERSON sued by CHWDNS for 500 pounds of tobavco or 50 shillings. Case dismissed 13 Mar 1770 "Not found"
26 May 1772	On 26 May 1772 the grand jury returned a presentment against Kezia HICKS for having a base born child\
26 May 1772	On 26 May 1772 the grand jury returned a presentment against Martha HALBERT for having a base born child
11 Nov 1773	On 11 Nov 1773 the grand jury returned a presentment against Ann FEARE for having a base born child
	Elizabeth SHELTON (CHELTON) – male b. 7 Feb 1780. William SMITH, adjudged father to pay 800 pounds of tabacco per yr for 5 yrs for support of child
14 Aug 1780	Mary HUSSEY – John BURNS gave bond for payment of 800 pounds of tobacco per yr for 4 yrs for support of child
15 Aug 1780	Sethey Simmons PALMER – Thomas COCKRILL Jr gave bond to pay 800 pounds of tobacco per yr for 4 yrs for support of child
15 May 1781	Katherine BROWN – child, George NICHOLS, adjudged father, to pay 1000 pounds of tobacco per yr for support of child
10 Jun 1782	Polly CLAIG – child, Phillip THOMAS, adjudged father to pay 800 pounds of tobacco per yr for 5 yrs for support of child

20 Mar 1783	Hannah HOWELL – child, William HOUGH, Jr, reputed father gave bond but failed to appear. Judgment 9 Jun 1795
14 Aug 1783	Margaret ENNIS complains on oath that James SMITH hath begotten on her body a child
13 Oct 1783	Ellis (Alice) DUNLAP – William STOKER gave bond to pay 8 pounds per yr for 4 yrs for support of child
	Sarah VEALE – female b. 9 Dec 1784. Reuben REED, adjudged father to pay 8 pounds per yr for 7 yrs for support of child
14 Feb 1785	Martha HESSE – child. Joseph LAY, adjudged father to pay 16 pounds per yr for support of child
	Kesiah BRIDGEWATER – two males b. 10 Jul 1785 at the house of Jacob SOWERS in Frederick Co. Mahlon COMBS, reputed father. Nov 1786 case dismissed being brought illegally
12 Jun 1786	Rachel KIDD – child. John Hawkins, adjudged father, to pay 6 pounds per yr for support of child until discharged by order of court
12 Jun 1786	Catharine HENDERSON – child. Samuel TILLETT, Jr adjudged father, to pay 8 pounds per yr for support of child until discharged by order of court
29 Jul 1786	Abigail FORGISON – child. Thomas HART gave bond to pay 17 pounds 10 shillings by paying 3 pounds 10 shillings on Jan 1 each yr until fully paid
11 Sep 1787	Lettice PILLER – 2 children, one 4 yrs and one 17 mo. Enoch FURR adjudged father, to pay 600 pounds tobacco per yr for each until 6 yrs old
9 Feb 1789	Sarah COSTILLO – child. Ellis HEART to pay for maintenance of child
14 Apr 1789	Mary SMITH – child. Thomas MCINTOSH, adjudged father to pay 8 pounds per yr for 6 yrs for support of child
	Catharine PALMER – children b. Mar 1790 and b. Feb 1793. John DEBELL, reputed father. 13 Aug 1793 discontinued
10 May 1790	Ann TETRICK – 2 children. James ROBERTSON, adjudged father to pay 7 pounds per yr for each child until 6 yrs old
14 Sep 1790	Mary (Mica) KIRK – child. Jonathan TREBBE, adjudged father to pay 8 pounds per yr for support of child until 5 yrs old
	Margaret POULTON – male b. 9 Apr 1791 at her father's house. Dr. John NICKLIN, Jr reputed father

Apprentices, Poor Children and Bastards   153

12 Nov 1792	Nancy ROOKARD – child. Joseph LEWIS, Sr, adjudged father to pay 6 pounds per yr for 3 yrs for support of child
	Elizabeth (Betsey) FOX – male b. 19 Nov 1792. James FITZSIMMONS, adjudged father, to pay 5 pounds per yr for 6 yrs for support of child
13 Mar 1793	Elizabeth HOLTSCLAW – child. William STEPHENS, adjudged father, to pay 6 pounds per yr for 6 yrs for support of child
	Hannah CAMPBELL – male b. June 1793 at the house of John CAMPBELL. Eli MCVAW (MCVEIGH), reputed father
14 Jun 1796	Nancy BOGGESS – at the house of Mary Ann BOGGESS, female b. 2 Feb 1794, called Amey, female b. 7 Mar 1796. John OWENS, adjudged father, to pay $30 per yr until Amey is 7 yrs old. To pay $30 per yr until __ is 7 yrs old
9 Dec 1794	Mary POPKINS – 2 children. Guynn (Gwynn) PAGE, adjudged father, to pay 11 pounds per yr until boy arrives at 6 yrs, then 5 pounds 10 shillings per yr until girl arrives at 8 yrs
13 Jan 1795	Polly BEASLEY – female. John Hewlett, reputed father
	Margaret POULSTON – female b. 16 Apr 1795. Thomas MARKS, adjudged father, to pay 7 pounds per yr until 6 yrs old, being 3 yrs old on 16 Apr 1798
9 Jun 1795	Sarah UPDIKE – child. George HUGHES, reputed father. Case dismissed
	Tamar MORRIS – child b. 7 Jan 1796. James SEATON, reputed father
14 Jun 1796	Sarah POPKINS – child. Jesse FOX, judgement for costs
	Esther MILLHOLLEN – male b. 17 Dec 1796 at house of Patrick MILLHOLLEN. David PHILLIPS, adjudged father, to pay 5 pounds per yr for 5 yrs for support of child
	Hannah BEANS – female b. 7 Jan 1797 at the house of William BEANS. James BEST, Jr reputed father
13 Feb 1797	Winifred URTON – child. Andrew HENDERSON, reputed father
	Tamar POULTON – male b. 15 Feb 1797. William CHAMBLIN, reputed father. Nov 1798 case dismissed
	Ann COOCK – female b. 24 Feb 1797 at the house of Jonathan COOCK. William COCKERILL, reputed father

	Lidia BALES (BAYLES)(BEALE) – female b. 3 Mar 1797. Thomas DRAKE Jr, adjudged father, to pay 7 pounds per yr until 6 yrs old
14 Nov 1797	Mary THOMAS – female b. 17 Jun 1797. Jesse JAMES, adjudged father, to pay 8 pounds per yr for 8 yrs
11 Jul 1797	Sarah BOND – child. Samuel FERGUSON, reputed father. 11 Jul 1797 case dismissed
	Nancy (Ann) STREET – female called Molly b. 27 Sep 1797 at the house of George HARDY. Richard DAVIS, reputed father. 12 Mar 1798 case dismissed agreed
	Cathern STEAGLER – female b. 3 Oct 1797 at the house of Benjamin HOLLEM. Jacob MILLER, adjudged father, to pay 6 pounds per yr for 6 yrs from 3 Oct 1797
	Elizabeth TRITIPAU – child b. 28 Jan 1798. John FORBES, millwright, reputed father. Nov 1799 case dismissed agreed
	Sarah CUMMINGS – male b. 5 Jun 1798 at the house of James CUMMINGS, her father. Benjamin WHEELER, reputed father. June 1800 case dismissed
13 Aug 1798	Elizabeth MCABOY – child. Thomas KIDWELL, reputed father
	Lydia SILCOTT – female b. 14 Dec 1798. John CHAMBLIN, reputed father
	Sarah HALBERT – female b. 22 Apr 1799 at the house of Robert BEAVERS. Robert COOPER, adjudged father, to pay 6 pounds per yr for 4 yrs. Sep 1800 – thereupon Robert COOPER married Sarah HALBERT
	Ruth DYER – male b. 10 May 1799 at the house of James BURSON. John REED, reputed father
	Sarah PHILLIPS – female (now 4 mo old Sept 1799). John PEACOCK, adjudged father, to pay $25 per yr until 5 yrs old
	Nancy DAVIS – female b. 25 Jul 1799. John OLDACRE, adjudged father, to pay $20 per yr for 4 yrs
10 Dec 1799	Mary MARTIN – female. James MCGETH, adjudged father, to pay $20 per yr until she is 6 yrs old
	Hannah DARR – male b. 14 Mar 1800 called Aaron MATTHEWS (or DARR). John MATTHEWS, adjudged father to pay 6 pounds for 4 yrs for support of child
	Elizabeth MACABOY – female b. 7 Sep 1800 at the house of George SMITH. Thomas KIDWELL, adjudged father, to pay $20 per yr for 6 yrs from the birth of the child

Apprentices, Poor Children and Bastards   155

                Catharine CREAMER – child. John SOWDER (SOUDER), reputed father. 14 Oct 1800 case abates, defendant (Sowder) dead

10 Nov 1800   Milley MARKS – female. William CHAMBLIN to pay $20 per yr for 6 yrs for support of child

                Nancy HICKMAN – male b. 29 Apr 1801. George YOUNG, adjudged father, to pay $140 for the 6 yrs from date of birth

                Sarah BOND – male b. 30 Dec 1801 at the house of Theophilus HOFF. Samuel NICHOLS, miller, adjudged father, to pay $20 per yr for 6 yrs

11 Jan 1802   Sarah RICHARDSON – child. William LACEY, adjudged father, to pay 8 pounds per yr for 6 yrs for support of child

                Sarah RYNE – female b. 30 Jan 1802, at her own dwelling rented from Benjamin H. Canby. William MCMACHEN (MCMICKENS), reputed father, served with summons in Sep 1807 – a resident of KY but now in Loudoun Co. 15 Sep 1807 case dismissed, agreed

                Polly MCNABB – female b. 11 Jun 1802 at the house of John Sears. Robert COMBS, alias ATHEL, adjudged father, to pay 6 pounds per yr for 5 yrs for support of the child

                Ann (Anna) WHITACRE – female b. 18 Jul 1802. Ebenezer PIGGOTT, adjudged father, to pay 6 pounds per yr for 5 yrs for support of the child

                Sarah ROMINE – male b. 18 Mar 1803. John OVERFIELD, reputed father

                Hannah ROACH – male b. 15 Apr 1803. Joseph BALDWIN, adjudged father, to pay 6 pounds per yr for 4 yrs for support of the child

15 Jun 1803   Mary POPKINS – female. Guynn (Gwynn) PAGE – CHWDNS to recover 5 pounds 16 shillings for maintenance of child from 9 Jun 1801 to 5 Jul 1802

                Phebe HOWELL – female b. 25 Nov 1803. George GIBSON, reputed father. Jun 1804 case dismissed agreed

                Deborah COPELAND – male b. 22 Feb 1804. David LOVETT, adjudged father, to pay 8 pounds per yr until 7 yrs old

                Frances BROUGHNER (BRAWNER) – male b. 13 Apr 1804. James SANDERS (SAUNDERS), adjudged father, to pay $25 per yr for 5 yrs for support of the child

                Euphemy SMITH – female b. May 1804. William BEST, reputed father. June 1805 dismissed agreed

Mary TOBIN – male b. Aug 1804. Henry HOWELL, reputed father

Nancy FURGUSON – male b. 8 Nov 1804. William TORBERT (TALBERT), adjudged father, to pay $20 per yr for 5 yrs from 9 Dec 1805 for support of child

15 Jan 1805 Nancy BROOKS – male. John CAMPBELL, adjudged father to pay 8 pounds per yr until 7 yrs old

Martha HEPBURN – female b. 22 Apr 1805. Nicholas OSBURN, adjudged father, to pay $20 per yr until she is 7 yrs old

Agnes POULSON – female b. 20 Apr 1806 at the house of Jasher POULSON. William LICKEY, adjudged father, to pay $20 per yr for 6 yrs for support of the child

Susannah MILLER – male b. 12 May 1806 at the house of John HUNT. George WILLETT, reputed father. Case dismissed 11 Jan 1808

Sarah BONHAM – female b. 9 Aug 1806. Jacob BROWN, adjudged father, to pay $23 1/3 per yr for 6 yrs for support of the child

Ann BEAL – male b. 26 Jan 1807 at the house of William THOMPSON. Jesse SMITH, adjudged father, to pay $20 per yr for 7 yrs for support of the child

Hannah SMITH – female b. 11 Aug 1807. John TOBIN, adjudged father to pay $23.33 1/3 per yr for 8 yrs for support of the child

Mildred RIGSBY – female b. 15 Sep 1807. Edward DAWES, reputed father. Case dismissed, she being a married woman

Sarah POWEL – female b. 2 Nov 1807. Thomas BEST, reputed father. Case dismissed 14 Dec 1807

Mary (Polly) SILCOTT – female b. 15 Nov 1807 at the house of George EARNEST. Henson ELLIOTT, acknowledged father in June 1811 to pay a total of $60 – $5 in advance and $20 per yr until fully paid

Jane JAMES – male b. 25 Mar 1808. Adam SMITLEY, reputed father

Anne (Anna) PEACOCK – male b. 3 Jul 1808. Isaac WORKMAN, Jr, adjudged father to pay $20 per yr for 7 yrs for support of the child

Susannah FRY (FRYE) – male b. 19 Sep 1808. Peter WYER (WIRE) adjudged father to pay #22 per yr for 7 yrs for support of the child

Mary HUNT – male b. 11 Nov 1808 at the house of Stephen TRIPLETT. Mahlon CRAVEN, adjudged father to pay $22 per yr for 7 yrs for support of the child

Ann WILSON – male b. 17 Jun 1809. William BRANHAM, reputed father

Mary MCCARTY – twins: 1 male, 1 female, b. 21 Oct 1809 at the house of her father, Timoth MCCARTY. William DAVIS, acknowledged father to pay $30 per yr each for 7 yrs for support of the children

Mary WRIGHT – female b. 15 Dec 1809 at the house of James MCKIMM. Henry MCGARVICK, adjudged father to pay $22 per yr for 7 yrs for support of the child

Rachel WORKMAN – female b. 24 Jan 1810 at the house of David HEAR. Clemince BATEMAN reputed father

Susanna CASEY – male b. 3 Jun 1810 at the House of David EFLIN (EVELAND). David EFLIN (EVELAND) adjudged father to pay $20 per yr for 5 yrs for support of the child

Pleasant LIVINGSTON – male b. 3 Jun 1810 at the house of John YOUNG. John GRIFFITH, acknowledged father, to pay $25 per yr for 2 yrs and $20 per yr for 3 more yrs for support of the child

Catharine GREEN – female b. 8 Aug 1810 at the house of Mackey TOTTON. Jonah HAGUE, reputed father

Christiana MORELAND – male b. 27 Oct 1810 at the house of William MORELAND. Henry DUNKIN, adjudged father, to pay $20 per yr for __ years for support of the child

Nancy LAWSON, free black – male b. Nov 1810 at the house of Charles LAWSON. Daniel SMITH, free black acknowledged father

Mary HOWELL – female b. 9 Dec 1810 at the house of Deborah MCKNIGHT. Jonathan HART, acknowledged father, to pay $20 per yr for 7 yrs for support of the child

Sarah TRACY – female b. 1 Feb 1811 at the house of Nancy THORNTON. Gerard URTON, adjudged father to pay $25 per yr for 7 yrs for support of the child

Sarah COWGILL – female b. 4 May 1811. William BATSON, adjudged father, to pay $25 per yr for 3 yrs from 4 May 1816 – Child not likely to be chargeable to the parish – is supported by grandfather

Polly HARPER of Jefferson Co. – male b. 10 May 1811 at the house of John HARPER in Loudoun Co. Jeremiah BYRNE, reputed father. Polly recently moved to Jefferson Co.

Bastard Children

10 Jun 1811 — Elizabeth MCGINNIS – female. John NIXON, Jr, adjudged father ordered to pay $20 per yr for 6 yrs for support of the child

Frances SHECKELS – female b. 14 Dec 1811. Thomas SEERS, adjudged father to pay $22 2/3 per yr for 6 yrs for support of the child

Margaret BRYANT – male b. 4 May 1812. Thomas LOWE, confessed father, to pay $20 per yr for 6 yrs 9 mo from 10 Aug 1812 for support of the child

10 Aug 1812 — Hannah SMITH – child. Edmund CARTER, adjudged father, to pay $20 per yr for 6 yrs for support of the child

Mary Ann YOUNG – male b. 11 Aug 1812. William CUMMINGS, adjudged father agreed to pay $30 per yr for 3 yrs from 14 Jan 1817 for support of the child

Lydia WATS – female b. 23 Sep 1812. John DOWNS, adjudged father, to pay $20 per yr for 7 yrs for support of the child

Elizabeth MOLDING (MORELAND) – female b. 16 Dec 1812. William RHODES adjudged father

8 Feb 1813 — Mary WILDMAN – male. Charles BINNS, Jr, adjudged father, to pay $20 per yr for 7 yrs from the birth of the child, payable at the end of each year

Susanna STUCK – male b. 2 Mar 1813 at the house of John SHORT. Frederick HEFFNER, adjudged father to pay $20 per yr for 7 yrs for support of the child

Mary E. COLE – child b. 20 Mar 1813. Joseph HANES adjudged father

Elizabeth BELLARD – male b. 8 Apr 1813 at the house of Ralph SMITH. Robert CUMMINGS, reputed father, contested suit and was discharged

Mary THOMAS – male b. 17 Jan 1814. Sandford CLEMONS acknoledged father

11 Jul 1814 — Elizabeth SEARS – male. David BEATTY (BATY) adjudged father to pay $24 per yr for 7 yrs from 30 Apr 1814 for support of the child

Elizabeth FRANCE – male b. 27 Oct 1814 at the house of James ALLDER. Richard SCAGGS acknowledged father

Nancy MCFARLING, a free woman – 2 males b. 20 Nov 1814 at the house of Thomas TRIBBY, Sr. William PHILIPS alias William BUFFINGTON confessed father, to pay $25 per child for 7 yrs for support of the children

Mary WILDMAN – female b. 4 Dec 1814. Charles BINNS, Jr., adjudged father, to pay $25 per yr for support of the child

Apprentices, Poor Children and Bastards 159

Nancy TAYLOR – female b. 26 Jan 1815. Ignatius ELGIN, adjudged father, to pay $24 per yr for 6 yrs for support of the child

Isabella TAVENOR – male b. 13 Mar 1815. William WILDMAN, confessed father to pay $20 per yr for 6 yrs for support of the child

Sarah HOLLIDAY – male b. 20 May 1815. Robert MARTIN, adjudged father to pay $24 per yr for 5 yrs 9 mo (order of 16 Aug 1816) for support of the child

Nancy CROSS – male b. 1 Sep 1815. George ROBERTSON, acknowledged father to pay $25 per yr for support of the child

8 Nov 1815 Catharine HUFFMAN – male (8 Nov 1815 says "lately delivered"). William HUNT, reputed father. Case dismissed on 11 Dec 1815

Sally HAYNES (Sarah HAINES) – male b. 18 Dec 1815 at the house of William BROWN. Henry BROOKBANK, reputed father

Rachel RUSE – male b. 3 Apr 1816 at her father's house, Frederic STATES (SLATES), reputed father

Elizabeth FRANCE – male b. 7 Sep 1816 at the house of Isaiah ROMINE, Richard SCAGGS acknowledged father

Ann VICKERS – female b. 27 Jun 1817 at the house of William NICHOLS, Lewis BERRY, adjudged father to pay $25 per yr for 5 yrs for support of the child

Sarah KENT – male b. 15 Mar 1818 at the house of Elizabeth NOLAND, William MCCAFFREY, reputed father. Case quashed Feb, 1820.

Jane RUSSELL – male b. 6 Jun 1818 at the house of Mason MARKS. Mason MARKS, acknowledged father to pay $20 per yr for 6 yrs from 10 Sep 1818 for support of the child

Ann GOVER – male b. 13 Oct 1818 at the house of Garrat HOUGH, Andrew ANDERSON, cabinet maker, reputed father

Susan NISEWANGER – male b. 3 Dec 1818 at the house of Mason SHIPMAN. Robert POWELL, carpenter acknowledged father. He gave birth date as 1 Dec 1819

Pleasant MATTHEWS – female b. 16 Jan 1819 at the house of Richard MATTHEWS, Newton FURR, reputed father

Sarah MUSGROVE – child b. 9 Feb 1819. John UNDERWOOD confessed father. Judgement for $120 payable in quarterly yearly payments from 13 Jun 1821

Bastard Children

8 Nov 1819

Catherine CRIDER (CRIDLER) – female b. 2 Mar 1819 at the house of Elizabeth PRICE. Elias THRASHER Jr., farmer, adjudged father to pay $25 per yr for 7 yrs for support of the child

Sally HOLLIDAY – male b. 18 Apr 1819 at the house of John WINGROVE, Stephen LEWIS reputed father

Christiana WRIGHT – child, Bennett MARKS, reputed father. 16 Feb 1820, case dismissed

Mary OGDEN – male b. 17 Jan 1820 at the house of Hezekiah OGDEN. James T. HOPE, miller, confessed father to pay $20 per yr for 7 yrs for suport of the child

Susannah MAHAUNY – female b. 27 Mar 1820. James MERCHANT, reputed father. Case dismissed 12 Feb 1821

Mary BEARD – male b. 10 May 1820 at the house of William BEARD. Elijah VERMILLION, adjudged father, to pay $20 per yr for 6 yrs from 11 Sep 1820 for support of the child

Tamson QUEEN – female b. 10 Oct 1820, Enos BROOMHALL, reputed father

Elizabeth WEBSTER – female b. 25 Dec 1820, Peter FRY, reputed father

Delilah MCKNIGHT – male b. 20 Jun 1821 at the house of William JONES, John HUGHES, confessed father. Judgement for $120 payable quarterly commencing 20 Jun 1820[sic]

Leatha EDMONDSON – male b. 8 Dec 1821 at the house of George REED, John COLE, adjudged father to pay $20 per yr for 6 yrs from 8 Dec 1821 for support of the child

Margaret WHITMORE – male b. 3 Apr 1822 (date given by Margaret Whitmore, order shows 9 Jan 1822), Caldwell WRIGHT, acknowledged father to pay $20 per yr for 4 yrs 6 mo from 8 Jun 1824 for support of the child

Mary WADE – female b. 11 Apr 1822 at the house of her mother, Joseph CAROLES, stonecutter, confessed father to pay $25 per yr for 7 yrs for support of the child

Melinda FOX – female b. 27 Apr 1822 at the house of Gracy FOX, Thompson ATWELL, carpenter, adjudged father to pay $20 per yr for 7 yrs for support of the child

Elizabeth MAGINNIS – male b. 4 May 1822, Greenberry M. MCDANIEL, shoemaker, acknowledged father to pay $20 per yr for 6 yrs from 14 May 1822 for support of the child

Apprentices, Poor Children and Bastards   161

Rebecca HARVIN – female b. 1 Jun 1822, William WILDMAN, confessed father, to pay $20 per yr for 4 yrs from 16 Nov 1825 for support of the child

Elizabeth SHRY – male b. 29 Jun 1822 at the house of Joshua PANCOAST, Elum JACOBS, acknowledged father to pay $20 per yr for 7 yrs for support of the child

Providence HAMILTON – female b. 30 Jan 1823 at the house of Charles KANE, Landon TAVENNER, reputed father

Mary SLACK – male b. 11 Jul 1823 at the house of Jane SLACK, James MERCHANT, adjudged father to pay $14.28 per yr for 7 yrs from date of birth for support of the child

8 Sep 1823   Martha VIRTS – child, John COOPER, acknowledged father to pay $25 per yr for 6 yrs from birth of child

Martha EVERHART – female b. 22 Nov 1823 at the house of her father, Jonathan CUNNARD, reputed father. Case dismissed 8 Mar 1824

Marianda (Marinda) BRADY, free woman of color, female b. 22 Dec 1823 at the house of Susan TURNER, Thornton MORIN, alias CHICHESTER, free man of color, acknowledged father to pay $25 per yr for 6 yrs for support of the child

Margaret WHITMORE – male b. 9 Jan 1824 (date given by Margaret Whitmore, order shows 3 Apr 1824), Caldwell WRIGHT, acknowledged father to pay $20 per yr for 7 yrs from date of birth for support of the child

Malinda FOX – female b. 18 Feb 1824 at the house of Wm. MIDDLETON, John HOLMES, adjudged father to pay $20 per yr for 4 yrs 9 mo from 6 Apr 1825 for support of the child

Rebecca HARVEY – male b. 6 Nov 1824 at the house of William MIDDLETON, Richard JONES, reputed father

13 Jun 1825   Nancy MORELAND – child, William YOUNG, adjudged father to pay $20 per yr for 7 yrs from 3 Jan 1825 for support of the child

Caroline MCARTOR – male b. 31 Jul 1825 at the house of Richard RILEY, Mahlon THOMPSON, acknowledged father, to pay $25 per yr for 6 yrs from 11 Sep 1826 for support of the child

Emily POULTON – female b. 26 Dec 1825 at the house of her mother, Thamer TRIBBY. Macka (Mackey) TARLTON, acknowledged father to pay $25 per yr for 6½ years for support of the child

Elizabeth HAGUE – female b. 30 Jan 1826 at the house of her mother, Amelia HAGUE, John SAMPLE, reputed father. Case dismissed 13 Aug 1827

Frances CARLILE – male b. 22 Jan 1827 at the house of Robert CARLILE, George W. PETTIT, reputed father. Case dismissed 14 Mar 1827, "not the father"

Nancy FULTZ – male b. 2 Apr 1827 at the house of Miriam HOLE, John FIELDS, reputed father

Pleasant SHOPE – female b. 4 Apr 1827 at the house of her mother in Jefferson Co., Va. Jeremiah C. FURR, reputed father, Jefferson Co., sued for support of the child

Jane RUSSELL – male b. 31 Aug 1827, Alfred SHIELDS, reputed father

Euphamy GREEN – male b. 10 Sep 1827 (she said 10 Oct 1827) at the house of Abraham ANDERSON, Elias POOLE, reputed father

Annzey THOMPSON – female b. 6 Jun 1829, Benjamin JACKSON, reputed father

Nancy SILCOTT – female b. 7 Aug 1829, Reubin TRIPLETT, reputed father

Octavia VANHORN – male b. 15 Jul 1829, Ryland JACOBS, confessed father to pay $25 per yr for 4 yrs from 11 Oct 1831 for support of the child

Susannah EARNEST – male b. 4 Jan 1830 at the house of George EARNEST, Lewis GIDEON, alias GORE, reputed father

Phebe HERRILL – male b. 26 Jul 1830 and male b. 6 May 1833, at her own house, Martin BUTCHER, adjudged father to pay $20 per yr for each until 7 yrs old for their support

Elizabeth LEWIS – male b. 27 Aug 1830, Charles BARTON, reputed father

Ann BEATTY – male b. 19 Nov 1830, Joab EVELAND, reputed father

Lucinda POWER – female b. 23 Dec 1830 at the house of John FIELDS, William FULTON, reputed father

Margaret MYERS – male b. (1830 or 1831), William FRYE, adjudged father to pay $20 per yr for 4 yrs 6 mo from 11 May 1833 for support of the child

Malinda BUTLER – male b. 20 Jul 1831 at the Poor House, William COHAGEN, reputed father

Matilda GIBSON – child b. (1831 or 1832), Samuel CARTER, blacksmith, adjudged father to pay $20 per yr until 26 Nov 1838 for support of child

Susanan EARNIST – female b. 15 Apr 1833 at the house of George EARNIST, Lewis GORE, alias GIDEON, confessed father, to pay $25 per yr for 4 yrs from 23 Mar 1835 for support of the child

Sarah DAWES – male b. 28 Apr 1834 at the house of Mary DAWES, William A. CHICK, adjudged father to pay $20 per yr for 7 yrs from 28 Apr 1834 for support of the child

Hannah MILLER – child b. 14 Apr 1837 at the house of James ROACH, Samuel EDWARDS, confessed father, to pay $25 per yr for 3 yrs 6 mo from 12 Oct 1840 for support of the child

Phebe Ann MOORE – child b. 12 Nov 1838, William HUNT, adjudged father to pay $25 per yr for 7 yrs for support of the child

Catharine MOSS – female b. 2 Dec 1838, Henry GLASGOW, adjudged father, to pay $20 per yr for 6 yrs from 9 Sep 1839 for support of the child

Elizabeth SANBOWER – male b. 12 May 1842 at the house of Micle SANBOWER, William WENNER (of George) adjudged father

Phebe CARTER – female b. 19 Jun 1843 at the house of her mother, Philip GRIFFITH, reputed father. Case dismissed 15 Aug 1843

Agnes SEWELL – male b. 6 Jun 1844, James SMITH, (son of William), reputed father

Sarah DERRY – male b. 7 Mar 1845 at the house of George WISSINGER, Thomas W. SHRIVER, reputed father. Case dismissed August, 1845

Elizabeth BRADLEY – female b. 3 Feb 1846 at a house in John Moore's field, Edmund ROSE, reputed father

Ruth HAMILTON – female b. 22 Jul 1846 and male b. 21 Apr 1848, David WOOD, reputed father

Hannah A. ARNET – male b. 13 Mar 1850, Turner H. GALLAHER, adjudged father to pay $20 per yr for 8 yrs from 9 Dec 1850 for support of the child

Index

No Surname
- Affee 46
- Agnes 139
- Amey 153
- Amos 139
- Andrew 57, 69, 90
- Ann Amelia 135
- Betsey 69
- Betty 75
- Bill 74, 139
- Caroline 140
- Catharine ... 134, 140
- Charles ... 54, 65, 127
- Daniel 65
- Dilley 57
- Elisha 142
- Eliza 142
- Emily 124, 142
- George 57
- Hannah 57
- Harriot 143
- Harry 76, 143
- Henry 87, 138
- James 143
- Jefferson 117
- Joannah 126
- Jonathan 54
- Judy 142
- Kitty 144
- Leroi 106
- Lydia 144
- Lynna 95
- Maria 144
- Mary 54
- Nancy 145
- Norvel 145, 146
- Owen 117
- Peter 149
- Peyton 146
- Phillip 146
- Pleasant 97
- Polly 69
- Priscilla ... 26, 49, 134
- Richard 36
- Salathiel 56
- Sally 147
- Samuel 59
- Sophia 67
- Stephen 54
- Suckey 65
- Uriah 36
- Venus 68
- Wallace ..... 120, 121, ... 148
- William 116, 139

A

Abbott
- Mary 66
- Nancy 66

Aby
- Jonas 108

Acres
- James 66
- Mary 66

Adam
- Andrew 12

Adams
- Andrew 3
- David C. 138
- Edward 38
- Elizabeth 114, 119
- James 119
- John 78, 114
- Jos. 119
- Josiah 125
- Nathaniel 37
- Samuel 104
- Thomas 55
- William ... 13, 54, 104

Adison
- Jos. N. 137

Aggleton
- Anne 34
- John 34
- William 34

Aldridge
- James 5, 7

Alexander
- Henry 139
- Mary 70

Alford
- Alcy 19
- Alice 10, 12
- Joseph 12

Alfred

- Hanah 19

Allan
- Perregrin 4
- Tobias 4, 6

Allder
- James 158

Allen
- Joseph 57

Allensworth
- Joseph Henry 137
- Kitty 137

Allison
- Hilleary 120
- Nathaniel ... 119, 120

Amand
- Anthony 58
- Laurence 53

Amos
- Thomas 11

Anders
- Linton 124

Anderson
- Abraham 37, 162
- Andrew 159
- Betty 82
- Eliakim 93
- Eliakim, Jr. 95, 98
- Henry 28, 29
- John 45
- Lydia 82
- Margaret 28
- Mary 27, 31
- Richard 30

Andres
Sanford McNealy 139

Andrews
Sandford McNealy 121

Annason
- Margaret 47
- William 47

Ansley
- Ann 70, 71
- William 14
- William & Ann 54

Armstead
- William 40

Index

Arnet
  Hannah A. ...163
  John ...119
  Mary Ann ...119
  Moses ...118
  Ruth ...9
  Samuel ...9
  Sarah ...9
  Thomas ...9
  Wm. ...119
Arnold
  George ...11
Arnot
  Catharine ...118
  Wm. & Ann ...118
Arnott
  Samuel ...45
Arters
  John ...14
Arwin
  Samuel ...7
Ashbey
  Tince ...139
Ashford
  Michael ...82
Ashton
  Buley ...72
Askin
  John ...69
Askren
  Elizabeth ...14, 18
Athel
  Robert ...155
Atkins
  Sarah ...28
Atwell
  Thompson ...160
Auber
  John ...20
Awbrey
  Samuel ...2
  Thomas ...1, 2, 4
  William ...23
Axline
  David ...72
  Jacob ...90
  John ...21, 75

B

Bagley
  Benjamin ...76, 110
  Catherine ...76
  Maria ...69
Bails
  Abner ...79
  Marey ...78
  Margaret ...86
  Polley ...82
Baily
  Andrew ...28
  Sarah ...28
Baker
  Mary ...59
  William ...13
Baldwin
  Joseph ...155
Bales
  Amar ...139
  Lydia ...154
Ball
  (nameless) ...135
  Eliza ...135
  Elizabeth ...17
  Farlan ...7
  Farling ...16, 25
  Hester ...123
  James ...135
  Jane ...29
  John ...13, 90
  Leah ...74
  Nepolian ...116
  Samuel ...18, 34, ...123, 127
  Stephen ...116
  William ...13, 115
Ballinger
  Charles ...123
  Henson ...123
  William ...123
Banning
  James ...30, 32
Barber
  James ...93
  John ...93, 99
  Mary ...93
  Samuel ...60
Barbour
  James ...102
  Mary Ann ...102
Bare
  Amey ...2
Barker
  Nathaniel ...17
  William ...34, 51
Barkley
  Thomas ...73
Barnes
  Samuel ...133
Barnett
  Jos. ...112
  Joseph ...116
  Mary ...112
Barns
  Samuel ...139
Barr
  Nimrod ...114
Barret
  James Carr ...5
Barrett
  Elizabeth ...7
  James Carr ...3
  John ...64
  John F. ...131
Barrott
  John ...63
Barthart
  Jean ...47
Barthast
  Anna Muriah ...36
Bartholomew
  Hannah ...28
Bartlett
  John ...47
Barton
  Benjamin ...68
  Charles ...162
Bassel
  Felix ...139
Bast
  James ...13
Bateman
  Clemince ...157
Bates
  John ...28
Batson
  James ...19, 61
  John ...101
  Mary ...45
  Rebeckah ...76, 84
  Richard ...45, 84
  Thomas ...61
  William ...157
Battson
  James ...100
Baugh
  Jacob ...63

Apprentices, Poor Children and Bastards 167

Baxter
  Elizabeth 37
  Margaret 37
Bayles
  Daniel 22
  Lydia 154
  Mary 84, 85
  Tamason 85
Bayly
  Mary Cammell 82
  Robert 139, 140
Bayne
  Henry T. 119, 134
Bazill
  Benjamin 60
Beach
  Joel 40
  John W.B............138
Beal
  Ann 156
Beale
  Abner 87
  Amos 70
  Frances 79, 87
  Lydia 154
Beales
  Amos 143
Beall
  Brooke 16
  Tebby 22
  Thomas H...........139
Bealle
  Joseph 89
Beamer
  Ann 62
  Soury 62
Beans
  Absolom 119
  Hannah 153
  Uriah 135
  William 153
Beard
  Joseph 79, 80, 86,
  ....89, 90, 93, 94,
  ....97, 104, 139
  Mary 160
  Nancy 8
  Stephen 139
  William 160
Beasix
  Precilla 145
Beasley
  Polly 153

Beattey
  David 24
Beatty
  Ann 162
  John 71
  Lawson 139
  Robert 90
  William 90
Beatty (Baty)
  David 158
Beaty
  Eliza 139
  Robert 33
Beavers
  John 57, 142,
  ..... 143, 145, 148
  John A. 147
  Robert 154
  Thomas 136
  Washington 144
  William 31, 62, 95
Beck
  Eleanor 121
  William 121
Beeson
  Jacob 2
Beezely
  Elizabeth 66
  Milley 70
Beezer
  John 66
Bell
  John 124
Bellamy
  Robert 63
Bellard
  Elizabeth 158
Bemardorfer
  Peter 106
Benham
  James 32
  Lydia 36
  Nathaniel 32
  Peter 32, 36
Bennett
  Charles, Jr. 55
  Chas. 121
  Edward 40
  Lucey 23
  Sydney/Sydnor ... 121
Bentley
  Banner 42
  John 2

Joseph 74, 88
Berkby
  Thomas 93
Berkely
  Sarah 67
Berkett
  Henry 58, 62
Berkin
  John 40
Berkins
  John 33
Berkley
  William 13
Berkly
  John 45
Berry
  Lewis 159
  William 11
Beshers 77
Best
  Enos 140
  James 47, 72, 84
  James, Jr. 153
  Michael 58
  Thomas 156
  William 74, 155
Betts (Belts)
  Peter 56
Beveridge
  William 78
  Wm. 73
Bidwell
  Jonathan 14
Biggs
  Reuben 14, 16, 20
Bimer
  Ann 53
  George 53
Binks
  James 4
Binns
  Charles 8, 21
  Charles, Jr. ...46, 117,
  158
  John A. 129
  John Alexander.... 57
  Simon A. 65
  Susanna Pearson 65
  Thomas 92
  Thomas N. 83
Binston (Bentson)
  William 51

Index

Birchett
  Hannah ...53
Bird
  Thomas ...23, 25
Birdsall
  Andrew ...104, 105
  Benjamin ...138
Birkby
  Thomas ...108, 128, ...132
Birkitt
  Henry ...58
Biscoe
  Thomas ...81, 86, ...120, 121
Bishop
  Mahlon ...139
Bitzer
  Conrod ...37
Bitzett
  Dublin ...75
Bivite (Bivet)
  Nicolle (Nicholas) ...7
Black
  Elizabeth ...150
  Thomas ...21
Blacknell
  Wm. ...123
Blakeley
  William ...98
Blinco
  James ...61, 62
Blincoe
  Joseph ...37
  Thomas ...21
Blinstone
  John ...47
Blockson
  Thomson ...98
Blockston
  James ...99
Blockstone
  James ...98
Board
  John ...56
Boardley
  Jacob ...57
  Mary ...57
Boardly
  Jacob ...54
  Judah ...53
  Mariah ...139

Mary ...54
Sarah ...54
Bodine
  Henry ...54
  John ...39
Bogar
  Michael ...39
Bogess
  Lydia Jane ...139
Boggess
  Mary Ann ...153
  Nancy ...153
Bogue
  Frances ...119
  Francis ...119
  Francis L. ...128
  John ...88, 91, 119
Boide
  Charity ...39
Bolin
  Catharin ...139
  William ...108
Boling
  Elizabeth ...30
Bollen
  Sarah ...137
Bolton
  Amos ...87
  Eliza ...139
  William ...3
Bond
  Bennett ...107
  Hannah ...86
  Sarah ...154, 155
Bonham
  Amariah ...36
  Samuel ...23
  Sarah ...156
Bontz
  John ...146
Boos
  Adam ...45
Boram
  Aron ...50
Bord
  John ...64
Bordley
  Rachel ...52
Boswell
  George ...132
  Robert ...132
  Walter ...132
  William ...132

Botts
  Moses ...6
Boughman
  Aquilla ...139
Boulton
  Margaret ...33
Bouts
  Mary ...145
Bouzier
  John ...17
  John Ludwick ...17
Bowen
  Elizabeth ...74
  Francis ...73, 74
Bowling
  Joseph ...30
  Thos. ...105
Bowlins
  Ferdinando ...111
  John ...111
Bowman
  Elizabeth ...10
  George Washington ...123
  John ...123
Boyd
  Elizabeth ...24
  James Voloney ...140
  John ...77, 92
  Samuel ...27
  William ...28
Bozzell
  Walter ...89, 132
  William ...132
Brabham
  Rt. ...73
Brackenridge
  Alexander ...126
  Alexander P. ...129
Braden
  Joseph ...52
  Robert ...95
  Rodney C. ...130
Bradfield
  Benjamin ...122, 142
  John ...110
  Samuel ...43
  William ...118, 146
  Wm. ...120
Bradley
  Elizabeth ...163
Bradock
  Francis ...150

Apprentices, Poor Children and Bastards 169

Bradshaw
  Harrison 67
Brady
  Absolem 50
  Henson 140
  James 50, 65
  Jno. 131
  John 73, 99, 117,
    .... 118, 122,
    .... 124, 128
  Marianda (Marinda)
    161
  William 73, 140
  Willis 140
Brandon
  James 105
Brane
  Mary 6
Branham
  William 157
Branian
  Arthur 11
Brashears
  Colmore 96
Brawner
  James W. 133
  Mary 7
  William 30
Brewer
  Henry 2
  William 2
Brian
  Charles & Sarah Ann
    55
Brickell
  Daniel 47
Brickle
  Daniel 57
Bridges
  Dennis 82
  John 82
Bridgewater
  Kesiah 152
Bridgman
  Ann 13, 23, 39
  Elizabeth Chelton
    .... 31, 39
  Peter Pelter 33
Briggs
  Robert 122
Bright
  William 91

Brigland
  James 8
Brisco
  Aquila 102
  Samuel 42
Brohon
  James 27
Brookbank
  Eliza 140
  George 140
  Henry 159
  Josiah 140
Brooke
  Hannah 15
  Rose 46
Brookhead
  Margaret 44
Brooks
  Geo. 134
  James 107
  John 131, 135
  Nancy 156
  Thomas W. 126
  Thos. W. 130
Broomhall
  Enos 160
Broomhill
  Rebekah 72
Broughner (Brawner)
  Frances 155
Brown
  Abraham 70, 114
  Andrew 36, 50
  Asa 114
  Benjamin 13, 31
  Fielding 107, 115
  George 59, 68
  Henry 37
  Isaac 114
  Issachar 140
  Issacher 142
  Jacob 78, 156
  James .. 23, 113, 120
  James, Sr. 64
  John 51, 64, 65,
    .... 98, 116
  John D. 109
  Joseph . 99, 103, 109
  Katherine 151
  Nathan 90
  Richard .. 44, 48, 101
  Robert 82
  Sarah 40
  Thomas 40, 120, 148

William 1, 86, 90,
  ..... 140, 141, 159
  William, Jr. 106
  Wm. 108
Brumback
  Peter 14
  Tapley 140
Bryan
  Daniel 92
  William 55
  Zaphaniah 17
Bryant
  Henry 24
  James 12, 23
  Margaret 158
Buck
  Samuel 105, 109
Buckley
  James 6
  John 48
  Mary 16
  Sarah 67
  William 6, 10, 27
Buffington
  William 70, 158
Burch
  James 67
  Linny 67
Burdine
  Henry 76
Burgoin
  Arnold 140
Burgoyne
  Duanna 78
Burguoin
  Sarah 78
Burguoyne
  Duanna 99
Burks
  Philip 81
Burn
  Elizabeth 56
Burnes
  Frederick 94
  Susanna 44
Burns
  Dennis 21
  Jeremiah 30
  John 15, 18, 151
  Patrick 118
Burns (Byrns)
  Thomas 52
Bursley

Index

Ann 33
Burson
  Benjamin 8
  Cyrus 144
  James 154
  Joseph 141
  Rachael 10
  Thomas 26
Burton
  ___ 32
  Elizabeth 30, 35
Burwell
  Robert 16
Bussell
  John 75
Bussle
  John 75
Butcher
  Martin 162
  Samuel 26
Butler
  Ann 55
  Ann Matilda 140
  Geo. 130
  Jacob & Sarah 84
  James 14, 29, 130
  Malinda 162
  Matilda 117
  Ruth 140
  Sarah 55
  William 84
  Wm. 126
Byrd
  Lina 16
  Thomas 13
Byrne
  Jeremiah 157
Byrne (Byrns)
  Susanna 52
Byrns
  Thomas 27, 38

C

Cadwallader
  Rees 11
Cafferty
  Nancy 42
Cagier
  Catharine 43
  Rachell 43
Cahill
  John 24

Caldwell
  Moses 37
Caler
  Nancy Anna 119
Callihan
  Catherine 67
  Edward 17
Calor
  Andrew 35
  Jacob 77
Cambel
  Jane 84
Camel
  Jane 110
  Robert 86, 110
Camell
  James 71
Cameron
  Thomas 46
Cammell
  Alexander 51
  Elizabeth 51
  George 51
  John 66, 84
Camp
  Reuben 42, 47
Campbell
  Addison 131
  Aeneas 2
  Andrew 118
  Elizabeth 54
  Hannah 153
  Henry 127
  James 71, 73
  James M. 129
  Jane 68, 118
  John 88, 140,
  .... 153, 156
  Joseph 127, 131
  Polly 81
  Robert 85, 86, 143
  Wm. 118
Camron
  Thomas 143
Canary
  Benjamin 33
  James 62
  Nancy 33
  Richard 33
Canby
  Benjamin H. .. 72, 155
  Samuel ... 16, 20, 23,
  .... 24, 36, 44

Cann
  William 72
Canter
  Ada 58
  Betsey 58
Carley
  John 14
Carlile
  Frances 162
  Robert 162
Carmichael
  Daniel 96
  Douglas 96
  Mary 96
Carn
  Henry 96
Carnell
  John 64
Carnes
  Jacob 74, 90
  John 88, 89
  Sarah 88, 96
Carney
  John 111
Carnickle
  John 51
Carns
  Henry 96
  Sarah 89
Caroles
  Joseph 160
Carr
  Elizabeth 73
  Isaaiah 73
  Izack 73
  John 4, 101
  John, Jr. 21
  Mary 101
  Peter 79, 82, 86
  Thomas 8
  William 58, 60,
  .... 144, 145
Carrigan
  Margaret 10
Carrol
  Dempsey 17
Carroll
  Dempsey 36
Carson
  Isabella 13
Carter
  Edmund 158
  Elam 79

Apprentices, Poor Children and Bastards 171

Eli 63
Hannah..............79
Jane 8
Jesse...............19
Jonathan 107
Phebe..............163
Richard.............29
Samuel.............163
William 60, 141
Cartright
 Elizabeth 54
Cartwright
 Betty...............71
 Elizabeth 70
 Fenton Lewis......140
Carty
 Madison M.........125
Caruthers
 John 1
Casey
 Susanna...........157
Caslo
 Jane 84
Cassell
 George 41
Cassey
 S. 112
Caster
 James 59
 Mary...............59
Castor
 James 140
 Mary.............34, 95
 Richard.............95
 Vincent.............34
 William 52
Catlett
 Jemima 71
 Lydia 71
Cavan
 James 90
 Michael..........90, 93
 Patrick 46, 50
Cavens
 John 6
 Joseph 52
 William 29
Cavins
 Edward 27, 34
 John 34
Chamblin
 Albert G. 131
 Jas. 121

John 154
William 153, 155
Chambling
 Wm. 121
Champ
 John, Jr. 5
Chapilier
 Levi 108
Chapman
 Eleanor 61
 Thomas......... 17, 68
Chappalear
 Wm. 109
Chappelier
 Elias.................54
 Zacheriah............54
Chelton
 Elizabeth 151
Cherry
 Richard 89
Chichester
 Thornton 161
Chick
 Elisha 111
 William A. 163
Childs
 Eleanor 10
 John.................10
Chilton
 Catherine 140
 George................2
Chriesman
 Elizabeth 64
Chrisman
 Elizabeth 64
Chun
 Mary.................39
Chunn
 Samuel 39
Church
 Jonathan 27
Claig
 Polly................151
Clandening
 Samuel 45
Clapham
 Josias .. 3, 31, 57, 69
 Samuel & Eliza.....83
Clark
 Alice................43
 Ann 17
 Elizabeth 42

George........ 24, 30
James Marks 17
Thomas 17
Clarke
 Albert G.C. 130
 George 138
 John F. 130
 Susan.............. 138
 Wm. F................ 128
Clasby
 Armistead 140
Clayton
 Stephen............. 98
Clearke
 Addison Harding .. 87
Clements
 Peter S. 137
Clemmons
 George H. 54
Clemons
 Sandford........... 158
Clency
 Daniel................. 12
Clendenning
 William................ 92
Clendinon
 William................ 97
Clifford
 Obadiah............ 106
 Thomas Obadiah 106
Cline
 William................ 12
Clinedienst
 John 144
Clinton
 George 19, 140
Clowes
 Joseph............. 140
Coates
 Elizabeth 85
 John 85
Coats
 John 5
 Thomas 81
Cochran
 James............... 109
Cocke
 William................ 23
Cockerill
 Daniel 108
 Elias 26
 Joseph.........71, 116
 Mahlon 68, 140

Index

Sarah 109
William 153
Cockerille
  Mary Ann 109
Cocklin
  Thomas 137
Cockrane
  James 71, 76
  Nathan 39
Cockreal
  Sebithery 37
Cockrell
  Daniel 147
  Elias 92
Cockrill
  Daniel 92, 146
  Elizabeth 44
  Jean 92
  John 37
  Thomas, Jr. 151
Coffey
  John 15, 38
Cohagen
  William 162
Cohorne
  James 31
  Robert 31
Cokely
  Elijah 49
Colclough
  Robert 47
Cole
  John 160
  Mary E. 158
Coleman
  Eleanor 17
  James 22, 33
  John 141
  Peter 37, 70
  Peter & Hagar 46
  Richard 46
Collens
  Thomas 29
Collier
  Francis 78
Collings
  John 86
Collins
  Ann 27
  Elizabeth 81
  John 29, 86
  Joseph 9, 29
  Patrick 10

Thomas 47, 67,
  .... 86, 102
William 27, 56
Colquhoon
  John Nisbet 9
Colsen
  Rawleigh 22
Colson
  Rawleigh 22
Combs
  Alex 111
  Joseph 72, 80, 84
  Mahlon ... 49, 83, 152
  Robert 155
  Samuel 2, 3, 5
Compher
  Peter 144
Compton
  Ezekiel 49, 56
  Mary 33
  Nancy 42
Connard
  Anthony 61
  Jonathan 15, 47
Connell
  Darby 18
  Jeremiah 10
  Jesse 10
  John 10
  Thomas 4
  Zachariah 10
Connelly
  John 60
  Peggy 66
Conner
  Ann 121
  Bridget 29, 33
  David 133
  Mary 5
  Michael 21
  Reuben 91
  Richard 76, 87,
  .... 141, 143
  William 123, 141
Connolly
  Thomas C. 137
Connor
  Bridget 28
  David 126
  Samuel 107
Coock
  Ann 153
  Jonathan 153

Cook
  Chloe 44
  John 40
  William 19
  Wm. 105
Cooke
  Stephen 91
Coombs
  Richard 8
  Samuel 10
Cooney
  James 64
Coonts
  Nicholas 43
Cooper
  John 141, 161
  Philip 95
  Robert 154
Cootes
  Eliza 91
Copeland
  David .. 105, 110, 145
  Deborah 155
  Jane 117
  Jno. 112
  Susan 117
  Wm. 117
Copper
  Thomas 26
Coprey
  John 35
Cordall
  Jacob 56
Cordell
  Collin 120
  Martha 133
  Martin 133
  Martin & Martha .. 111
  Pressley 89
  Wm. Martin 133
Cornwell
  Ann 150
  Louisa 99
Correll
  Abraham 120
Corry
  John 53
Coss
  Jacob 80
Cost
  Jonathan 141
Costelo
  Elizabeth 83

Apprentices, Poor Children and Bastards

Costillo
  Sarah 152
Costlo
  Crs. 83
  Jane 84
Cotteril
  Linney 34
Counse
  Adam 41
Coutsman
  Jacob 46
Cowgill
  Isaac 141
  Mariah 141
  Sarah 157
Cox
  Joseph 33
  Samuel 27, 28,
  .... 32, 130
  Stephen 6
  Thomas 130
Crady
  John 19
Crage
  Anne 73
Craig
  Jane 74, 81
  Rebecca 4
Craine
  Henry 88
Cramer
  Elizabeth 35
Crane
  Henry 82
Crauford
  Peter 18
Craven
  Abner 73
  Giles 63
  James 85
  Josiah 92
  Mahlon 156
  William H. 85
Crawford
  George 141
  William 2, 5
Creagor
  George 127
Creamer
  Bernard 33
  Catharine 155

Creamour
  Elizabeth 95
  Jacob 35
  Thomas 35
Crider
  David 53
  Frederick 114
  William 119
  Wm. 114
Crider (Cridler)
  Catherine 160
Crim
  Jacob 136
  John 140
Cromly
  Elizabeth 80
Crook
  Chloe 44
  Samuel 142
  Sarah 44
Cross
  Betty 85
  Catharine 140
  Eli 141
  Elijah 38
  James 27
  John 29
  Joseph 38
  Joseph & Maryan . 64
  Mary 141
  Nancy 64, 159
  Sarah 64, 141
  Violet 125
  Wesley 125
  William 67, 141
Crouse
  John W. 121
Crowse
  John W. 123
Crozier
  Lydia 88, 90
  Sarah 88
Crumbaker
  Jacob 94
Crupper
  John 18, 126
Cuisar
  Cassandra 83
  Jacintha 83
Cummin
  William 100
Cummings
  Geo. 108

Gideon 69, 71
Harrison 108
James 154
Jane 20
Robert 158
Sarah 154
William 158
Cummins
  Bridget 7
  Charles 141
  Joseph 100
  William 7
Cunnard
  Jonathan 161
Curans
  Sarah 100
Curran
  Stephen 100
Currey
  Terence 9
Cusine
  Catharin 67

D

Dade
  Francis 9
Dagg
  Robert 51
Dailey
  John W. 137
Dale
  Thomas 11
Dalihan
  Mary 46
Dalihon (Dillahon)
  Letty 46
Dalkin
  Catherine 34
  John 34
Damewood
  Jacob 69
Daniel
  Benjamin 141
  James M. 121
  Samuel & Sarah .. 97
  Stephen 101
  William 64
  William, Jr. 118
Danniel
  Samuel 97

Index

Darnal
  Christopher 63
Darr
  Eliza 57
  Hannah 154
  John 57
  Sally 57
Davidson
  John 124
  Mary Catharine ... 124
  William 61, 124
Davis
  Asaph 76
  Benjamin 14, 58
  Casander 58
  Catharine ... 109, 114
  Catherine 111
  Daniel 2
  David 2
  Elizabeth 3
  Francis 51
  Hannah 32
  Harriet 141
  Henry 44, 111
  John 3, 42, 55,
  .... 62, 66, 72
  John W. 144
  Jonathan 14, 31
  Joseph L. 131
  Martha (Patty) 48
  Nancy 141, 154
  Peyton H. 132
  Richard 58, 154
  Saml 74
  Samuel106, 111, 114
  Sanford 141
  Thomas 75
  Walter 48
  William 55, 56, 58,
  .... 109, 157
Dawes
  Benj. 122
  Benjamin 122
  Edward 156
  Henry 114
  Mary 163
  Sarah 163
Dawlin
  Thomas 120
Daws
  Henry . 112, 113, 141
Day
  George 127

Dayley
  John 88
Dean
  Ignatius 114
Deane
  Robert 31
Debell
  John 152
Decker
  John Lawson 82
  Mary 82
  William 82
Dehaven
  Jacob 30
  Jesse 44
Demsey
  Edward 49
Denty
  Susanna 131
Derrey
  Ann 71
Derry
  Sarah 163
Dial
  Nancy 51
Diall
  Elizabeth 51
Dickey
  James 22
Dicks
  John 51
Dickson
  William 7, 10
Dillon
  Ezar 79
  James 39, 54
  Josiah 53, 54
  Samuel 53
Divers
  John 62
Divine
  Aaron 88, 130
  Catherine 95
  Sarah 50
  Uphama 50
  William W. 130
Dixson
  Samuel 141
Dobbins
  Eleanor 98
  James 98
  John 97, 104

Dodd
  Jesse 74
  John, Jr. 70
  Lydia 149, 150
  William 1, 95
  Wm. 105
Dodson
  Mary 31
  Thomas, Jr. 31
Donaldson
  Bayly 63
  James 25, 32
  John 25
  Stehen, Jr. 94
  Stephen 24, 25,
  .... 32, 33, 37
  Stephen, Jr. 93
Donham
  Amos 29, 69, 74
Doniphan (Donivan)
  Richard 50
Donohoe
  John 64
  Samuel 59
  Stephen J. 130
Dood
  William 81
Dorning
  Andrew 60
  Mary 60
Dornon
  Andrew 141
Dorrell
  George W. 137
Dorsey
  Edward . 91, 107, 141
Dorst
  John 53
Dougan
  Robert 113
Dougherty
  Mary 28
  Thomas 28
Doughty
  Thomas 14, 18
Douglas
  Hugh 85, 86
  Joseph 83, 94
  Robert Harrison 92
Douglass
  Hugh 51
  William 6, 17

Apprentices, Poor Children and Bastards 175

Douling
James 20
Dove
William 78
Dow
Peter 47, 48
Dowdell
James 128
John 128
Moses 142
Dowling
Thomas 87
Downer
Henry 28
Downs
Benjamin 28
Henry 38
Henry B. 101
John 158
Margaret 97
Nancy 100
Walter 100
William 100
Drake
James 34
Thomas 42
Thomas, Jr. 139, 154
Dreane
John 44
Drish
Charles 36
John ... 37, 63, 69, 76
William 34
Drumgold
Alexander 28
Dulaney
John 119
Dulap
Barbary 12
Dulin
John 74
Duncan
Rachel 149
Duncomb
Henry 21
Dunham
Amos 17
Hamton 141
John 52
Dunkin
Henry 157
Samuel 103

Dunlap
Ellis (Alice) 152
Zeebar 73
Dunlop
John 50
Tacy 78
Dunn
George 94
Dunsmore
Mary 72
Duty
Hiram 111
Simpson 66
Duval
Alexander 129
Harriet 129
Duvall
Aaron 125
Amon 141
Benjamin 125
Dyall
Edward 27
Leonard 4
Dyer
Ruth 154
Dyers
Joseph 35

E

Eades
John 52
Earnest
George 156, 162
Susannah 162
Earnist
George 163
Susanan 163
Earp
Verlinda 110
Washington 110
Eaton
Henry 21
Isaac 7
James 70, 84
Rebeckah 65
Shepherd 84
Eblin
Elizabeth 52
Isaac 56
John 9
Peter .. 12, 35, 42, 52

Eckart
Casper & Nancy .. 93
Eckhart
Casper 67
Eckman
Jacob 130
Edding
John 98
Eddings
John 48
Edgsworth
Jane 16
Edi
Thomas 61
Edmonds
John 60
Sandford 108
Edmondson
Leatha 160
Edward
David 5
Edwards
Arthur 21
Benjamin 6
Edward R. 131
Elizabeth 19
Elizha 58
Jacob 92
John 22
Joseph 89
Samuel 163
Thomas 47
Edwins
John 41
Eflin (Eveland)
David 157
Egleton
John 17
Eidson
Jos. 119
Joseph 94, 119
Elgin
Gustavus 42
Ignatius 159
Wm. 128
Elias
John 40
Elijah
James 124
Elliot
John 142
William 69, 105

Index

Elliott
  Hanson 133
  Henson 156
  James 75
  John 133
  William 34, 35
Ellis
  Elias 19
  John 40
  Joseph 103
  Lewis 103
  Samuel 103
Ellzey
  John 45
  Lewis 102
Emerson
  R.D. 127
  Richard D. 127
English
  David 83
  Mary 149
  Sarah 55
  Susana 55
  Winifred 4
Ennes
  Sarah 36
Ennis
  Margaret 152
  William 38
Enzer
  John 113
Erskins
  John 75
Erton
  Elijah 142
Ervin
  Samuel 44
Erwin
  Francis 19, 20
Eskridge
  Charles 18, 25, 27
  Selina 107
Essex
  Elizabeth 36, 48
Ethell
  John 1
Evans
  Alexander 38
  Asahel 118
  David 49
  Eliezer 41
  Henry 114
  John ... 9, 11, 41, 101

John Bennett 118
Joshua 13, 15,
        .... 17, 18
Mary ...25, 27, 28, 44
Samuel 37, 51
Thomas 74, 126
Thos. 124
William 29, 46
Eveland
  Joab 162
Evens
  Even 136
Everhart
  Martha 161
Everheart
  Abraham 135
  Jacob 107
  Joseph 137
  Michael 82, 86
  Philip 72
Ewers
  John 87
  Jonathan 21, 63
  Jonathan, Jr. 71
  Thomas ... 68, 81, 94

F

Fackler
  Elizabeth 111, 112
  Franklin John 112
  Michael Wm. 111
Fadely
  Chs. F. 136
  Jacob 132
Fadly
  Jacob 82
Fagan
  Nancy 101
  Sarah 101
Fairhurst
  George 40, 95
Ferguson
  Malinda 142
Farmer
  George 142
Farnsworth
  Daniel 71
  David 86
  Hannah 71
  Henry 12
Farrel
  William 40

Farris
  Samuel 99
Feagins
  Mary 97
Feare
  Ann 151
Featherstone
  Thomas 27
Fegg
  Joseph 44
Fegins
  Daniel 17
Fenton
  Charles 133
Ferguson
  Abner 49
  Ann 50
  Elijah 53
  Henry 8
  James 79
  Marey 79
  Mary 73
  Samuel ... 43, 46, 154
Fergusson
  Elijah 66
  Elisha 73
  William 64
Ferril
  Sanford 142
Ferris
  Jonathan 102
Ficklin
  William 18
Fiddes
  Christopher 11
Fielder
  William 4
Fields
  Jemima 42
  Jemimah 55
  John 162
  Thomas 1, 3, 13,
        .... 20, 30
Figh
  Lewis 113
Filler
  Fred 106
Filpott
  John 74
Finass
  Sarah 6
Finican
  Elizabeth 150

Apprentices, Poor Children and Bastards 177

Fishback
  James N. 71, 75
Fisher
  Christopher..........20
  Dawson 87
  Stephen................25
  William Hampton ..25
Fitch
  Adolphus Descletian
 136
Fitzgerald
  Rachel..................75
Fitzsimmons
  James 153
  Samuel.................91
Fleetwood
  Isaac 20, 23
Fleming
  Archibald, Sr........82
  William 3
Fletcher
  Christopher..........19
  John.....................93
Fling
  Owen....................63
  Richard.................55
Flood
  Thomas................62
Floyd
  Sinah....................11
Foley
  Andrew...............119
Follin
  Bathsheba...........77
  Thomas................78
Forbes
  John...................154
Forgison
  Abigail 152
  Malinda...............142
  Samuel.................43
Forler
  Nathaniel..............45
Forrest
  Thomas..............136
Fortney
  George 87, 91,
  .... 128, 130
  John...................128
Foster
  Edmond................90
  Willis....................90

Fouch
  Isaac.....................9
  Jacob...................91
  John...................128
  Thomas................65
Fouche
  Daniel 138
Fox
  Ann......................31
  Bartleson.............60
  Charles..............111
  Daniel 101
  Elizabeth Betsey 153
  Ezra 140
  Gabriel.................10
  Gracy.........111, 160
  James......31, 45, 77
  Jesse 153
  Joseph B............128
  Malinda..............161
  Melinda..............160
  William 27, 52
  William, Jr. 19
Fraizor
  William 142
France
  Bennet 142
  Elizabeth....158, 159
  Fanny.................142
  Sinthy.................142
Francis
  Enoch 62, 73, 78,
  ....93, 94
  Mary...................142
  Pressly................142
  Richard 142
  Thomas....11, 61,65,
  ....68, 72, 78,
  .... 106, 107, 133,
  .... 139, 143
Franks
  Henry 3
  Mary...................149
Frazier
  Thomas..............123
Fred
  Joseph, Jr. & Hannah
 146
  Thomas..............134
Fredd
  Joseph 58, 114
Freeland
  James 4

Freeman
  Richard......... 80, 81
French
  James D. 141
  Wm. H. 133
Frits
  Any A................ 137
Fros
  Mary Ann............ 84
Frost
  Martha............... 142
  Marthew............. 79
  Matty 84
Fry
  Catharine............ 37
  John 147
  Mary 37
  Peter................. 160
Fry (Frye)
  Susannah 156
Frye
  Jacob............ 67, 70
  John 81
  Philip 39
  William............... 162
  Wm.................... 112
Fryer
  George 60, 63
  James................... 9
  Jeremiah 6
  Jesse............ 60, 63
  John 1
  Robert 9, 10, 26
  William................... 1
Fryrear
  Aaron................. 31
  Francis 32
  Jeremiah 32
Fulton
  David 55, 59, 106,
  ....119, 121,
  ....123, 125
  John 126
  Rachel.............. 142
  Robert 73, 82
  Susanna 142
  William............... 162
Fultz
  Nancy 162
Furguson
  Nancy 156

Index

Furr
Enoch 152
Jeremiah C. 162
Newton 159
Fye
John 110
William Henry 110

G

Gale
Henry 132
Gallagher
Caleb 101
Gallahar
Caleb 103
Gallaher
Turner H. 163
Galleher
David 105
William 147
William & Margery
.... 147
Galliher
John 127
William 127
Galt
William 90
Gant
Amelia 137
Charles 138, 142
Joanna 129
Robert 138
Wilson 137
Gardener
Joseph 96
Gardner
___ 89
Josep, Jr. 23
Robert 103
Garner
Henry 108
James 92
John 63, 66
Joseph 59
Robert 103
Samuel 23
Garrett
Nicholas 88
Silas 122
Garrison
James 116, 117, 132

Gaskins
Betsey 143
James 143
Nelly 143
Geeasling
Anderson 101
Geen
James 118
George
John 14, 80, 81
John, Jr. 94
German
Eleanor 110
George 110
John 110
Peter 110
Sarah 110
Gheen
Jas. 118
Wm. 118
Gibbs
Joseph 60
Margaret 3
William 60
Gibson
Aaron 12
Amos 103, 111
David 99
Esther 82
George 155
Isaac 15, 64
James 12
John 1, 20
Levi 96
Matilda 163
Thomas 9, 26, 44,
.... 66, 67
William 137
Gideon
Lewis 162, 163
Gilbert
Jefferson 138
Margaret 138
Wm. 137
Gilder
Benjamin 109
Giles
John 86
Ludwell 86, 92
Gill
Daniel 119
Uriah 119
Vincent 82, 98

Gilmore
James 120
Gilpin
Samuel 120, 124
Gist
John 3, 4
Thomas 44
Gladdell
Thomas 92
Gladhill
Mary 72
Thomas 92
William 72
Glasgow
Catharine 120
George 116
Henry . 103, 106, 163
Henry & Catharine
.... 116
Wm. 120
Glassgow
Henry 92, 98
Gleeson
Edward 76
Glibbing
Ann 29
Glibrey
Ann 45
Elizabeth 45
Goddard
John 5
Goens
Catharine 140
Goff
Adam 120, 121,
..... 122, 124, 143
Elleanor S. 120
Ellen 122
George 124
George L. 120
Hannah 121
Hannah Binns 120
Margaret 122
Margaret Douglas
.... 143
Nancy 122
Gohagan
Ann 29
Gohogin
Mary 17
Rose 17
Goines
George 148

Apprentices, Poor Children and Bastards 179

Going
  Elihu 59, 143
  Elihue 80
  Joseph 16
  Leitha 59
  Levi 59
  Luke 59, 70
  Mary 59
  Samuel 57
  Thomas 59
  Zacheriah 54
Going: 66
Goings
  Lewis 133
  Luke 130
  Mary 133
  Patrick 143
  Polly 105, 109
  Thomas 88, 93
Golding
  John 38
Gooden
  David 74, 75
Goodhart
  John 81
Goodheart
  Henry 86
  Jacob 78
Goodwin
  William 23, 91,
   .... 96, 99
  Wm. 98
Goram
  John 7
Gorden
  Charles 104
Gordon
  Silas 122
Gore
  Jonas 49
  Joseph, Jr. 139
  Lewis 162, 163
  Thomas 2, 4
  Truman 112
Gorham
  Ann 16
  Mary 18
Goughner
  Jacob 117
Gover
  Ann 159
  Jesse 107, 111
  Robert 109, 129

Robert H. 141
Governeur
  Samuel L. 135
Gowen
  Madison 138
  Martha Ann 138
Gowing (Going)
  Zachariah 52
Graham
  Andrew 145
  Peter 26
  Robert 65
  Samuel 37, 44
Granger
  Sarah 29
Graves
  Joshua 104
  Lott 113
  Mary Ann 52
Gray
  Abraham 24
  John 8, 23
  Ralph 83, 85
Grayson
  Amy 143
  Dennis 143
  Jesse 135
  Willis 143
Green
  Catharine 157
  Elias M. 133
  Elias Mason 129
  Elizabeth 48
  Euphamy 162
  Harrison 129
  Henry George 3
  John 65, 102,
   .... 129, 133
  Joseph 1
  Mary 1, 129
  Mary Ann 23, 25
  Nelly 44
  Nelson 148
  Richard 79
  Wm. 105
Greenlease
  James 91
Greenlees
  James 47
Gregg
  Aaron 51
  Caleb 76
  Joseph 86
  Joshua 80, 91, 95

Joshua & Lydia .. 142
Reasin 112
Richard 26
Samuel 49, 53,
   .... 54, 56
Samuel, Jr. 70
Samuel, Sr. 83
Thomas 66
William .. 84, 107, 108
William & Rebeckah
   107
William & Rebekah,
   his wife 55
Gregory
  Henry 9
  John 143
Griffin
  Ann 150
Griffith
  John 157
  Philip 163
  Thomas William . 135
  William 83
Grigsby
  Nathaniel 9, 29
Grim
  John 14
Grimes
  Ann 11
  Elizabeth 11
  George 41
  Isaac 100
  Nathaniel 51
  Nicholas 86
  Nicholas, Jr. 63
  Susanna 3
Grimsley
  Jemimah 40
  Sally 40
Grooms
  Mary 95
Grubb
  Adam 107
  John 88, 93, 146
  Joseph 104
  Susannah 89
Grymes
  Daniel 34
  Nathaniel 34
Guider
  Charles & Kate
   .... 129, 133
  Eli 143
  John 129, 133

Index

Richard 136
Sarah 129
Gullat
  Charles 83
Gullatt
  Charles .. 87, 91, 112
Gunn
  James 76
  John 63
Gunnell
  John 45, 51
  William, Jr. 11
Guy
  Samuel 22, 77, 78
  William 90

H

Hachet
  Ann 83
  Thomas 83
Hacket
  Ann 83
  Thomas 83
Hackett
  Ann 90
  Ann (Nancy) 75
  Nancy 75
  Thomas 75
Hagarman
  James 76
Hagerly
  George 32
Hagerman
  Benj. 108
  Benjamin 112
  Leven 112
Hague
  Amelia 162
  Amos 18
  Elizabeth 162
  Francis 11, 18, 45
  Hannah 54
  James 39
  Jonah 62, 157
  Samuel 32
  Sarah 39
  Thomas 18, 34
Haines
  Edward 139, 148
  Joseph 123
  Mandly M. 123
  Sarah 159

Stacey 123
Hains
  Armstead Thompson
    Mason 128
  Charles Fenton .. 128
  Edward W. 123
  Joseph & Mary ... 128
  Simeon 40, 100
Halbert
  James 69
  Martha 151
  Michael 69
  Sarah 154
  Thomas 69
  William 69
Hale
  James 8
Hall
  Eliza 136
  George 19
  Jesse 4, 9
  John 4
  Jonathan 3
  Letitia 136, 138
  Rachel 11, 150
  Thomas 75
  William 17, 85
Halsey
  Asa 102
Hambleton
  Mahala 106
Hamerly
  Jno. 128
  John 129
  Mandly 128
Hamilton
  Alexander 126
  Elizabeth 126
  Henry 126
  James .2, 5, 9, 13, 40
  Jeremiah 53
  John 126
  Presley 126, 127
  Providence 161
  Robert 15
  Ruth 163
  Samuel G. 121
  Washington 126
  William 58, 59
Hammat
  Edward 130
  George 105
Hammerley
  John 84

Hammerly
  Jno. 110
  Mandly 137
  Wm. 105
Hammett
  George ... 30, 38, 109
  Samuel 122
Hammontree
  Samuel 120
  William W. 122
  Wm. 124
Hampton
  Jeremiah 86, 147
Hanby
  John 42
  Wm. J. 121
Hancher
  James W. 141
Hanes
  Edward 136
  Joseph 158
Hanks
  John 25
Hannah
  Robert 48
  William 123
  Wm. 123
Hanrick
  Samuel 30
Hany
  Ann 52
Harbert
  Thomas 29
Harbout
  Peter 24
Hardin
  Catharine 31
  Thomas 31
Harding
  James 69
Hardy
  George 154
  John 113, 115
  Joshua 101, 109
  Thos. 100
Harle
  Jemima 150
Harley
  Silvester 8
Harman
  Peter 14, 58
Harmon
  Peter 32, 34

Apprentices, Poor Children and Bastards 181

Harned
  Kerzia 113
  Moses 117
  Nathaniel 113,
  .... 115, 117
  William 115
Harper
  Anna Muriah 36
  John 157
  Polly 157
  Samuel 83, 92
  William 81
Harris
  Ann 10, 18
  Eliza 132
  Isaac 73, 74, 95,
  ..... 107, 112, 141
  Jacob 10
  Jesse 10
  Jno. 123
  John 14, 25, 43,
  .... 84, 112, 122
  Mary 14
  Middleton 76, 93
  Obed 1
  Richard 36
  Ruth Young 18
  Samuel 9, 73
  Sarah 25
  William 9, 21, 26
Harrison
  Addison 86, 89
  Alexander 55
  John Peyton 8
Harriss
  Ann 20
  Jacob 20
Harrop
  James 40
Harrover
  Cassandra 127
  George 127
  Thomas & Sinah .127
Hart
  Ellender 103
  Jonathan 157
  Thomas 152
  Wm. 107
Harvey
  Amos 106, 107
  Amos & Elizabeth
  142
  Nathan 62
  Rebecca 161

Samuel 62
Harvin
  Rebecca 161
Hassett
  Thomas 92
Hatch
  Daniel 7, 16
Hatcher
  Catherine 141
  James 80, 139
  John 147
  Thomas 68, 139
  William 2, 17, 57
  William & Mary 57
Hatchett
  Thomas 95
Havenner
  John 82
Haverlin
  Hannah 106
  Rebecca 101
Hawkings
  Rebekah 65
Hawkins
  John 70, 152
  Joseph 61, 72
  Samuel 63
  Sarah 65
Haynes
  John 26
  Sally 159
Hays
  Ann 149, 150
  John Winn 4
  Leven Powell 9
Hazell
  Elisha 26
Head
  Geo. 128
  George 105, 127
  George, Jr. 103
  John 71
Headon
  George 11
  George, Sr. 14, 15
  Richard 22
  Samuel 11
  William 22
Hear
  David 157
Heart
  Ellis 152

Heath
  Jeremiah 24
Heaton
  Joseph 77
Heator
  John 52
Heblin
  Ann 112
  Eliza 112
  Rebecca 112
Heffner
  Frederick 158
Hefner
  Jacob 15
Helpon
  John 120
  Michael 120
Hemmery
  Christian 35
Henard
  Robert 29
Hencher
  J.S. 112
Henderson
  Andrew 153
  Catharine 152
  Elizabeth 36, 90
  James 4
  Jemima 82
  Richard H. .. 105, 140
  Samuel 53
  Thomas 33
  Westley 90
Henry
  George W. 96
  James 101
  John 122
  John, Jr. 29, 32
  John, Sr. 32
  Stephen 122
  William 113
Hepburn
  Martha 156
Hepburne
  Delilah 66
Herbert
  Ellender 52
  Josiah 47, 57
  Thomas 16
Herle
  Ruth 150
Herrill
  Phebe 162

Index

Herryford
  John ... 18
Hervey
  David ... 95
  Henry ... 95
  Jacob ... 95
  Viney ... 95
  William ... 95
Hesse
  Martha ... 152
  Polly ... 65
Hesser
  Peter ... 57
Hetherlin
  Benjamin ... 35
  Hewin ... 35
  James ... 35
  John ... 35
  Nathan ... 35
Hevelin
  Ann ... 112
  Eliza ... 112
  Rebecca ... 112
Hewlett
  John ... 153
Hibbs
  Amos ... 31
Hickman
  Conrade ... 47
  Nancy ... 155
Hicks
  Eliakim ... 95, 98
  Israel ... 81, 85
  Kezia ... 151
  Levi ... 103
  Moses ... 95
Hide
  Elizabeth ... 83
Higby
  James ... 124
Hildrop
  John ... 19
Hill
  Ann ... 12
  Catherine ... 12
  Costolon Dorson .. 77
  George Dorson ... 77
  Roseanna ... 77
  Sally ... 21
  Samuel ... 12
Hilliard
  John ... 58
  Joseph ... 105, 116

Hinds
  David ... 19
  Edward ... 58
Hines
  Daniel ... 114
  John ... 114
Hinksman
  Samuel ... 76
Hinton
  Robert ... 128
Hirkly
  Peter ... 46
Hirst
  Jesse ... 90
  John ... 40, 41
  Martha ... 40, 41
  Mary ... 41
  Nancy ... 41
  Richard ... 41
  Sarah ... 41
Hix
  Levi ... 111
Hixon
  Reuben ... 72
  Timothy ... 56, 92
Hockley
  John ... 44, 48
  Peter ... 46
Hoff
  Theophilus ... 155
Hoge
  Miller ... 32
  Morgan ... 32, 35
  Solomon ... 80
  William ... 5, 6, 32, 35
Hogland
  Phillip ... 23
Hogue
  Isaac ... 134
  Joseph ... 32, 37, 70
  Miller ... 26
Holaday
  Isabella ... 136
Holding
  John ... 67, 144
Holdren
  Patk ... 25
Hole
  Abalino ... 124
  Miriam ... 100, 162
  Washington ... 125
Holiday
  Harvey ... 143

Holifield
  Voluntine ... 6
Holladay
  Mahala ... 138
  Thomas ... 137
Hollam
  Samuel ... 76
Holland
  Elonder ... 34
  John ... 34
Hollem
  Benjamin ... 154
Holliday
  Dardana ... 138
  Sally ... 160
  Sarah ... 159
  Virginia ... 134
  William ... 39
Hollum
  Samuel ... 51
Holmes
  Henry ... 132
  Jacob ... 132
  John ... 161
  Joseph ... 77
  Joseph D. ... 132
  Martha ... 89
  Sarah ... 37
  William Barnes ... 89
Holtsclaw
  Elizabeth ... 153
Holyday
  Ann ... 39
Homan
  Joseph ... 15
  Samuel ... 15
Hood
  Linny ... 97
  Sarah ... 97
Hook
  Elizabeth ... 99
  Isaac ... 99, 106
  Keziah ... 102
  Martha ... 99, 106
  William ... 124
Hooke
  Isaac ... 107
Hope
  Christian ... 78, 79, ... 91, 93
  Christopher ... 87
  Hannah ... 87
  Henry ... 91, 93

James T. 160	Howard	Humfrey
Hopewell	Amanda 134	Isaac............. 60, 62
Dennis................33	Caty....................47	Humphrey
Mary....................23	Charles 47	Abner.............. 40
Samuel.........21, 23	Laban................108	Charles............... 80
Hopkins	Michael...............47	Isaac............. 45, 68
Billy 75	Howdershell	John 102
Minty 75	Jacob 46	John G............. 103
Horn	Howell	Thomas 10, 76
Mary 13, 28	Armstead 143	Thomas G......... 143
Horns	Hannah 58, 152	Thomas M. .139, 147
Mary....................22	Henry 156	Humphreys
Horton	John..............67, 73	Thomas 53
William 50	Levin 109	Humphries
Hough	Mahlon 66	Thomas, Jr. 49
Amasa........115, 142	Mary..................157	Hunt
Barnard 27	Phebe 155	Alexander 74
Dr. Isaac..............99	Polly...................65	Elizabeth 78
Garrat................159	Rebekah 66	Hannah................ 66
Isaac 130	Sarah 58	James.................. 78
Jane 144	Howser	John 156
John 6, 14, 20,	William 89	Joseph......82, 88, 89
..........38, 39, 52,	Huddlestone	Lewis 66, 89
..........56,77, 100	Nathan 43	Martha 74
John, Jr. 21, 27	Hudson	Mary 156
Joseph 119	David 2	William..........66, 116
Mahlon ...46, 69, 140	Huet	..............159, 163
Mary A................134	Rachel 65, 68	Winifred 75
Moses 38, 54, 56	Sally....................78	Hunter
Peyton...............106	Huff	Elizabeth 30
R.R......................114	George................87	John 22
Robt. R..............109	Huffman	Joseph................. 30
Samuel....41, 46, 48,	Catharine 159	William........... 76, 97
.69, 96, 121, 122	Charles 59	Hurdle
Samuel..............121	Huffty	John 143
Theophilus...........69	Benjamin.............31	Hurley
Thomas 94	Hughes	Cornelius 9
William 18, 52, 59,	Amey 101	Hurst
..........71, 87, 96	Constan 71	David 68
William, Jr...........152	Constant 58	Fanny 48
Wm. H. 137	Constantine 108	Jesse................... 95
Houghman	George........58, 153	Richard 28
John, Jr. 53	John 160	Hussey
Houpt	Mary....................77	Mary 151
Dennis 40	Hughley	Hutchinson
Householder	Charles 11	Ann...................... 65
Adam..................115	Hughs	Hutchison
Houser	Constantine..........81	Benjamin 30
William 89	Hugh 99	Beverly 129
Housholder	Mary...................29	Daniel 56
Adam, Jr..............78	Theophilus 67, 68	Henry 87
Gideon 126	Hulls	Joshua................. 87
	Richard 19	Moses................. 48
		Neilson 87

Index

Nelson 110
Nelson H. 109
Robert 65
Thomas 59, 67
William 31, 51
Hutson
  Richard 19

I

Ingeldue
  Ebener 44
  William 44
Ingledew
  Ann 57
  Blackstone 57
Ingledoe
  Ann 57
Ingmyer
  Robert 45
Irey
  John 49, 75
Irwin
  Francis 17

J

Jackson
  Alexander 129
  Alfred 119
  Benjamin 162
  Carline 129
  Chs. 130
  Fanny 134
  George C. 143
  Georgianna 130
  Jno. W. & Polly ... 130
  Joseph 143
  Mary 4, 134
  Nelly 129
  Robert 72, 129
  S.A. 115, 143
  Samuel 13
  Samuel A. 116
Jacobs
  Charles William .. 126
  Elizabeth 104
  Elum 161
  John 48, 57
  Joshua 90, 93
  Peter 95, 104
  Polly 71
  Price 67

Ryland 162
Thomas 52, 121,
.... 124, 126
Thos. 123
William 44
James
  Benjamin 96
  Daniel 50
  Elias 21, 23, 26
  Elijah 84
  James 61
  Jane 51, 53,
.... 60, 156
  Jesse 53, 58, 154
  John 72
  Levi 53, 95
  Matson 134
  Sarah 48
  Smith 125
  Thomas 51
  William 8, 66
Janey
  Mary 1
Janney
  Aaron 113
  Abel 4, 14
  Blackstone 89
  Daniel 93, 144
  David 95, 100
  Eli 97
  Elisha 37, 111
  Elisha, Jr. 106
  Israel 32, 41, 142
  Jonas 24, 88,
.....107, 111, 144
  Joseph ... 5, 8, 11, 18
  Lot T. 145
  Mahlon 10, 99
  Ruth 93
Janny
  Mahlon 115
Jared
  John 23
  Susannah 105
Jarvis
  Washington 109
Jay
  William 83
Jefferson
  John 97
  Thomas 104
Jenkins
  Ann 151
  Charles 50

Elizabeth 2
Ellis 100
Hamilton 50
Harness 6
Jacob 68
Job 6
John 38
Margaret 6, 113
Reuben 131
Thomas 29
Zachariah ... 7, 16, 18
Jenners
  Abiel 86
Jennings
  Peter 1
Jerard
  Sophia 105
Jett
  Birket 144
Jew
  Jane 150
Jewell
  Martha 34
  Thomas 30
  Winifred 30
  Zachariah 34
Jinkins
  David 145
John
  Daniel 48
  Elizabeth 40, 42
  Sally 42
  William 40
Johns
  Eneas 26
Johnson
  Casper 112
  Charles 77, 82
  Charles A. 129
  Elisha 9
  George 137, 143
  James 112
  James Hanson ... 131
  John 112, 115,
.... 138, 145
  Noah 75
  Sally 138
  Sarah 13
Johnston
  Baldwin 103
  Charles 71
  Chloe 36
  John 67, 113
  Noah 65

William 88, 94	Keene	Kibby
Jones	Newton............. 127	Alexander 58
Abel...................128	Keith	John 52
Alfred.................100,	William 7	Kid
............103, 115	Kelley	John 43
Clarissa 69	John..................... 34	Kidd
Clary....................68	Vincent................. 98	Rachel 152
Cleareny...............71	Kelly	Kidwell
Dennis Gillum.......92	An 19	Amelia 82
Elizabeth 97,	Ann 12, 29	Emly 80
............111, 115	Elizabeth............. 42	Fanny 138
Ellender................71	John..................... 27	Hannah............... 143
Henry 123	Mary............... 27, 42	James Edward... 138
Isaac 80	Thomas........... 4, 25,	Jonathan 102
Jesse....................71	.... 27, 149	Thomas 143, 154
John 13	William 49	Kile
Joshua 7	Kellyham	Albert................. 144
Levi 99, 103,	Dennis 48	Elizabeth 144
............104, 111	Kelsey	John 77, 143
Lewis..............63, 64	Elizabeth............. 22	Nicholas & Mary .. 67
Mahala 71	Kempe	Kilgore
Martha 41, 42	Mary..................... 31	George 28
Mary....................51	Kendall	Killihare
Richard..............161	Adam 101	Michael............... 24
Ruth 13	Wm. 101	Killimare
Sarah 81	Kennan	Matthew............... 23
Thomas 69	William 42	King
William 22, 26, 37,	Kenneday	David 43
.........89, 90, 160	Mary..................... 53	Osborn 47
Jordan	Kennedy	Patrick 113
Silas 123	Jonathan........ 56, 62	William........104, 111
Jorden	Mary..................... 56	Wm....111, 112, 113,
Thornton.............104	Kenner	......114, 120, 127
Wm. 104	John..................... 20	Kington
Jurey	Kennerly	Betty 79
David & Mary........41	Samuel 143	William 79
Jury	Kenny	Kipheart
David...........60, 121	John..................... 23	Godfrey 41
	Kent	Kirby
K	Jane..................... 90	Thomas H...119, 121
	June..................... 66	Kirk
Kabrick	Samuel 87	James................ 36
George 132	Sarah 159	Mary 51
Kabridge	William 66	Mary(Mica) 152
George 132	Kerby	Meca 51
Kalb	Thomas H. 116	William................. 99
Samuel...............119	Kern	Wm. 103
Kane	Valentine............. 14	Kitsmiller
Charles...............161	Kevan	Martin 84, 86, 87
Kean	Samuel 72	Kittle
George 143	Kibbe	James................ 129
Kebb	William 52	
Molly....................72		

Index

Kitzmiller
  Martin 92, 96, 97,
  .... 100, 101, 102,
  .... 109, 110, 117,
  .... 123, 141
  William 123
  William W. 125
Klein
  Lewis 103
Kline
  John N. 104
  Lewis 102
Knighting
  Betty 68
Knighton
  Betty 79
Knott
  Julia 128
  Lewis 125
  Violinda 51
  Zachariah 125
Knox
  Joseph 78, 80,
  .... 83, 89
Kye
  Mary 57
Kyser
  Cassandra 93
  Marten 88
  Martin 90, 93

L

Lacey
  Benjamin 52, 60
  Elizabeth 36, 52
  Ephraim 61
  Israel 50
  Joseph 14, 28, 29,
  .... 50, 63, 70
  Margaret 22, 70
  Mesheck 83
  Stacy 94, 95
  Thomas 101
  William 36, 61,
  .... 63, 155
Lacy
  Mesheck 80
  Stacy 97
  William 82
Lafaber
  Wm. 121

Lafaver
  Wm. 139
Lafever
  Henry 90
Lafevers
  Henry 33
Laggax
  Thomas 22
Lair
  Abraham 73
Lambag
  Anthony 65, 104
  Neomi 104
Landers
  Betty 35
  George 35
  Roger 35
Landy
  Edward 112
Lane
  Ann 30
  Carr Wilson 39
  Hardage 14, 29
  James 3, 10
  Jesse 144
  Rachel 58, 59
  Samuel 59
  William 51, 53,
  .... 58, 59
Langley
  Elick 120
  Henry 120
  Sarah 75
  Walker 75
  Walter 85, 140
Lanham
  Henry 7
  Jane 7
  Stacey 7
Lappington
  Abraham .. 28, 44, 53
  Elizabeth 25, 27
  George 34
  Thomas 47
Latham
  Robert 65
Lauder(Lander)
  William 13
Lawson
  Charles 157
  Nancy 157
  Nero 62, 77

Lay
  Emanuel 65
  Joseph 27, 63,
  .... 93, 152
Layer
  Catharine 74, 75
Leach
  Burrell 118
Leaich
  Mary 59
Lee
  Dr. Geo. 131
  Edward 24
  Elizabeth 144
  Peter 130
  Simon 144
  William 144
Leech
  James 63
  Mary 63
Leese
  Bartholomew 37
Leeson
  Margaret 27
Lester
  Jesse 22
  Sarah 75
  William 75
Lewelling
  Thomas 3
Lewis
  Abraham 31
  Albert 134
  Capt. Joseph 38
  Charles 92
  Daniel 24
  Elizabeth 134, 162
  George 38, 40, 63
  John 19, 143
  John W. 144
  Joseph 17
  Joseph, Sr. 153
  Mary 38
  Nancy 115
  Sarah 64
  Stephen 160
  Thomas 8, 19
  Vincent 9, 29
  William 28, 71
  Wm. 79
  Wm. 116
  Zachairah 116
  Zachariah 115

Apprentices, Poor Children and Bastards 187

Lickey
 John W. 133
 William 156
Likins
 John 15
 William 15
Lindsey
 Samuel 140
Linn
 Joseph 11
Lishman
 Jane 59
 Janett 59
Little
 Sary.......................98
 Squire....................98
Littlejohn
 John 29, 31, 34,
 ....52, 70, 103
 Wm. M. 102
Littleton
 Charles............27, 66
 Sampson.............115
 Solomon......115, 144
 Thomas......125, 129,
 ....144, 146
 William 37, 44
Livingston
 Pleasant......100, 157
 Wm. 100
Livingstone
 Mary 88
Locker
 Jarrett....................96
Locklan
 Henry 4
 Joseph 3
 Priscilla..............3, 4
Lodge
 William 108, 111
Loflin
 George 34
Logan
 Alfred..................134
 John 78, 79
 John, Sr. 146
Long
 Adam....................35
 Armistead 85, 86,
148
 Chatherina 84
 Hannah.................84

Henry 83, 85,
 ....86, 97, 99
Philip.....................42
Phillip....................64
Losh
 Daniel 56
Love
 John 145
 Samuel 11, 65
Lovet
 Edmund 84
Lovett
 Daniel 50, 58, 62
 David 50, 52,
 ....132, 155
 Edmond 65
 Elias.....................50
Lowe
 Edward...............121
 Henson 124
 Sarah R. 117
 Thomas..............158
 Thos...................121
Loyd
 Edward & Dorinda 55
 Henry 6
Lucas
 Anthony 113, 115
 Barton 94
 Charles & Delia ..134
 Charles William ..134
 George.................52
 Jeffrey................127
 Samuel 8, 18
 Thomas..............127
 Wilson................127
Lucus
 Cndora 79
 Volney................144
Lyder
 Jacob 120
 Landon 120
 Letitia 120
Lynch
 Thomas..............133
Lynimier
 Casper................66
Lynimyer
 Casper................65
Lynn
 Adam...................74
 Jane 71
 Thomas...............71

Lyons
 Hugh Franklin.... 115
 Jos. 115
 Joseph................ 115
 Robert 115

M

Macaboy
 Elizabeth 154
Mackey
 Anthony 33
 Mary 33
Macklaw
 James................ 104
Macon
 Rebecca 1
Macro
 Mary 40
Magess
 Elizabeth 1
 Henry..................... 1
Maginnis
 Elizabeth 160
Mahauny
 Susannah 160
Mahon
 John 8
Mahoney
 John 67, 144
 Riner.................... 67
 Thomas 67, 144
Mahue
 John 44, 58
 Leviston............... 60
 Nancy 58
Mains
 William......58, 65, 66
Males
 Enoch 26
Malone
 Martha 12, 24
 Rhody 24
Manley
 Phillis..................... 1
 Sarah............. 31, 96
 Susanna 96
Manly
 Ann...................... 32
 Benjamin 31, 132
 Dorcas................. 31
 Edy...................... 56

Index

Fanny..........72, 125
Francis..........42, 55
George..........144
Hannah..........58, 63
Henny..........32
Jemima..........34
Peter..........63, 93
Susanna..........72
Susannah..........56
Thomas..........63
Vincent..........29, 31
Wesley..........125
Mann
  Bernard..........33, 35,
  ....93, 99
  Jacob..........118, 147
Mansfield
  James..........80, 128
  John..........80
  Stephen..........81, 92
Manuel
  Isaac..........2
Marbury
  Mary..........8
Mark
  John..........18
Marker
  John..........144
Marks
  Bennett..........160
  Elisha..........46
  John..........11, 145
  John, Jr...........26
  John, Sr...........26
  Mason..........159
  Milley..........155
  Polly..........81
  Thomas..........153
Marlbrough
  Elizabeth..........151
Marlow
  Thomas J...........146
Maroney
  William..........42
Marr
  Rachel..........59, 65, 68
Marshall
  David..........33
  James..........35
  John..........91
  Samuel..........44
  William..........140

Martin
  Henry..........29
  Jacob..........106, 109,
  ....110, 111, 114
  James..........15, 25
  James L...........148
  Jas. L...........129
  John..........143
  Linny..........31
  Mary..........154
  Rachel..........87
  Ralph..........6
  Robert..........159
  Sarah..........21, 29, 46
  Thomas..........6
Mash
  Peter..........63, 86
Mashel
  Thomas..........4
Maskel
  Thomas..........4
Mason
  Abraham Barnes
    Thomson..........46
  Benjamin..........47
  Elijah..........93, 115
  George..........41
  Henry A...........144
  Jesse..........144
  Nancy..........144
  Thompson..........27, 32
  Thomson..........11, 22, 30
  Wesly..........144
Mass
  Catherine..........112, 118
  Mary..........112
Massey
  Lewis..........31, 85
Mastell
  William..........14
Matheney
  Sarah..........151
Mathias
  D.T...........126
Mattershard
  Charles..........43
  Christopher..........43
  Sarah..........43
Matthews
  Aaron..........154
  Daniel..........15
  David..........87
  John..........37, 154
  Joseph..........87

Pleasant..........159
Rachel..........51
Richard..........61, 67,
..........76, 86, 159
Samuel..........51, 59
Thomas..44, 51, 128
William..........51, 59
Maulsby
  Benj...........111
  Benjamin..........128, 133
Mavin
  Wm. & Robert..........133
McAboy
  Elizabeth..........154
  Emily..........101
  Emly..........80
McAffrey
  Catharine..........144
McAllister
  Daniel..........83
McArter
  Joseph..........41
McArtor
  Caroline..........161
McCabe
  Henry..........28
  John..........100
  Thomas..........53, 66
McCaffery
  Caterin..........20
  John..........20
McCaffrey
  William..........159
McCann
  Charity..........35
  John..........24, 65, 89
  William..........36
McCarty
  John..........27
  Mary..........35, 157
  Robert..........147
  Timoth..........157
McCastor
  Mason..........144
McCaulley
  Grace..........78
McClain
  Francis..........34
  James..........52
  John..........32
McClanachan
  James..........35

Apprentices, Poor Children and Bastards 189

McClaningham
  James 36
McClelan
  William 29
McClosky
  William 147
  Wm. 124, 125
McCluster
  Ann......................19
McColline
  Denis...................15
McConnahay
  Jesse................144
McCormck
  John A. 130
McCormick
  James 54
  John 79, 106
McCouatt
  Thomas 74
McCoy
  Ben....................109
  Henley...............110
  Henly.................109
  James 4
McCrackin
  Thomas 19
McCro
  Sarah 40
McCulla
  Robert 47, 54
McCulley
  Grace 78
McCullock
  Robert 87
McCutchen
  Samuel................48
McCutcheon
  Jonah 121
McDaniel
  Ann.....................72
  Greenberry M. 160
  James 76
  Jane 3, 151
  Jas. 118
  Stephen...............79
McDanniel
  John 33
McDevit
  Eleanor................65

McDonald
  Duncan 10
  Mary.....................45
McDonall
  James 96
McDonough
  James 133
McFarland
  Leven..................59
  William 79
McFarlane
  Eleanor 16
McFarling
  Ann 61
  Eleanor 21
  Elisha...................35
  Ezekiel.................56
  John 30, 42, 56
  Landon............... 145
  Leven....... 55, 59, 63
  Mary............. 55, 79
  Milton 145
  Nancy 158
  Rebekah 62
  Washington........ 145
  William 55
McGaha
  Elizabeth 107
  James 119
McGahey
  Curtis 68
  Daniel 55
  David 68
  Jeremiah. 38, 44, 55,
  .... 59, 62, 68
  John.....................68
McGarvick
  Henry 157
McGeath
  Gabriel 84
  James. 105
  Jane 93
  Madlin 26
McGee
  Charles 56
  Nelson 107
McGeth
  James 154
McGhee
  Sophia 107
McGinnia
  Elizabeth 158

McGinnis
  Charlotte............ 145
  Edward 81, 82
  Harriet Ann 145
  John 4
  John Haddock 13
McGoughey
  Rachel 31
McGraff
  Madlin 18, 28
McGuire
  Hugh..................... 2
  Isabella................ 45
  James................. 17
McGwin
  George 92, 101
  Rachel 92
McIlhaney
  James................ 130
McInerny
  Eleanor................ 26
McIntire
  Alexander 33
McIntosh
  Thomas 152
McIntyre
  Alexander 16, 20,
  ....28, 29, 54
  C.C. 143
  Charles................ 54
  Patrick 105, 106
McKay
  Catharine.............. 6
McKemey
  Eli...................... 145
McKensie
  James................... 9
  John 7, 17
  William............ 7, 17
McKenzey
  Henry................... 27
  John 7
McKim
  George 122
  James.............. 122
  Margaret 131
McKimm
  James................ 157
McKinzey
  James................ 40
McKnight
  Bridget................ 15
  Burniar................ 145

Index

Deborah 157
Delilah 160
Lydia 70
Nimrod 145
Ruth 35
McMachen
 (McMickens)
 William 155
McMaken
 Alexander 36, 37,
 .... 58, 70
McMakin
 Alexander............ 46
McMullen
 George 85, 101
 Nancy 44
 Rosannah............ 85
 Samuel................ 44
 William 85
McMullin
 George 86
 Rosannah............ 86
 William 86
McNab
 James 56
 Mary...................... 4
 Rachel................... 6
McNabb
 Polly 155
McNamara
 Peter 106
McNamare
 Dennis................ 48
McNeal
 Jesse 3
McNeally
 George 91, 106
McNeil
 Dominick 45
McNely
 George 82
McNulty
 Hugh 125
McPhearson
 Job 48
McPherson
 Daniel................. 47
 Henry M. 145
 Mary 138
 Peter William 145
 Samuel.......... 42, 86
 Sebastian 63
 Stephen 105, 141

Stephen, Jr. 34
William ... 44, 87, 145
McVaw (McVeigh)
 Eli 153
McVay
 Jesse 64
McVeigh
 Jesse 64, 69, 73,
 .... 75, 84, 140
McVickers
 Ann 63
McWharter
 Robert................. 28
Mead
 Aquilla............... 101
 Benjamin 46
 William 5, 6, 7
Meade
 Acquilla............. 111
Means
 William................ 58
Mecabe
 Catharine.............. 1
Meegeth
 Fanny 145
Mellan
 Eli 100
 Jesse 100
Mellon
 William 17
Melon
 John.................. 145
Melvin
 Jane...................... 7
 Winney 13
Menick
 John.................. 108
Menix
 Jemima............... 99
Mercer
 Cruse.................... 5
 Henry 116
 Richard 5
 Thomas 114
 William 116
Merchant
 James 160, 161
Meredith
 Elizabeth............. 71
Merrick
 Hannah 18
 Patrick 74

Merrill
 Nicholas 47
 Ruth 48
Merriott
 Samuel................17
Metcalf
 Asa 56
Mical
 Hannah 56
 Mary 56
Middleton
 Thomas.................6
 Thomas, Jr. 4, 6
 William 161
 Wm. 161
Milbourn
 Jonathan 73
Milburne
 El____ 71
 Rebecah..............71
Miles
 Josiah.................150
 Josias..................29
Milett
 Sarah 56
Milholland
 Henry 145
Millan
 Thomas 24
 William 36, 44
Millar
 Moses 82
Miller
 Anna Barberry 10
 David 63
 Elijah 14
 Hannah 163
 Henry 15
 Isaac 89
 Jacob 154
 James 113
 Jehu 71
 John ... 7, 10, 14, 113
 John Daniel 20, 55
 Moses 81
 Susannah 156
 William 113, 146
Millett
 Sarah 49
Millhollen
 Esther................153
 Patrick................153

Apprentices, Poor Children and Bastards 191

Mills
  Thomas 78
Milner
  John & Mary 37
Mina
  Thomas 142
Miner
  Nathaniel 77
  Samuel 77
Minich
  Elijah 88
  William 88
Minick
  Elijah 91
  Elizabeth 88
  William 91, 93
Minnix
  Elijah 108
  Elizabeth 108
Missetts
  Hannah 22
Mitchell
  Adam 24
  Benjamin 126
  Benjamin, Jr. 144
  James 79
  Mary 80, 84
  Matthew 100
  Robert 9
  William 80, 84, 86
Mobley
  Samuel 1
Mock
  Daniel 116
  Elizabeth 97, 99
  John Cornelius ... 135
  Kitty 135
  Nancy 99, 115
  Polly 99
  Tilghman 137
Moffett
  Benj. 108
  Daniel 117
  Nancy 123
  Robert 91
  Wm. 117
  Wm. B. 123
Molding (Moreland)
  Elizabeth 158
Money
  Alexander 12
Moninger
  Henry 95

Monkhouse
  Jonathan 19
Monroe
  Jno. 111
  John 113
  John H. 119
Monster
  Lucindy 145
Montawney
  Burgois 47
  Joseph 47
Montgomery
  Sarah 85, 92
Mooney
  Elizabeth 40
Moore
  Abner 121
  Amos 73
  Asa 40, 50, 52,
  .... 53, 61, 68,
  .... 70, 92, 109
  Bently 121
  Eaton 49
  Eden 113
  Edon B. 113
  Elizabeth 108
  Hannah 105, 108
  Isaac 113, 131
  Jacob 37
  James 35, 41, 50,
  .... 54, 69, 90,
  ..... 101, 102, 103
  James & Co. 104
  Jas. & Co. 104
  Jeptha 37
  John 49, 82, 108
  Jonathan 86
  Levenia 105
  Nancy 49
  Phebe Ann 163
  Polly 72
  Robert 107
  Samuel 99
  Thomas 41, 50,
  .... 53, 54, 58
  Thomas, Jr. 53
  William 91
  Wm. 113
Moore & Phillips ....
  93, 97, 102, 103, 106
Moore and Phillips:
  80

Moran
  John 117
  John M. 117
  Richard 126
  William 117
Moreland
  Bridget 114
  Christiana 157
  David 114
  Jason 25
  Kitty 114
  Mary 114
  Nancy 161
  William 157
Morgan
  Andrew 135
  Ann 77
  Charles 135
  James 16, 21
  Job 43
Morgert
  Peter 32
Morin
  Thornton 161
Morlan
  Jason 7
  William 11, 17
Morris
  Harriot 97
  Jacob 8
  Jno. 125
  John 2, 6, 28
  Tamar 153
Morrison
  Abel 107
  Archibald 72, 108
  John 55
Moss
  Catharine 163
  Gideon 40
  John 7, 17
  John, Jr. 5
  John, Sr. 4
  Mary 112
  Stephen 112
Mott
  Randolph 75
  Thoms R. 117
Moul
  George 49
Mount
  Elijah 53

Moxley
  Abigail 64
  John 45, 62
  Joshua 44
  William 41
Moyer
  Philip 145
Muckler
  Jacob 45
Muir
  John 52
Muirhead
  Andrew 19
  George 13, 24
  William 41
Mullen
  Catherine 112
  John 112
  Joseph 112, 116
  Mary 116
  Polly 116
  Richard 109, 110
  Samuel 113
Mullin
  Richard 108
Munks
  Henry 56
  Mary 56
Murphey
  Benjamin 88
  Charles 45
  George 45
  Jeremiah 38
  Mary 24, 69
  Samuel 69
  William 69
Murphy
  Mary 20
Murray
  Nancy 55
  Patrick 21
  Samuel 25
  Susannah 50
  William 50
Murrey
  Samuel 146
Murry
  Peggy 50
Muschet
  John 2
Muschett
  Bazill 57

Muse
  James H. 131
  Walker 131
Musgrove
  Cuthbert 41
  Sarah 159
Myers
  Basil 137
  Benjamin 94
  Elizabeth 94
  Israel 120
  Jacob 64
  John 56, 78, 91, 94
  Jonathan 17, 42
  Margaret 162
Myres
  Israel 120

N

Nailer
  Barton 38
Nanbe
  William 26
Nash
  Joseph 15
Neale
  Charles 108
  Daniel 32
  John 75
  Mary 24, 75
Neare
  John 92
Neilson
  James 129
  William 12, 21,
  .... 22, 27
Nelson
  Ann 149
Newhouse
  David 46
Newlin
  Martin 122
Newlon
  ___ 113
  Geo 113
  James 118
Newman
  David 46
  Joseph 66, 69
  Nash 27

Newton
  Alexander 126
  Henry 121
  Jno. C. 110
  Robert 126
Nicholes
  John 145
Nicholls
  Henry H. 136
  Thomas 16
Nichols
  Frederick 16
  George 151
  Henry 71
  Isaac 17, 47
  Isaac H. 148
  Isaiah 74
  James 18, 48
  Jonah 119
  Maria 138
  Nathan 94, 148
  Permelia 145
  Samuel 155
  William 74, 81,
  .... 139, 159
Nickens
  Richard 125
  Violett 125
Nicklin
  John, Jr. 152
Nickolls
  Isaac 18
  Isaac, Jr. 13
  James 23
Nickols
  Isaac 89
  Isaiah 81
Nighting
  Elizabeth 92
  William 92
Ninby
  William 27
Nisewanger
  James Henry 134
  Susan 159
Niswanger
  Susan 134
Nitre
  Gabriel 145
Nixon
  David 112
  George 56
  James 13, 73

Apprentices, Poor Children and Bastards 193

John, Jr. 158
Jonah 53, 56
Jonathan 80
Nixson
  George 38
Nodding
  William 1
Noding
  William 3
Noggins
  Amanda 135, 136
Noggle
  Jack 134
Noland
  Elizabeth 117, 159
  Geo. W. 134
  George W. 148
  Mary 3
  Philip 3, 19, 25, 58
  Philip, Jr. 34
  Phillip, Jr. 23
  Pierce 117
  Thomas 56
  Thomas J. 116
Norman
  George 1
Norris
  Lucy 126
  Milly 126
  William 45
  Wilson 138
Norton
  John 24, 41
Nucom
  James 10
Nutt
  Jonathan 72

O

O'Cain
  John 4
Oden
  James 78
  Nathaniel 78
Offutt
  Mary 92
Ogden
  Andrew 147
  Charles 106
  David 108, 112,
    ....117, 126
  Hezekiah 160
  Hugh 106
  Mary 160
Ogdon
  Cornelius 37
  Lucy 37
O'Harrow
  Frances 88
  Francis 91
  Hugh 90
  James 88
  Manasses 90
Oldacre
  John 154
Oldridge
  Rebecca 5
Oliver
  Thomas 28
O'Neal
  Elizabeth 79
  Lydia 70
  Nancy 52
Oneale
  Bernard 79
O'Neale
  Ferdinando 10
Oram
  Hiram 95, 112
  James 31, 33
Orr
  Tamar 134
  Wm. 134
Orrison
  Arthur 143
  David 94
  John 146
  Samuel 99
  Sarah 146
Orton
  Mary 2
  William 3
Osborn
  Herod 128
  John 27
  Joshua 94
Osborne
  John 26, 39
  William 26
Osburn
  Addison 133
  Franklin 136
  Joab 135, 136
  John 11
  Martha 136

Outon
  Elizabeth 12
Overfelt
  Peter 36
Overfield
  John 155
  Peter 48
Owens
  Evan J. 123
  John 153
Owsley
  Henry 29
  Sarah 150
  Thomas 1, 19
Oxley
  Ann 39
  Clare 14
  Everett 19
  Hannah 150, 151
  Henry, Jr. 9
  Jenkin 14
  Jeremiah 55
  Joel 39
  John 67, 73
  Mary 20

P

Page
  Ann 146
  Elizabeth 57
  Guynn (Gwynn)
    ....153, 155
  Robert 57, 146
Pain
  David 146
Paine
  David Batson 101
Painter
  John 9
Palmer
  Catharine 152
  Cornelius 80, 105
  Elijah 103
  John 24, 102
  John E. 106, 109
  Jonathan 53
  Jonathon 23
  Margarett 57

Nicholas 156
Richard 21
Turner 139
William 21

Index

Mary 57
Sethey Simmons 151
William 63
Pancoast
  John 101, 134
  John & Ruth 36
  John, Sr. 95
  Joshua 100, 161
  Simion 49
Parker
  Ann 101
  Anthony 1
  Charlotte 68
  Edward 22
  Elizabeth 76
  Hannah 18
  Joseph 7, 98
  Margaret 1
  Morris 111
  Presley 125
  Wm. 101
Parry
  John 27
  Thomas 15
Parsons
  Catharine 2
  John 2
Pascals
  Richard 5
Passmore
  Margaret 20
  Samuel 101
Patten
  Elizabeth 25, 32
Patterson
  Abner 84
  Fleming 8, 12,
  .... 13, 15, 16
  James 85
  James, Sr. 139
  John 5, 25
  Joseph 5, 111
  Sarah 82, 84
  Tamzon 78
  William 5, 20, 46
Paul
  Edward 56
Paxon
  James 59, 83
  William 48, 52,
  .... 60, 62
Paxson
  James 59, 83
  Samuel 135

William 52
Paxton
  Samuel 138
  William 49, 50
Payne
  Rachel 34
  William 34
Peacock
  Anne (Anna) 156
  John 73, 154
  Wm. 125
Peale
  Thomas H. 80
Pearce
  Abijah 47
  Amos 67
  Ann 47
  Griffith 12
  Herod B. 99
  John 99, 142
  Molly 45
  Sarah 47
Pearl
  William 8
Pearson
  Craven 136
  John 102
Pedicoart
  Thomas 34
Peel
  Mary 28
Peemy
  Azariah 45
  Benjamin 45
Pegg
  Nathaniel 31, 57
Penn(?)
  John 121
Perfect
  Christopher 5, 19
Perry
  Ann 60
  Benj. 104
  Benjamin ... 102, 110
  Edmond 68
  John 43, 68
Perryman
  John & Ann 43
Peterson
  Thomas 38
Petit
  Jacob 79
  Mary 36

Pettit
  George 139
  George W. 162
  Mary 48
  Nathaniel 42
  Samuel 22
Pettitt
  Joab 90
Pew
  John 62, 68
Peyton
  Craveñ 4, 11
  Francis 11
  Henry 8
  Henry, Jr. 8
  John 51
Phesil
  Jacob 24
Philips
  Asahel 61
  Benjamin 143
  Catharine 77
  Catherine 74
  Israel 79, 147
  John ... 30, 65, 72, 76
  Kitty 146
  Mary 57
  Thomas .. 78, 83, 143
  William 158
Phillips
  Ann 16
  Benjamin 141
  David 153
  Ester 70
  Isaac 10
  Jenkin 10, 23
  John 7, 10, 14, 16
  Mary 10
  Polley 78
  Sally 79
  Sarah 154
  Thomas 10, 87,
  .... 92, 112
  William 6
Phitzimons
  Wm. 108
Pickeley
  Thomas 47
Picken
  Robert 85
Pickler
  Mary Magdalene 6
  Peter 6

Apprentices, Poor Children and Bastards 195

Pierce
  Abijah 51
  Amos 76, 142
  Griffith 70
  John 71
Pierpoint
  Charity 9
  Charles 9
  Joseph 45
Piggott
  Ebenezer 155
  William 74
Pike
  Jonathan 8
Piles
  John 7
Piller
  Ellsey 46
  Lettice 46, 152
  Sally 46
Pinkham
  Ann 11
Piper
  Margaret 9
Plaister
  Henry, Jr. 116
Plaster
  James 147
Plummer
  Rebekah 60
Plymeall
  Barbara 26
  Jacob 26
Poland
  Alexander ... 127, 136
  America 136
  Elizabeth 30, 35
  Hannah 50
  William 53
Polen
  Elizabeth 53
Poling
  John 67
  Nathaniel 31
  William 31
Polon
  Amanda 134
Polton
  Ambrose 61
  Emily 116
  Thomas 62

Pomroy
  Armistead T. 128
  F. 128
  Nancy 128
Pool
  Alfred 117
  Amasa 53, 65, 75
  Ebur 39
  Elias 98, 99,
  .... 103, 162
  Elizabeth 53
  Israel 81
  John 102
  Joseph 101
  Martha 39
  Mary Ann 131
  Maryan 89
  Susanah 117
Poor
  Chloe 149
Popkins
  Ambrose 90, 94
  David 54
  John 9
  Mary 153, 155
  Robert 4, 5
  Sarah 153
Porter
  Mary 93
Poston
  Charles Martin 8
Potton
  Henry 35
Potts
  David 61
  Edward 59, 68
  Ezekial 73
  Isaac 15
  Jonas 84, 144
  Nathan 15
Poulson
  Agnes 156
  Jasher 156
Poulston
  Margaret 153
Poulton
  Adrain 118
  Alfred 146
  Ambrose 67
  Berkley 118
  Charles 72
  Emila 146
  Emily 161
  Eviline Ann 118

John 69, 118
Margaret 152
Martha 62, 69, 72
Reed 92
Tamar 153
Thomas 146
Powell
  Colvin 111
  James 81
  Leven 40, 146
  Levin 8, 53
  Mary 111
  Peyton 145
  Robert 159
  Sarah 156
  William Harrison .. 42
Power
  Joseph 12
  Lucinda 162
  Robert 49
Prescoat
  John 22
  Mary 23
Presley
  Charles 29
Preston
  Daniel 3
  John 41
  Martha 3
  Sarah 3
Price
  Elizabeth 160
  Jonathan 22, 30
  Oliver 14, 25
Prim
  James 4
  Kitchen 4
Prince
  John 56
  Levi 38, 146
  Matthias 146
Pritchard
  Sarah 52
  Thomas 53, 54
  Thomas, Jr. 57
Proctor
  John 4
  Mary 149
  Sarah 1
Prohen
  John 28
Prohon
  Christopher 34

Index

Prohorn
 Cateron 34
Proker
 Christopher 27
Pue
 John 68
Pugh
 John 39, 60
 Samuel 30
 Spencer 30
Puller
 Samuel 108
Pumcrats
 Lenard and Elenor 49
Purcel
 Edwin 135
Purcell
 John 99
 Joseph 93
Purdy
 Henry 79
Pursel
 Thomas 138
Pursell
 Ann 25
Pursley
 Daniel 21
 William 40
Pusey
 David 80
 Joshua . 95, 106, 121
Pyott
 Amos 50

Q

Queen
 Catherine 55
 Elizabeth 86, 89
 Nancy 86, 89
 Tamson 160
 Tamzin 86
Quick
 Armstead 127
 Maria 127

R

Rabbitt
 Bryan 15
Race
 Moses 43

Patty 64
Phebe 43
Pheby 64
 William 52, 71
Ralls
 Capt. George 42
Ralph
 J__ 66
 John 98
Ramey
 Barbary 149
 Jacob 20
 Sandford 76
Ramey(Remey)
 Barbara 149
Ramsey
 John 148
 Mary 73
 Richard 73
Rasler
 William 23
Ratcliff
 Ned 31
Rattee
 John B. 77
Rattekin
 James 33
Rattikin
 James 24
Raw (Rau)
 William 35
Rawdery
 John 4
Razor
 George, Jr. 141
 John 89, 90
Reader
 Christian 12
 John 12
 Nicholas 12
 William 12
Reagan
 Bazel 32
Rector
 Henry 132
 Hy. & Eliz. 128
 Solon 128, 132
Redman
 Lucindy 146
Redmon
 Andrew 46
 George 131
 John 131

Redmond
 Aaron 3, 8
 Andrew 65, 72
 Elizabeth 24
Redwood
 William 38, 61
Reecard
 Frances 5
Reece
 David 141, 146
 Thomas 62
Reed
 Charlotte 130
 George 130, 160
 James 38
 John 146, 154
 Joseph 34, 37, 47
 Mary 57, 64
 Minor 118
 Nancy 57
 Reuben 152
 Sampson 95
 William 56, 98
Reeder
 Lawrence 21
Reese
 David 47, 139
 Edward 50
 John ... 109, 110, 114
 Silas 57, 81
 Thomas 50
Reeves
 Chloe 9
Regor
 John 15
Reid
 Sampson 105
Reiger
 John 5, 7, 20
Reily
 Thomas 107
Rennick
 James 38
Revells
 James 67
Revely
 George 19
Rhine
 James 115
 Sarah 115
Rhodes
 George 52, 70,
 .... 91, 147

Apprentices, Poor Children and Bastards 197

Rice
  William 158
  Beninah 70, 104
Richard
  Geo. 132, 133
  George 131, 140
  Leven 133
Richards
  Richard 46
  Richards 48
  Samuel 64
Richardson
  Elisha 41
  John 54
  Sarah 155
Richcreek
  John 31
Rickett
  Simon 43
Ridenbaugh
  George 105
Rider
  Thomas 67, 70
Riegor
  John 17
Riely
  John 40
Riggs
  Allen 104
Right
  William 27
Rigney
  Isaac 36
  Mary 26
  William 38
Rigsby
  Mildred 156
Riley
  Patrick 18
  Richard 161
  Thomas 146
  Wm. 103
Rind
  Anne 26
Rine
  Harriott 100
  John 92
  Sarah 100
Risbey
  George W. 146
Risby
  Sally 141
  Samuel 141

Riticor
  Amasa 146
Rivers
  Charles 131
  Christopher 128
  Sarah 43
  Thomas 131
Roach
  Hannah 81, 155
  James 21, 36,
  .... 42, 72, 163
  Margaret 91
  Maria 94
  Melindy 81
  Owen R. 98
  Owen Rodgers 91
  Richard .. 40, 80, 114
  Richard & Hannah 66
Roads
  John 55
Roberts
  Griffith 82
  John 3, 60, 82
  John, Sr. 98
  Joseph 72, 75, 85
  Margaret 3, 85
  Mary 3, 47
  Owen 2, 10
  Peggy 82
  Samuel 96
  Sarah 149
  William 14, 39, 54,
  ..... 58, 70, 78, 97
  Wm. 104
Robertson
  Carter 146
  George 159
  James 152
  John 72, 107
  Sarah 107
  Sarah Frances ... 137
  Susan 146
Robey
  William 130
Robins
  Thomas 15
Robinson
  Elizabeth 48
  George & Ann 53
  Henry 38
  James 50
  Jane 38
  John 116
  Joseph 146

Thomas 18
William .. 2, 38, 85, 86
Robison
  George 59, 67
  Mary Ann 146
  Payton 147
Rodgers
  Elizabeth 140
  John H.G. 123
Roe
  Ellzey 60
  Mary 60
Rogers
  Archibald 60
  Arthur 43, 60, 69
  Hamilton 60
  Hugh 67
  John 28, 30, 123
  William 26
Romine
  Isaiah 159
  Sarah 155
Roof
  Betsey 72
  Catey 72
Rookard
  Nancy 153
Rose
  Edmund 163
  James 77, 80
  Jno. W. 110
  John 133
  William 131
Ross
  John 143
Roszel
  Stephen 16
Roth
  Christian 31
  John 31
Rowan
  George 78
Rowsey
  Reuben 102
Rozell
  Stephen 13, 15
Rucard
  Frances 5
Rule
  Mary 22
Runnells
  Lorenz M. 126

Index

Ruse
  John 114
  Rachel 159
Russell
  Aaron 147
  Anne 1
  George 63
  Hendley 94
  James 87, 89
  Jane 1, 159, 162
  Jas. 101
  John 20, 40, 112
  Jonathan 64
  Mahlon 140
  Samuel .. 41, 145, 146
  Sarah 36, 50, 112
  Thomas 64, 114,
    ..... 119, 120, 124,
    ..... 125, 126, 144
  William H. 147
Rust
  Peter 91
Rutherford
  Ann 22
Rutledge
  Richard 61
Ryan
  John 100
  Mary 16
  Rebecca 1
  Sarah 100
Ryley
  John 2
Ryne
  Sarah 155
Ryon
  John 97

S

Sample
  Diana 2
  John 81, 162
Samuels
  Shadrach 8, 12
Sanbower
  Elizabeth 163
  Micle 163
Sanders
  Daniel 149
  James 12
  Thomas 35, 36,
    .... 43, 48

William Gunnell 39
Sanders (Saunders)
  James 155
Sandford
  Robert 100
Sandiford
  James 142
Sands
  Abijah 72
  Edmund 10, 20
  Jacob 40
  Jonah 95
  Jonas 49
  Joseph 20
Sanford
  Robert 6
  Sibby 110
Sanns
  Jacob 75
Sap
  Mary 12
Sappington
  John 90, 91
  John F. 99
  John P. 88
Saunders
  Francis 10
  James 24, 132
  James William ... 132
  William 132
  William S. 143
Saxon
  Daniel 30
Saxton
  John 33
  Matthew 16
Scaggs
  Richard 158, 159
Scandling
  Catharine 18
Scatterday
  Aaron 49, 60, 105
Schachen
  Jacob 5
Schooley
  Aaron 132
  Dority 49
  Eli 129
  Elisha 44
  Jesse 49
  Jno. 126
  John 41, 65, 72,
    .... 76, 85

John Henry 132
John, Jr. 91
Reuben 100
William, Jr. 32
Wm. 120
Schry
  Jacob 90
Scott
  Elizabeth 74
  George 3
  Harriett 130
  Isaac 11
  John 14
  Joseph 3
  Stephen 75
Scrivener
  Benjamin 22
  John 96
Seager
  Ann 45
  Charles 45
  George 83
Sealock
  Thomas 48
Sear
  James L. 107
Sears
  Elizabeth 158
  Esther 94
  Isaias 109
  John 155
  William 96, 97
  William Bearnard .. 27
Seaton
  James 153
Secres
  Charles 5
Seeders
  Thomas T. 137
  William 137
Seekrest (Seekright)
  Charles 11
Seers
  Josiah 106
  Thomas 158
Segar
  Christian 82
Seirs
  William 97
Self
  Ann 65
  Elizabeth 33
  Nathan 65

Apprentices, Poor Children and Bastards

Presley 39, 54
Presly 31
Thomas 23
Settle
  Josiah J. 138
  Reuben 75
Sewell
  Agnes 163
Sexton
  Joseph 21
Seybold
  Jasper 43
Shanks
  Conrad 2
Shannon
  John 31, 38
  Mary 38
Sharo
  William 54
Sharp
  Virgilia 13
Shaver
  Adam 15
  John 87
Shavor (Shover)
  Jacob 38
Shaw
  Henry 21
  John 35
  Mary 35
Shawn
  Cornelius 93
Sheckels
  Frances 158
Shedacre
  Elizabeth 100
Shedd
  John 24
  Jonathan 28
Shell
  Barsheby 81
  John 81
Shelton
  Elizabeth 151
Shepard
  John 14
Shepherd
  Charles 44, 102
  Humphrey ... 134, 135
  John 36
  Leven 110
  Thomas 11, 90

Sheppard
  Chs. 103
  Leven 103, 104
Shervin
  James 71, 75
Shields
  Alfred 162
  John 46
  Margret 41
  Michael 41
  Thomas 30, 37
Shipes
  Daniel 109
Shipley
  Ann L. 130
  John 130
Shipman
  Deborah 94
  John 88
  Lydia 88
  Mason 94, 159
Shirlock
  John 61
Shively
  George 37, 70
  Mary 32
Shivers
  Hesther 54
  Mary 54, 64
Shockness
  Thomas 40
Shoemaker
  George B. ... 121, 123
Shope
  Pleasant 162
Shore
  Rebeckah 81
  Simon 81
Shores
  John W. 137
  Priscilla 137
Short
  Jemes 44
  John 37, 158
Shover
  John 105
Shreve
  Benjamin 6, 140
  Benjamin, Jr. 125
Shrieve
  Westley 147

Shrieves
  Benjamin 34
  Mary Ann 32
Shriver
  Thomas W. 163
Shrives
  James 2
Shry
  Elizabeth 161
  Jacob 89
  Powell 114
Shumach
  Betsey 127
Shuter
  William 21
Sigler
  Jacob 12
  John 12
Silcoat
  Jacob 69
Silcott
  Abraham 96, 132, 146
  Alcinda 132
  Jacob 69
  John 132
  Lydia 96, 154
  Mary (Polly) 156
  Micanda 95
  Nancy 162
  Peyton 96
Silket
  Abraham 80
Simcock
  Joseph 32
Simcocke
  Joseph 62
Simmonds
  Thomas 10
Simms
  Phebe 24
  Thomas 43
Simons
  Amey 33
  Ann 40
  Effie 98
  Joseph 32, 33, 98
  Simon 32, 33
Simpkins
  Elizabeth Gussett 33
Simpson
  Charles 99
  Henson 114
  Jas. 114

Index

John 29, 131
William 131
Sinclair
  Amos 53
  Amy 60
  Edith 97, 100
  George 100
  James 13, 44
  Linna 69
  Linney 60
  Samuel 55, 97
  Thomas McDowell
  97
Sinclar
  Robert 23
Singer
  Charles 45
Sinkler
  James 64
  John 22
Skillman
  Abraham 38
  Christopher 39
Skilman
  John 79
Skinner
  Charles 136
  Cornelius 39, 46
  Elijah 83
  James 87
  John Thomas 147
  Nathaniel .. 32, 33, 78
  Peter 93
  Phinehas 29
  Richard 76, 93
  William 76
Slack
  Jane 161
  Jeremiah 69
  Manly 125
  Mary 161
  Polly 125
Slator
  Jacob 33
Sloacomb
  Thomas 55
Smale
  Simon 131
Smalley
  William 83, 140
Smallwood
  Elijah 43
  George 82, 120

James 146
Jemima 43
Leven 90, 92
Mary 120
Tracey 59
Walter Bayne 65
Walter Bear 60
William Randolph 147
Smalwood
  James 144
Smarr
  James 100
  Robert 46
Smiley
  Mary 30
Smith
  Alexander 39
  Allen 38
  Andrew 32, 62
  Ben 135
  Betty 38
  Catharine 17
  Charles 62
  Daniel 68, 94, 157
  Daniel G. ... 127, 131
  Elizabeth 16, 17,
  .... 20, 91
  Erasmus 61
  Euphemy 155
  George .. 76, 94, 154
  Hannah .68, 156, 158
  Henry 26
  Howard P. 133
  Jacob 60, 84, 88, 124
  James ... 38, 152, 163
  Jesse 156
  John 21, 41, 61,
  .... 62, 118
  Joseph, Sr. 73
  Lemuel 124
  Mahlon 37
  Mary 61, 80, 93,
  .... 133, 152
  Meraia 60
  Polly 94
  Ralph 41, 158
  Samuel 6, 37,
  .... 81, 115
  Seth 115
  Thomas ... 48, 51, 77
  Thomas & Martha 48
  Wethers 33

William 3, 25, 27,
  28, 34, 35, 37, 47,
  48, 57, 60, 61, 66,
  70, 76,. 79, 85, 89,
  .... 94, 151
Winnifred 62
Withers 150
Smitley
  Adam 156
  Edmund 120
  Elijah 119
  Jane 119, 120
  Matthias 41, 43
Snider
  Jacob 96
  John 76
Snyder
  Mary 76
Songster
  John 27
Souder 95
  Philip 40
Sowder (Souder)
  John 155
Sower
  B.W. 123, 131
  Brook W. 133, 137
  John 137
  William P. 133
Sowers
  Jacob 152
Sparrow
  Caroline 147
  Dinah 147
Spates
  Charles W. 137
  Minor 147
  Thomas 130
Specht
  Andrew 33
  Daniel 67
Spence
  Georg 83
  George 89
  Hanson 117
  Henson 116
  James 107, 115
  Margaret 108
  Nancy 116
  Vincent 116
  William 116
  Wm. 125

Apprentices, Poor Children and Bastards 201

Spencer
  Cecilia 96
  John 96
  Nathan 16, 38
  Robert 36
  Samuel 38
  William 111
Spooner
  John 102
Squires
  George 38
  Reuben 38
Stabler
  Edward & Mary ...144
  William 49
Staley
  Jacob 41
Stall
  David 99
Standey
  Garret 58
Stanhope
  John 45
  William 22
Stapleton
  John 20
  Sarah 36
Stater
  Jacob 71
States (Slates)
  Frederic 159
Steagler
  Cathern 154
Steer
  Benjamin 87
  Isaac, Jr. 93
  John 37
  Joseph 111, 112
  William 133
Steere
  Isaac 35, 96
  Isaac, Jr. 88, 91
  Joseph 92
  Thomas 88, 91
Steers
  Joseph 16, 42
  Mary 85
Stephens
  Edward 39
  Henry 127
  James 39
  John 7
  Joseph 14

Levina 36
Richard 13, 25
Robert 38
William 57, 153
Stephenson
  William 42
Steuart
  Hugh 38
Stevens
  Hannah 14
Stevenson
  James 75
Steward
  Daniel 56
Stewart
  Catharine 124
  Catherine 150
  Christinia 26
  George 138
  Henry 101
  James H. 127
  James Henry
    .... 122, 124
  Wm, Jr. 121
  Wm. 122, 127
Stickler
  Mary 73
Stinchecombe
  John Henry 138
Stoker
  Elizabeth 151
  John 76
  William 152
Stone
  Davis 50
  Edward 82
  Elizabeth 94
  John 136
  Mary 97
Stoneburner
  Christopher 144, 145
Stonestreet
  Bazel 72
Storts
  Henry 69
Stotts
  Henry 50
Stoutsberger
  John 76
Stoutsenbarger
  John 66
Stover
  Edwin A. 130

Street
  Nancy (Ann) 154
Stuart
  Daniel 56
  William 65
Stubbs
  Sidina 11
Stuck
  Susanna 158
Stump
  Thomas 3
Styles
  Phillis 5
Suddith
  William 66
Sullivan
  John 117
Summers
  George 26
  Jacob 124
  Wm 118, 119, 120
Surgenor
  John 113
Surghnor
  Jno. 130
  John ..115, 120, 121,
  .....129, 130, 131,
  ......143, 145, 147
Surgnor
  John 88
Suthard
  John 66
  William 9, 64
Sutherland
  Caleb 105
  Caleb C. 127
  John A. 105
  Lavina 136
Sutton
  Amos 42
Swain
  John 72, 83
  Sihon 74
Swann
  Charles 50, 52
Swart
  John 45, 143
Swarts
  Elizabeth 70
  Henry 79
Swean
  John 79

Index

Swick
  Anthony 25

T

Talbert
  Henry 23
Talbot
  Rebekah 102
Talbott
  John 70, 102
  Joseph 94, 95, 97
  Thomas, Jr. 89
  William 41
Talbut
  John 7
Talley
  Josiah 89, 91
  Susannah 91
Tapin
  John 68
Tapmen
  Elizabeth 150
Tarlton
  Elijah 96
  Macka (Mackey) . 161
Tarman
  John William Strong
  22
Tarr
  Elizabeth 46
Tate
  William 131
Tavender
  James 80
  Susanah 80
Tavener
  George, Sr. 94
Tavenner
  Landon 161
Tavenor
  Elizabeth 147
  Isabella 159
  Mary 147
Taverner
  Alexander 36
  Mary 11
Tawner
  Jacob 108
Taylor
  Ambrose 68
  Anne 68

Bernard 74,
  .... 101, 135
Charles 134
Henry 25, 70, 142
Jane 105
Jesse 74
John 95
Jonathan 60
Joseph 103, 124,
  .... 146, 147
Mahlon 41
Nancy 159
Stacey 41, 44, 66
Stacy 143
Thomas 89, 126, 129
Timothy 96, 146
William 29
Wm. 104, 134
Templeton
  Isaac Spurr 33
  Margaret 23
Terrell
  Elizabeth 79
  Margaret 79
  Susanna 15
Terry
  Mary 125
Tetrick
  Ann 152
Tharp
  Ann 48
  David 45
  Hannah 48
Thatcher
  Abigail 149
  Amos 149
  Lurana 76
  Richard 23
  Samuel 54, 67
Thomas
  David 64
  Elizabeth 11
  Emet 13
  Enoch 29, 31
  Evan 14, 18
  Griffith 69
  Isaac P. 113
  James 101, 122,
  .... 124, 127
  Jason 16, 22
  Jeremiah 36
  John 40, 103, 104,
  .... 106, 108, 109
  John, Jr. 117

John, Sr. 117, 138
Joseph 12, 22, 23,
  .... 32, 82, 103
Joseph P. 110
Lindsey 93
Lindsy 82
Martha 139
Mary ... 109, 154, 158
Nan 26
Philip 108
Phillip 151
Robert 19, 138
Thadeus 135
William ... 13, 44, 135
Wm. 109
Thomkins
  Benjamin 64
Thompson
  Annzey 162
  Daniel 51
  Hugh 115, 144
  Isaac 23, 24
  Israel 15, 32, 33,
  .... 51, 54
  James 19
  Jane 29
  John 19
  Jonah 69
  Jonas 37
  Mahlon 161
  Morris 147
  William 156
Thomson
  James 28
  John 12, 28
Thornton
  James 104
  James Madison .. 147
  Jane 26
  John 20
  Jos. N. 137
  Mary 26, 137
  Mordecai 26
  Nancy 147, 157
  Thomas 51
Thrasher
  Elias, Jr. 160
Tillet
  Mason 69
Tillett
  James 58
  Mason 74
  Samuel, Jr. 152
  Sybbil 74

Apprentices, Poor Children and Bastards 203

Tilman
  Ebeline 147
Tilton
  Richard 13, 24
Timbers
  Alfred 147
  Joseph 135
  Nathan 125
  William 135
Timms
  James 129
Tinsman
  Henry 102
  Phebe 102
  Pheby 107
Tintzman
  Henry 107
  Phoebe 106
  Samuel 106
Titus
  Francis 60, 63
Tobin
  John 156
  Mary 156
Todd
  Samuel 83
Todhunter
  John 29, 31
Tomkins
  Jonah 60, 76
Tompkins
  Jonah 60
Toon
  Lott 44
Torbert
  Elizabeth 142
  Thomas 69, 142
Torbert (Talbert)
  William 156
Torrison
  Wm. 132
Totton
  Mackey 157
Tracey
  Alexander 60
Tracy
  Mary 147
  Ryland W. 136
  Sally 147
  Sarah 157
Trahern
  James 133
  James H. 133

James Henry 133
Pricila 133
Trahorn
  James 128
Trammel
  John 6
Trammell
  John 4, 34
  Samson 17, 35
Traverse
  Barrett 5
Trayhern
  Jas. 109
Trayhorn
  Enos 118
  Israel 111
  James 130
  Martha Ann 130
  Samuel 119
  Sarah 63
  William & Sarah ... 83
Trebbe
  John 52, 67
  Jonathan 152
  Joseph 50
  Thomas 70
Trebbee
  John 61
Trenary
  Manuel 137
Tribbe
  John 52
  Thomas 48
Tribbee
  Amandy 135
  Emily 135
Tribby
  Emily 115, 136
  Jesse 136
  John 39
  Joseph 136
  Mary 136
  Tamer 146
  Thamer 161
  Thomas 145
  Thomas, Sr. 158
Trip
  Joshua 67
  Sally 67
Triplet
  Mary 64
Triplett
  Enoch 66

Reubin 162
Stephen 156
Tritipau
  Elizabeth 154
Trost
  William 86
Tugwell
  Edward 32
Tully
  Nelly 29
Turley
  John 31
Turnbull
  John 124, 147
  Susan 147
Turner
  Agnes 147
  Alexander 50, 62,
  147
  Ann 43
  Fielding 7, 13
  John 43, 87, 113
  Lewis 77
  Major Feeldon 84
  Major Fielding 77
  Nathaniel 16
  Sarah 43
  Susan 161
Tustin
  Samuel 114
Tweedy
  George 30
Tyler
  Ann 25
  Benjamin 25
  Charles 25
Tytus
  Francis 55, 59

U

Underwood
  John 105, 159
Updike
  Sarah 153
Urten
  Joseph 147
Urton
  Gerard 157
  John 123
  William 64
  Winifred 153

Index

V

Valentine
  Jacob 101, 109
  Michael 109
Vanander
  George 89
  Jane 87
  Margaret..............80
Vandevanter
  Isaac 31, 33, 88
Vandevender
  Isaac 85
Vandeventer
  Isaac 75
Vanhorn
  Nancy 119
  Octavia 162
Vanhorne
  William 119
Vannander
  Esible 87
Vanover
  Henry 19, 140
Vanpelt
  Catherine 68,
  .... 69, 107
  Richard 110
Vansickle
  John 118
Vansickler
  John 137
Vaune
  Cornelius................3
Veale
  Sarah 152
Veatch
  Nancy 102
  William 99
Venanders
  Jane 102
  John 102
Vermillion
  Elijah 160
Vernon
  Daniel 115
Verts
  William 94
Vickers
  Abraham 74
  Ann 159
  Aquilla 74

Elizabeth 72, 80
Nancy 71
Nimrod 147
William 74
Vietch
  Jesse 102
Vincell
  John.................... 47
Vines
  Ann..................... 149
  Reuben 6
Violett
  Jemimah............. 66
  John.................... 14
  Lavitha................ 66
Virgin
  Keziah 37
  Thomas 35
Virts
  Conrod................ 86
  Martha 161
Vollum
  Margaret 117
  Samuel 77
Votaw
  Isaac............. 21, 37
Vowells
  John................... 52
  Phebe 52
Vowels
  Febey 56
  Jonathan............ 56

W

Wade
  Caleb 46
  John................... 127
  Joseph 134, 148
  Mary 160
  Nehemiah 72
  Robert 62, 85
Wagley
  George 56
Wagner
  Elizabeth 35
Waid
  Robert................ 73
Waigly
  George 64
Walentine
  George 50

Walker
  Aris.................... 113
  Ben. 103
  Benjamin 77
  Catharine............ 82
  Craven 113
  Garret........ 103, 141
  Garrett............... 136
  Henry 103
  Isaac 32, 107
  Peyton................ 85
  Robert 84, 102
  Thomas 78
  Thornton............ 104
  Wormly............... 113
Wallace
  David M. 124, 128
  John 34
  Joseph 36
Wallis
  David M. 128
Walters
  George 92
  James 80
Waltman
  David 119
  Jacob 70, 92, 97
  John 102
  John Melcher...... 107
War
  Benjamin 132
  John 81
  William 132
Ward
  James 131
  Patrick 58
  Thomas 36
  William 131
Ware
  Robert 90, 94
Warford
  Abraham 7, 57, 69
Warfurd
  William 12
Warman
  Thomas 42
Warner
  George 139
  Peter 58
Warrant
  Walter S. 75
Warren
  Walter S. 75

Apprentices, Poor Children and Bastards 205

Warrenburg
  Mary 61
Warters
  Enos 110, 148
  George 110
Warwick
  Middleton 94
Waters
  George 105
  Ishmael 99
  Mary 99
Watkins
  John 79
  Peyton 148
Wats
  Lydia 158
Watson
  Benjamin 73
  Lemuel 130
  Margaret 3
  Richard 55
  Robert 5, 6, 7
  Thomas 3, 6
  Thomas Weldon ... 30
Watters
  Mahlon 106
Watts
  Elizabeth 5
  James 5
  Mandy 119
  Manly 121
Waugh
  Benjamin 107
  Diana 111
  John 80
  Polley 94
  Polly 93, 111
  Samuel 148
Weadon
  John 144
  Margaret 109
Weast
  John 78
Weatherby
  Matthew 42
Weathers
  Pashent 42
Weaver
  Elizabeth 39
  John 36, 65
  Mary 39

Webb
  Cressey 91
  John 61
Webster
  Elizabeth 160
Wedgeworth
  Jane 15
Weedon
  Frederick 109, 117
Weisner
  Jacob 58
Welcome
  Anthony ......,..... 113,
  .... 115, 116
  James 113
Wells
  Isaac 51
  Jane 7
Wenner
  William 163
Werts
  Adam 99
Wertz
  William 93
West
  Charles 28
  John 74
  Joseph 48
  Thomas 15, 17,
  .... 19, 20
Westby
  John 3
Wetherby
  Matthew 72
Whaley
  James 3
  James, Jr. 149
Wharton
  Anthony 9
  Jesse 13
Wheeler
  Benjamin 154
  John 125
  Maddison 148
  Nancy 102
Wheese (Whuse?)
  Liney 27
Whitacre
  Ann (Anna) 155
  Benjamin 47
  Caleb 44, 45, 62
  Caleb, Jr. 41
  Caleb, Sr. 41

Elizabeth 49
Enoch 74
Esther 55
George 45, 62
James 55
Joseph 55
Martha 44
Robert 47, 49,
  ....64, 122
Ruth 47, 49
Whitaker
  Robert 31
White
  Ann 31
  Benjamin 61
  Daniel 75
  Joseph 46
  Josiah 66
  Matthew 28
  Richard 8, 40
  Robert 56
  Thomas 43
Whitecor
  George 23
Whitecotten
  James 61
Whitley
  Mary 64
Whitmore
  Margaret 160, 161
Widner
  Alexander 5
Wigginton
  John 136
  Wm 136
Wilcox
  Nathan 49
Wilday
  Thos. 106
Wilding
  Jacob 54
Wildman
  Ann 32
  Jacob 36
  Mary 158
  William 159, 161
Wiley
  Hugh, Jr. 146
  James 49
Wilkerson
  Asa 61
  Israel 43
  Joseph 55

Mary 151
Sarah 39
Wilkins
  Thomas 20
Wilkinson
  James 98
  Joseph 99
  Thomas 116
Wilkison
  Thomas 72
Wilks
  Francis 2, 9
  John 15
Willard
  Reuben 2
Willett
  George 156
Williams
  Abner 65
  Benjamin 20, 80
  Catherine 9
  Elijah 73, 78
  Israel 49, 76, 77
  James 29
  Jane 28, 40
  John 40, 105, 132
  John & Lydia 95
  Joseph 20
  Samuel 42
  Thomas 1
  William 19, 148
  Wm. 105
Williamson
  James 28
  William 28
Williard
  William 53
Willis
  George 37
Wills
  Benjamin 98
  Thomas C. 97
  Thomas Cradill 73
Willson
  James 65
Willyard
  William 37
Wilson
  Aaron 38
  Alexander 71
  Amos 41
  Ann 157
  Caleb 96

Catherine 30
David 15
Eli 106
Elizabeth 42
Fleming 8, 36
George 24
Israel 81, 82
James 38, 42,
  .... 48, 56
Jane 8
Jesse 19
John 39, 132
Joshua 26
Mahlon 85
Margaret 8
Mary 8, 151
Orpha 96
Peter 3
Rebekah 96
Robert 62, 92
Samuel 41, 49
Susanna 53
Thomas 66, 97
William 139
Wm. 117, 132
Wilt
  Susanna 70
Wilyard
  Catharin 37
Windgrove
  John 39
Windsor
  Hezekiah Butler 6
  Mary 28
  Sarah 61
Winegrove
  John 83
  Nancy 83
Wingrove
  John 58, 160
Winn
  John 103, 142, 149
  Minor 4, 5
  Minor, Jr. 6
Winsor
  Mary 150
  Thomas 4
Winters
  Mary 148
Wise
  Joseph 136, 148
Wisheart
  Henry 11

Wissinger
  George 163
Wofter
  Boston 83
  John 83
Wolcard
  William 70
Wolf
  Henry 35
  John 14, 60
Wollard
  William 35
Wood
  David 163
  James 8
  Joseph . 62, 111, 147
Wooddy
  Samuel 131
  Sarah 140
  William & Elizabeth
  105
Woodford
  Joseph 39
  Thomas 19
  William 43, 54,
  .... 64, 65, 89
Woodhouse
  Christian 4, 150
  Moren 5
Woofter
  Sebastian & Mary . 84
Woolcard
  James 70
Woollard
  Joseph 51
  William 39
Workman
  Isaac, Jr. 156
  Rachel 157
Worran
  Francis 122
  Spencer 122
Worthington
  Frederick 94
Wren
  John 39
  Sandford 76
Wright
  Alfred 77, 138
  Caldwell 160, 161
  Catherine 117
  Christiana .. 114, 117,
  .... 122, 160

Apprentices, Poor Children and Bastards

Daniel Thomas ...133
Eliza Ann............111
Elizabeth 117
Fanney 11
Isaac .. 116, 125, 133
James 114
Jane Ann............111
Jno. 122
John 62, 71
John Mason..........33
Jotham 96, 97,
............109, 112,
............118, 129
Mary.............33, 157
Robert 17
Thomas Daniel ...133
William 80, 86, 87,
........88, 89, 101,
.............109, 146
Wm. 108, 109
Wyatt
Abner 19

Wyckoff
Nicholas...............18
William 35
Wycoff
Nicholas... 27, 28, 50
Wyer (Wire)
Peter..................156
Wynn
Clement 98
John L.... 98, 99, 100

Y

Yagey
Simon 92
Yakey
Simon 92
Yates
Lydia 11
Yeats(Yates)
Joseph..............141

Young
George 142, 155
Harrison Douglas
.... 148
Isaac................. 145
Isaiah................. 104
Isak 104
John 43, 52, 54,
.................62, 157
John & Lois........ 145
John B. 140
Landon 95
Leticia................. 95
MaryAnn 158
Rebecca 28
Susanna 16, 24
William............... 161

Z

Zabra
Thompson 148
Zimmerman
Adam................. 101

www.ingramcontent.com/pod-product-compliance
Lightning Source LLC
Chambersburg PA
CBHW071415160426
43195CB00013B/1701